Ryanair

*How a
Small Irish Airline
Conquered Europe*

SIOBHAN CREATON

Aurum

First published in Great Britain
2004 by Aurum Press Ltd
25 Bedford Avenue, London WC1B 3AT

Designed in Minion by Geoff Green Book Design

Printed in Britain by MPG Books Ltd, Bodmin

Contents

Acknowledgements

This is the unauthorised account of how a small Irish airline founded by Tony Ryan grew to become Europe's biggest low-fares carrier. The story has been constructed from many hours of interviews and conversations with individuals who were central to the story. Others associated with the airline and the industry generously gave advice, help, guidance and insights into the workings of Ryanair and the management style of its colourful chief executive, Michael O'Leary. I would like to express my sincere thanks to all of them.

CHAPTER ONE

Don't Forget Your Passport

I t was another busy day at Stansted Airport. Thousands of passengers were grinding their way towards the head of their check-in lines, browsing in the shops, scanning the monitors for flight information. But those bound for Cork on Ryanair were restless and bored. Their flight had been delayed. And as the minutes turned to hours they grew frustrated. One Irish man was particularly agitated. Suddenly, out of the corner of his eye, he spotted a face familiar to him from television and newspapers.

It was Michael O'Leary. The Ryanair chief executive, dressed down as usual in an open-necked shirt, was boasting into a television camera about how his airline was going to become the biggest in Europe. The burly would-be passenger saw his chance. Striding over towards the airline supremo, he fixed him with a stare. Mark Davison, Stansted's media relations manager, saw it all as if it was slow motion. Terrified that O'Leary was going to get punched on live television, he got ready to call security.

The interview ended, and the clearly irate passenger moved menacingly close to O'Leary. The airline boss looked up. 'What can I do for you?' he asked him. The man vented his spleen, long and loud, about the delay, claiming that Ryanair was keeping its customers in the dark about when they might actually reach their destination. He was livid. Ryanair had ruined his weekend, and cut short the time he was hoping to spend with his family.

O'Leary listened, then inquired calmly: 'How often do you visit them?'

'Maybe every few months,' the man replied.

'And how often did you see your family before Ryanair?' O'Leary asked.

After a brief pause the man said he used to return to Ireland only about once a year, maybe less.

O'Leary threw his eyes up to heaven, shook his head and declared: 'That's what I've done for you – and you're here complaining about a delay?' There was a pause. Then the media relations man watched agog as the two Irishmen slowly smiled and shook each other by the hand. Within a few seconds, the formerly disgruntled passenger was summoning his friends to meet the forty-three-year-old man from Mullingar, County Westmeath who had revolutionised air travel.

Ryanair pioneered low-cost air travel in Europe. It is the airline that will sell you a ticket to Paris, Brussels, Rome, Frankfurt or Stockholm for as little as a penny but will actually take you to Beauvais, Charleroi, Ciampino, Hahn or Skavsta, an hour or two down the road. In 2004 O'Leary expected to carry 24 million people to its rapidly expanding range of destinations. By the end of the decade he believes Ryanair will carry 50 million passengers and that about half of its seats will be free, with passengers paying just the local taxes. As part of his efforts to achieve this he intends to save money by paring the comforts on board Ryanair planes to the bare minimum, dispensing with window blinds, reclining seats, velcro-anchored headrest covers and even the seat pockets where customers normally find a safety notice and free magazines. Sick bags will be handed out only on demand and O'Leary has suggested that passengers could carry their own baggage on board to save handling costs.

Ryanair has become one of the best-known brands in the world. A survey by Google, the Internet search engine, found that Ryanair was in the top five leading brands alongside names such as Sony and Ferrari. The tails of its blue and white planes carry its trademark yellow angel and harp motif. O'Leary has ordered breast enhancements for the angels on its new planes; a spokesman said it wanted to offer its customers a more uplifting experience.

The low-cost revolution has reduced the price of air travel to below the fares charged on buses and trains and given millions of people the opportunity to regularly visit friends and relatives across Europe. 'Doing a Ryanair' has become the generic term for buying a cheap ticket to some out-of-the-way destination over the Internet. Sometimes it can be hard to find a bargain, although O'Leary says if you can't find a cheap deal with Ryanair 'you're a moron'.

Those travelling midweek and who can be flexible about their arrangements are guaranteed the best prices. Buying a Ryanair ticket at the last minute or en route to a popular sporting fixture can be expensive. Fans travelling to Seville to support Celtic Football Club's bid for the UEFA Cup Final in 2003 were horrified when Ryanair charged a £601 fare from Stansted on a special football flight. Advertising standards authorities in Britain and Ireland have censured the airline for misleading sales promotions. The Irish authority upheld a complaint about a Ryanair newspaper advertisement carrying the banner 'EASTER SPECIALS!' that offered flight to various cities in Britain from the end of April until 14 June 2003. A footnote explained that the offer 'excludes Easter travel'.

'Doing a Ryanair' is also used to describe a sometimes fraught and difficult experience that, at its worst, leaves people swearing they will never do it again. During the trip many will keep their fingers crossed that everything will run smoothly because, if things go wrong, flying with Ryanair can be a nightmare. If a flight is delayed or cancelled passengers risk being stranded in remote airports, usually where Ryanair is the only airline offering flights. The next flight might be due a day later but sometimes you might have to wait a couple of days or even a week to return. During that time you are on your own. No one from Ryanair will offer you a cup of tea or a bed for the night. Tabitha Dmochowska told the *Guardian* how it had cost her, her husband and three children £716 to find their own way back to Britain after Ryanair left them stranded at Vasteras airport, 100km from Stockholm. Another hundred people were also abandoned when the airline cancelled the flight.

Ryanair has also become famous for imposing surcharges for wheelchair users. When Bob Ross, a cerebral-palsy sufferer, arrived to check in for a flight from Stansted to Perpignan in France he was told he would have to pay £18 for the use of a wheelchair. He took the case to court and in January 2004 won a landmark ruling against Ryanair. When these stories appear in the national media they prompt many more travellers to relay their experiences of flying with Ryanair. The sheer volume of complaints in Britain has swelled to such an extent that some newspapers now have columns dedicated solely to Ryanair customer gripes. O'Leary claims the airline receives fewer customer complaints than any of its rivals, and that Ryanair is 'Britain's favourite airline'.

It is committed to publishing monthly customer-service statistics, and its figures for February 2004 showed that 92 per cent of its more than 14,000 flights had arrived on time. Ryanair received on average 'less than one' complaint per thousand passengers and said that all complaints had been answered within seven days. Disaffected passengers would say the low level of complaints is due to Ryanair's insistence that customers must raise any issues in writing. 'Most people know by now that Ryanair will probably just tell them where to get off, so they wouldn't waste the stamp,' one source in the airline industry suggested.

The *Guardian*'s City Diary has christened the airline 'Eire O'Flot' and has run 'My Ryanair Hell' and 'Ryanair-Miles' competitions. The latter asked readers to guess which of Ryanair's airports was farthest from its ostensible destination – Frankfurt (Hahn), Oslo (Torp), Stockholm (Skavsta), Reims (Disneyland) or Helsinki (Pirkkala). The winner was offered a trip to Ireland to visit O'Leary's farm and palatial home in Mullingar. It was a popular competition to which Reims (Disneyland), hundreds of miles from EuroDisney, was deemed the correct answer, though Frankfurt (Hahn), two hours' journey by road from Germany's financial centre, was also the choice of many. Amongst others, an Irish reader, Micheàl O'Laoire from Mullingar, had submitted that answer; the newspaper suspected the airline chief himself had participated in the competition, using the Irish version of his name.

Forbes Magazine has ranked Michael O'Leary, the man acclaimed for transforming a small cash-strapped Irish airline into Europe's biggest low-fares carrier, one of the world's top twenty-five business leaders. He claims to have little interest in such accolades. On winning an award as Business Leader of the Year he said: 'It usually tends to lead to complacency in the company or from the gobshite who wins it. But I was a gobshite anyway.'

He talks with great conviction about Ryanair ultimately becoming the world's biggest airline. 'There is no shortage of ambition here. We bow to nobody. We'll stuff every one of them in Europe, we won't be second or third and saying "Didn't we do well?"' To celebrate that milestone O'Leary has promised to run a new advertising campaign featuring 'a drunken Paddy' saying, 'Howya Boss, I'm flying Ryanair – the world's favourite airline.'

O'Leary enjoys publicly taunting other airlines either through cheeky advertising or by staging outrageous publicity stunts. In 2003 he donned combat fatigues and drove a Second World War tank to Luton Airport, leading a battalion of Ryanair staff in a high-profile attack on its low-fares rival, easyJet. Claiming to be on a mission to 'liberate the public' from its rival's fares, he roused his troops with a loud-hailer to join in a rendition of a platoon-march song: 'I've been told and it's no lie, easyJet's fares are way too high!'

O'Leary loves to tell people 'where to get off' and will usually use the most colourful language possible in the process. He has said he would have no qualms about telling people looking for a refund on a Ryanair ticket to 'fuck off'. His favourite insult is to call someone a 'wanker' and he has branded some of Europe's politicians 'loonies' and 'Communists', and the European Commission 'an Evil Empire'. O'Leary has also coined his own expletive, 'bolloxology', to enrich the English language. The Ryanair.com website suggests the term should be 'liberally used in one-to-one print media interviews when referring to any procedure that other airlines claim is complex', such as 'Aer Lingus's inability to publish its punctuality figures'.

It was O'Leary's idea to insist that passengers had to carry a passport if they wanted to fly with Ryanair. He decided this was the only form of identification that was acceptable and ordered the airline's staff to strictly enforce his policy. And they did.

Socialite Tara Palmer-Tompkinson, star of reality television series *I'm A Celebrity! Get Me Out Of Here*, was enraged to be told she couldn't board a flight from Stansted to Blackpool because she didn't have her passport. 'When I got to Stansted I signed photos for all the cabin crew going on the flight,' she told the media. 'But when it came to getting on the plane the woman on the check-in desk said I could not go on board. She said I needed a passport – a passport to go to Blackpool! I could not believe what I was hearing. They said a passport was needed as formal identity of who I was. I was not even leaving England. I hadn't got anything else they would accept – not even a copy of *Hello!* with my picture in.' A month earlier, Ryanair had given another television star, Jeremy Beadle, his marching orders for the same reason. Ryanair's sales manager, Kathryn Munro, explained that the airline enforced its policy without exceptions. 'It doesn't matter whether you are Jeremy Beadle, Tara Palmer-Tompkinson, or His Holiness the Pope: if you don't have the right ID, you won't get on our aircraft.' One former Ryanair employee recalled O'Leary saying that even if someone turned up at the check-in desk without a passport and said they knew him, they had his full permission to tell them 'where to get off'. 'We could have turned his mother away and he wouldn't have flinched,' the ex-crew member said. 'He was as good as his word in that regard.'

Today O'Leary and his deliberate rudeness are virtually synonymous with Ryanair. Since he first joined the board of directors in 1988, he has become more and more central to the airline's fortunes, becoming chief executive in 1993. But the man who founded Ryanair and who guided it through its difficult early years was someone quite different – the iconoclastic businessman Tony Ryan.

CHAPTER TWO

Learning to Fly

T ony Ryan claims his family has been in the transport business for a thousand years. His grandfather was a station master, his father a train driver and he himself went on to found Ryanair for his sons, Cathal, Declan and Shane. And while a thousand years may be exaggerating the longevity of the Ryan family's association with various modes of transport, it is no exaggeration to say that Tony Ryan has scaled the heights and plumbed the depths of the aviation business.

Born in County Tipperary in 1936, he grew up in the town of Thurles. His mother used to say that Tony had always been a very focused child who managed to finish his homework more speedily than his siblings, something that frequently got him into trouble with his father, who thought he wasn't doing it properly. He attended the local Christian Brothers school and went on to work at the Irish national airline Aer Lingus as a clerk at Shannon airport in County Clare, a role that included working behind the counter dealing with customers – he described himself as a 'counter jumper'. Another new recruit in Shannon the same day was Christy Ryan from County Waterford. The two Ryans weren't related but quickly forged a firm friendship.

Tony Ryan married his childhood sweetheart, Mairead, and in the mid-1960s he moved with his wife and sons to the US to work as the Aer Lingus station manager at New York's JFK airport. Around 1972 Aer Lingus advertised for a leasing manager in Dublin. The position caught Ryan's attention. He applied for the job and was supported by the Aer Lingus US operations head, David Kennedy, who would shortly become the airline's chief executive.

Airlines across the world had the problem that many of the aircraft they needed in the busy summer season were unused during the winter. Aer Lingus was among the first airlines to lease out its surplus aircraft during the quiet winter months. A leasing department was established in the mid-1960s and the first lease, to Trans Caribbean Airlines, lasted five years, earning much-needed additional cash for the national airline.

'It was very. much part of our ethos to have this fairly aggressive approach to leasing out aircraft at times when they weren't needed,' Kennedy recalled. In 1972 the escalating troubles in Northern Ireland kept tourists away. Aer Lingus realised that one of its Boeing 747 aircraft would now be idle that summer and winter, and began to look for a home for it. The airline industry itself was suffering from the effects of a period of economic slow-down, making the leasing manager's task all the more daunting. 'Tony Ryan was given the assignment to try to find an arrangement that would allow our aircraft to be productive,' Kennedy said. 'He literally went around the world. It was a very tough assignment and frankly very few people gave him much of a chance of success.'

In his travels, Ryan stumbled upon Thailand's Air Siam, which was just about to start up and was looking for aircraft. Its financial position was precarious and it could provide little in the way of security for Aer Lingus' $10m aircraft. But Ryan argued the business case persuasively and agreed to base himself in Asia for the duration of the lease. It worked well for the first three years, earning millions of extra cash for Ireland's national airline. Air Siam's finances plunged into the red shortly afterwards leaving Aer Lingus a couple of million dollars shy of its contractual agreement but Ryan's arrangement, and the safe return of the jet, had been a success.

While in Asia Ryan closely studied the burgeoning aviation market and began to formulate a plan for a new venture when he returned to Ireland. 'One evening in 1974 when I lived in Asia, I stopped to watch a street food vendor whom I passed each day,' he told the Irish Management Institute's national conference in 1992. 'He was a banana-chip-maker. His business was to slice, cook and sell banana chips to passers by. He was extraordinarily skilful, not only in slicing hundreds of bananas into thousands of perfect pieces but also at selling his product. He impressed me and made me think. I felt it a pity that such marketing, technical talent and energy were devoted to a process which sold for a mere penny. There and then I determined that when I went into business on my own account I would apply my energies to developing and marketing a big-ticket product which could sell for vastly more. It could have been property, ships or aircraft. Given my background, the choice was inevitable.'

From his experience leasing Aer Lingus aircraft in Asia, Ryan realised there was a demand for aircraft that could not be met simply from temporary over-capacity, when airlines sought short-term homes for what were inevitably the least attractive planes in their fleet. In 1973 members of the Hungarian Gonda and Udvar-Hazy families had set up the International Lease Finance Corporation in California, to supply aircraft to international airlines. Ryan returned to Dublin in 1975 enthusiastic about developing such a business, but he claims to have found it difficult to sell the idea to Aer Lingus. David Kennedy, Aer Lingus' chief executive, remembers things differently. He pointed to the airline's policy of investing in businesses beyond the aviation industry. In 1972 the airline took a five per cent shareholding in the London-based Guinness Peat bank, and Jerry Dempsey, an Aer Lingus executive, was working with the bank's chairman on potential joint ventures. Kennedy said aircraft leasing was top of that list.

'Aer Lingus had all the technical and operational skills,' he pointed out. 'We believed that there must be an opportunity for acting as a broker for aircraft in any part of the world, not just the odd surplus aircraft that we had ourselves, but that there could be opportunities elsewhere. There was some debate internally about why don't we do it ourselves. The argument for bringing in the Guinness Peat group was that it had financial resources that we didn't have. We also wanted to have it out of house because we felt it would develop in a better way.

'We knew what we wanted to do, the only question was who would actually run it for us. At the same time Tony had been in Bangkok, doing an excellent job there, and had developed even further the strong entrepreneurial streak that he had. He had seen the way in which things were done in the Far East and was coming back to Ireland and he was the obvious choice to run the company. The only question then was to negotiate a deal with Tony.'

They were difficult negotiations, with Ryan demanding a substantial stake in the new business. He had spoken to Guinness Peat and to Air Canada and threatened to forge ahead and establish the company himself if his terms weren't met. Some at Aer Lingus formed the impression that Kennedy resented Ryan's demand for a shareholding. 'He would not have viewed this as appropriate behaviour,' one said. 'Having to accede to Ryan's demand would have left a very bad taste. It probably set the tone for what happened next.' Others also pointed to a poor relationship between the two men. 'Tony Ryan was too good a businessman to be curtailed by David Kennedy,' another source thought. 'Kennedy was a mathematician and chess player, a patrician. It was a bit like old money versus new money.'

For its part, Aer Lingus reminded the enthusiastic entrepreneur that its presence at the new aircraft leasing company could prove essential to getting the business, to be called Guinness Peat Aviation, off the ground. 'Aer Lingus' involvement was that it was contributing a lot more than capital and this was part of the negotiations with Tony,' Kennedy emphasised. 'It was contributing respectability and its name within the airline industry. GPA was nothing. It was just a start-up company. There was a lot of one man [companies] – somewhat dodgy characters in some cases – trading around the world trying to do leasing at the time, and it wasn't the most respectable business. So it was important for GPA that it had the backing of a well-known international airline and also a bank behind it.'

It was eventually agreed that Ryan would get a 10 per cent shareholding in GPA, with Aer Lingus and Guinness Peat each taking a 45 per cent stake. The company was established with a total investment of £50,000. Ryan remortgaged his home to chip in his £5000 share.

The Irish Government encouraged GPA to base its business at Shannon, in County Clare, where it could benefit from a range of tax incentives designed to attract new industry to the region. As its major shareholders were in Dublin and London, Ryan believed the Shannon base would give the firm operational independence, and it was also close to his native Tipperary. 'We consciously decided not to apply for state grants because I believed these would engender a sense of protection from the commercial realities in the market place,' Ryan said later.

And so GPA went into the business of facilitating the placing of surplus aircraft for airlines across the world, acting as an arranger for airlines that had a surplus and those that needed planes. The tax advantages at Shannon also encouraged employees to participate as shareholders, giving generous tax relief on dividends earned from businesses based there. 'I was determined from the beginning to give all our employees the opportunity to own part of GPA and to share fully in the company's success,' Ryan has said. The staff were awarded options to purchase shares in GPA based on their contribution to the firm's success. James King, a former GPA director and friend of Ryan's, explained that 'you got nothing for free. You never got anything for free from Tony'.

GPA had three employees when it opened for business. One, Peter Swift, a professional long-term planner, had read a Ford Foundation report that noted that companies with written objectives tended to be the most profitable. Ryan, determined not to miss a single trick, reacted to this discovery by saying, 'Peter, GPA needs written objectives urgently and badly so that we can make a profit this year.'

When speaking publicly about GPA's formation Ryan has quoted former Chinese Communist leader Deng Xiaoping's reason for establishing the Shenzhen industrial tax-free zone to attract international investment in the 1970s: 'Some people have to get rich first, otherwise we will all remain poor together.' Ryan believed he was entirely right. He described Shannon as Ireland's 'Shenzhen' and was extremely proud to have created a 'small zone of wealth' in that region.

Commercial aircraft leasing was an innovative concept. Traditionally airlines liked to own and design their own fleet, which meant there was no common aircraft specification, but rather a huge number of models with different engines and different take-off and landing weights. Finding the right aircraft to suit different airlines was hugely challenging. King believes GPA's great success was due to its mastery of that art.

In 1978 GPA reported a $1.1 million profit and was preparing to purchase its first aircraft, a secondhand Boeing 737^{8}200. In the US President Jimmy Carter signed the Airline Deregulation Act, opening up the US skies to competition. Thousands of new routes were opened and the demand for aircraft soared. New airlines were burgeoning and cheaper airfares were increasingly being offered to US consumers. A brash low-cost carrier, Southwest Airlines, had taken to the Texas skies in 1971 offering flights between Dallas, Houston and San Antonio for $20. It was founded by an Irish-American lawyer, Herb Kelleher, who would become a personal friend of Ryan's. There was fierce competition between the many new carriers and titans such as American Airlines and TWA. There were also tremendous opportunities for GPA to provide aircraft to entrepreneurs who dared to establish new airlines, and the firm kept an eye on the casualties who were crushed by deregulation – creating opportunities for GPA to purchase or source aircraft. Braniff, Southwest Airlines' bitter rival in Texas, was the first major US carrier to go bankrupt, filing for Chapter 11 protection from creditors in 1981. Its planes were grounded and were parked in long lines at its headquarters in Dallas, a sight that would have caught Ryan's attention when he met with the lawyers handling the bankruptcy proceedings – who included a former civil-rights specialist, David Bonderman, who was getting his first taste for the aviation business.

Ryan is described as an 'Olympic' salesman, and he circled the globe in search of new business for GPA. He gathered intelligence from within the aviation industry and furiously networked with key figures. He would note the names of individuals who impressed him with a view to recruiting them in the future. Many people have acknowledged Ryan's great ability to recruit talented people to work with him. Aer Lingus senior executives Jerry Dempsey and Maurice Foley represented the national airline on the GPA board of directors. Foley would later join GPA, as would Ryan's close friend from Aer Lingus, Christy Ryan. 'One of Tony's strengths was his ability to build a good team around him,' Kennedy recalled. 'He needed someone like Maurice Foley who was absolutely meticulous and very highly organised, who would know all the details of all of the leases and would intellectually cover all of the risks associated with the business. He was a

very good partner in management terms to Tony's more entrepreneurial visionary style.'

Ryan was extraordinarily hard working and a very difficult
taskmaster. His friend James King believed that his strong personality meant that he would never have been considered for a
top management post at Aer Lingus. 'He has a prickliness, an
inability to accept bullshit and could not accept the promotion of
individuals on grounds other than their ability. He starts with a
few and then he entrusts them to bring on board those that they
need for their particular area of expertise.'

GPA grew rapidly and generated large profits every year. By
1983 it reported an $8 million profit and was building a fleet of
aircraft. New shareholders, Air Canada and the US General Electric Capital Corporation, had come on board, adding greater
prestige to its operations. It was doing business in places like
Iran, Africa and Thailand ahead of its competitors and was well
on its way towards achieving its primary objective – becoming
the world's biggest leaser of aircraft.

Around August or September every year Ryan would start
writing down the ten objectives he wanted to achieve both for
himself and for GPA, and he encouraged his colleagues to do the
same. He managed by strategic objectives. 'By the time we came
to the end of the year when we had a conference he would present the objectives for the following year, and of course he would
always raise those objectives,' King said. 'He was one of those
people who could make those who worked for him achieve far
more than they ever believed they were capable of themselves. He
goaded them on and encouraged them. One of the great qualities
he had was for open debate. He had famous Monday morning
meetings that started at precisely 8.30. He would arrive a shade
just before 8.30, which was so teasing to the rest of us who would
have been in an hour early preparing. He would arrive with a
small briefcase, sometimes his driver would carry it, or sometimes he would come into the meetings with nothing other than
a cigar. He would know everything about what had happened the
previous week and everything about what we needed to do the
following week. It took a while for us to realise that he did all of
this on a Sunday evening. In the early years I remember thinking
I had done a splendid job last week and that I was probably going

to get a compliment on Monday morning. But no one ever got a compliment. What you were asked to do was to say what you proposed to do the following week. The bar was always lifted.'

These legendary occasions became known as 'seagull meetings' – according to one executive, because Ryan 'swoops in, shits on everyone from a height and swoops away again'. King dismissed this description but acknowledged that Ryan could be ferocious. 'He could be absolutely scalding at these meetings, never unfairly, but sometimes with unnecessary barb. It was probably warranted but maybe not the rudeness. It was all forgotten by the end of that day or certainly by the end of the week, when those of us who worked closely with him would all repair to Dirty Nelly's [a nearby public house] on a Friday evening. Somebody who had particularly got the wire brush treatment during the week would be singled out and asked to go with him.'

King said Ryan would always find a subtle way of smoothing feathers that he might have ruffled. 'He valued creativity, energy and initiative more than anything else. He forgave mistakes. If you made a genuine mistake that was it, you explained it, you learned from it and we wouldn't do it again.' Many would readily embrace the demanding and extraordinarily well-paid jobs at the thriving international aircraft-leasing group. Others would burn out or fall out of favour with Ryan and exit with a bitter taste in their mouths.

As GPA chairman and chief executive, Ryan was accumulating a fortune from the generous dividends paid to shareholders. He became one of Ireland's wealthiest entrepreneurs; some estimated he was worth more than £50 million. Ryan and GPA's management and staff owned 16 per cent of the company, and they were all enriched by the dividends. Ryan had dabbled in a number of private investments and began to formulate potential new aviation ventures based on his in-depth knowledge of the industry. In particular, he saw the possibilities of appealing directly to the passenger market.

In August 1980 Ryan and some associates put a proposal to the Irish Government for an airline that would provide a 'cheap, no-frills and efficient service' for Irish consumers. The airline, which would be substantially funded by Ryan, was to be called 'Irelandia' and would be headquartered at Shannon Airport. If approved, Irelandia expected to get airborne by 1982, operating scheduled flights to New York for £99 one way, and to London for £25. 'The keystone of Irelandia's proposal will be low overheads, efficient operation and forceful marketing,' the proposal stated. 'It would compete aggressively with the foreign airlines which will otherwise dominate this aspect of Irish air travel and which cannot be successfully opposed at present.'

The document noted the growing acceptance amongst the European Economic Community's Council of Ministers of the need for a more liberal aviation service throughout Europe, like that which had developed in the US. In the UK, aviation entrepreneur Freddie Laker had launched his Skytrain, offering low fares to the public on transatlantic routes. But he was constantly at war with Europe's aviation authorities and other airlines that seemed determined to thwart his every move. 'Deregulation is a word that appears offensive to most national airlines,' Ryan told the Irish Government. 'Nevertheless, in the long term, deregulation combined with competition is the only method by which the travelling public will enjoy low fares.' The proposal stated that low fares could only be achieved if airlines had low overheads and were efficient or if the state was prepared to subsidise the operating losses that would mount from the cutting of airfares.

Looking forward, the document suggested that European nations were likely to follow the US style of deregulation and drop or relax what were known as 'fifth freedom' traffic rights. This would clear the way for airlines to operate services from other European states, allowing Ireland's national airline to launch services from UK airports to other European destinations and foreign airlines to open new routes out of Ireland. The proposal concluded by telling the Government that 'Ireland must have an airline capable of taking advantage of this situation whilst competing effectively against foreign opponents'. But Ryan was ahead of his time. His plan was ultimately rejected, leaving Aer Lingus and Pan Am still in control of the routes from Ireland to the US.

Ryan wasn't alone in his desire to take on the national airline. In the early 1980s, Avair, an airline established by Irish businessman Gerry Connolly, began to operate executive charter flights before branching out to offer scheduled flights on domestic routes, with the ultimate ambition of offering flights from Dublin to Blackpool and the East Midlands. Aer Lingus didn't broach a huge objection to Avair flying within Ireland, believing that such a service would be beneficial, as passengers would transfer on to Aer Lingus to travel further afield. It was adamant, though, that Avair should not be allowed to operate between Ireland and the UK. While Aer Lingus didn't fly to the airports Avair was targeting, it was concerned that its rival might attract traffic from the adjacent Dublin to Manchester and Birmingham routes and provided a detailed analysis of the reasons why Avair should be denied these routes to the Department of Transport. The Minister for Communications, Jim Mitchell, overrode Aer Lingus' objections and gave Avair a licence to fly scheduled services to Blackpool and the East Midlands in March 1983. It was the first Irish carrier to be granted a licence to operate scheduled international services against the wishes of Aer Lingus. But Avair struggled to compete with the national airline and never managed to gain a foothold in those markets. It closed down in 1984.

Avair's experience had shown that it was virtually impossible to muscle in on the Dublin to London route. The Irish and British governments had a bilateral agreement that governed this route and effectively controlled the air fares charged by Aer Lingus and British Airways. This made it virtually impossible for a small airline to take on the state-owned monopolies on the most profitable route out of Ireland. Anyone thinking about setting up an airline would need to have very deep pockets both to fund the start-up costs and to weather the Aer Lingus retaliation.

Meanwhile, despite Ryan's failure to set up a passenger airline, his public profile was growing rapidly. He had a lavish home, Kilboy House, and a 200-acre farm in County Tipperary, but spent most of his time travelling, clocking up thousands of air miles for GPA. Some of his wealth had gone into backing the re-launch of the *Sunday Tribune* newspaper, and he had an interest in a nearby public house, Matt the Thresher's. Newspaper articles that highlighted Ryan's achievements at GPA impressed one ambitious young banker, Dubliner Denis O'Brien, who wrote to Ryan expressing his ambition to work with him. 'If you were out of college in the late '70s or early '80s and you were looking to join a dynamic company there were only a few options in Ireland,' O'Brien said later. 'I had read about how Tony Ryan had started GPA with a small amount of money and I said, "Jesus, he's the guy to work for."'

Declaring his great admiration for Ryan's business acumen and his willingness to learn, O'Brien cheekily suggested: 'I hear you are an early riser. I will meet you in Shannon some morning.' Within a week Ryan's accountant met O'Brien, and when the young banker passed muster the GPA chief deigned to follow suit. 'I was hired as his personal assistant and paid the princely sum of £10,000 a year.' O'Brien's brief was to establish some of Ryan's investments outside GPA, including managing the farm, getting Matt the Thresher's up and running and, later, becoming company secretary to the *Sunday Tribune*.

'I used to live in Kilboy House,' O'Brien recalled. 'At seven in the morning I would be sitting in the back of the car with Tony and he would be asking questions in unbelievable detail. Everything had to be done quickly. He didn't believe in waiting around. I suppose that was why he was such a dealmaker. If he wanted to do something he would just go and do it. That was his philosophy.'

Ryan made copious lists of tasks for his assistant and would diligently go through each one on a weekly basis. 'He is an unbelievable lateral thinker. He would say, "I want you to go and buy this for me. But when you are having the conversation with that person you are to say the following words" – and make me write them down. He could think of all of the emotional things that would make a buyer sell. He would say, "I want you to say this to him, then I want you to say that, then you should finish up by saying X, Y and Z." He was a bit like a good jockey. He could see the jumps half a mile down the track and know how he was going to jump them. He has a terrific brain. And he has balls of iron.'

O'Brien was very impressed by Ryan's ability to spot potentially lucrative business opportunities far beyond the aviation world. One example was his idea to get into satellites in the late 1980s. A consortium of GPA, Allied Irish Investment Bank, the Irish state-owned telecommunications company, Telecom Eireann, and the national broadcaster, Radio Telefis Eireann, was assembled to bid for the licence to build a high-powered satellite. O'Brien was the project manager. The bid was rejected because the Government felt it was too risky for Telecom and RTE, but the satellite was later built by a Luxembourg company, Astra, and it provided the footprint for the modern European satellite business. 'Tony's idea, to launch a satellite that had a footprint all over Europe that would allow anyone with a small sixty-metre dish to receive signals, was fairly brilliant,' O'Brien pointed out.

Today he still remembers the many tongue-lashings he received from Ryan, and in particular one of the last terse exchanges that his father overheard. 'Tony was burying me on the phone. It was difficult. I was trying to get off the call and my father smelt it. He said, "Look, it's time for you to go before you get bought and wrapped, before you take on all of the trappings. Get out and set up your own business."' O'Brien took that advice and went on to set up numerous businesses, the most successful being Esat Telecom, the mobile-phone company he sold to British Telecom for £200 million in 2000. He believed that one of Ryan's greatest strengths was that he spawned a really great risk-taking culture out of GPA. 'I walked out the door saying: "You might be based in Ireland and you might be Irish but what's stopping you?" He had an attitude that nothing could stop us and that's how he went on to turn GPA into the biggest leasing company in the world.'

The young personal assistant had quickly realised that his mentor wanted to be in the passenger airline business and had attended many meetings with politicians with Ryan, who expressed his desire to go into competition with Aer Lingus. Ryan spotted an opportunity to acquire a licence from a struggling Irish cargo operator, Aer Turas and made an offer for it. The price had been agreed and the deal was done when it was scuppered at the last minute by Aer Lingus. News of the deal had filtered to the airline chiefs and suddenly Aer Lingus decided it would buy the Aer Turas licence and pay a much higher price for it than Ryan had offered. Again Ryan's plans had been thwarted at the last minute. But things were about to change.

CHAPTER THREE

Ryanair

I t's hard to imagine that Ryanair could have achieved European domination in quite the same way if it had been called Trans Tipperary. But that's nearly what happened. One of Denis O'Brien's last tasks was to arrange a lease agreement for a Bandeirante aircraft that was sitting on the tarmac in Shannon, acquired as part of a deal with the Danish shipping and transport group Maersk. Ryan decided that he would finally take the plunge and set up a new airline. He had the Bandeirante extensively refurbished and fitted out with fifteen seats, with the intention of using it for charter work, ferrying small groups of business and leisure passengers between Ireland and the UK.

While Ryan was making these plans, his old friend Christy Ryan, godfather to Tony's second son Declan and now working for GPA on the sales team, was also preparing to launch a new airline. The proposal was to fly between Waterford and London's Gatwick Airport with three other associates, and two English businessmen had agreed to provide the financial backing. But the plan unravelled, and Christy Ryan was left without funding. Keen not to give up his idea, he met Tony Ryan in a pub close to the latter's County Tipperary home to discuss putting their ventures together.

At the same time, Liam Lonergan, who had established the Dublin firm Club Travel, had the idea to seek a licence to fly between Dublin and Luton Airport as a new gateway to London. Luton Airport was the home of charter flights, and from it airlines including Monarch and Britannia ferried thousands of passengers to package holiday destinations. It came to national attention through the 'Luton Airport' song recorded by the band

Cats UK in 1979, which was used in a Campari advertisement featuring the estuarine accent of Lorraine Chase. The route between Dublin and Luton wouldn't be covered by the bilateral agreement and Lonergan would be free to set his own airfares.

Lonergan also needed a financial backer for his airline and he turned to Tony Ryan. The three men pooled their ideas, and it was decided that Christy Ryan would apply to the Department of Transport for an air, sea and customs licence. The name of the new airline was a source of disagreement. Tony Ryan still favoured his original idea, Trans Tipperary, but the Waterford man was insistent that his name should be lent to the new carrier. Eventually the GPA chief agreed that Ryan was indeed a good name and the new airline was christened Ryanair.

Aer Lingus learned about its potential new rival when senior civil servants at the Department of Transport asked the national airline to provide its expert opinion on Ryanair's licence application. Once again, it was opposed to allowing any new carrier onto the Ireland-UK routes. But the Minister for Transport, Fine Gael's Jim Mitchell, took a different view and granted the licence to Christy Ryan, handing it to him at ten o'clock at night in Dublin's Ashling Hotel.

Ryanair, born on 28 November 1985, was registered 'to carry on the business of general carriers and forwarding agents and to use machines of all kinds capable of being flown in the air'. It had an address in Dublin and its business grew up out of the tiny Waterford Airport on the south-east coast of Ireland, ninety miles from Ireland's capital city. Waterford is Christy Ryan's hometown, and it was his idea to fly between there and London. But he feels that his part in establishing Ryanair has never been publicly acknowledged; nearly two decades later, he is still angry.

Tony Ryan was providing the seed capital to get the company off the ground and had established a trust through which his three sons would be the airline's major shareholders. GPA had assisted many airlines to go into business, and the firm would hire experienced executives on secondment from Aer Lingus and British Airways to aid them. Ryan was obliged to declare his outside investments to the GPA board, which still included Aer Lingus representatives. Sources suggest that the Aer Lingus directors 'weren't wild' about the notion, but as the GPA chief wasn't directly involved with the new airline there was nothing they could do about it.

O'Brien had found a potential replacement to step into his shoes as Ryan's personal assistant: his brother-in-law, Eugene O'Neill, who was then working at Citibank. Ryan was impressed by O'Neill and hired him immediately. Before he left, O'Brien was sent to Waterford to put up hoarding to advertise the arrival of the new airline. Its staff would soon realise that its financial backer wasn't a passive investor but would direct its every move. They knew Ryan as 'the man from Del Monte', likening him to the fruit-company boss portrayed in its television advertisements. He was never seen but he had the final say on everything.

And so, much to Aer Lingus' chagrin, a second airline had been born. Tony Ryan put just over £1 million into it through the trust he had established for his three sons, Cathal, Declan and Shane. Cathal had trained as a pilot and was based in Malaysia. Declan was working for the America West airline in the US. Their youngest brother, Shane, was still at school. As soon as Christy Ryan returned with the licence telex messages were sent to the two older Ryan brothers telling them to get back to Dublin – Ryanair had been cleared for take-off.

The new airline could now open for business. It took a small suite of offices in the arrivals hall of Dublin Airport and began to charter its fifteen-seater Bandeirante to bring small groups on business and leisure trips. Its first pilot, George White, went to Shannon to fly the aircraft to Dublin. The media was invited to Dublin Airport to report on the new venture and to board a short flight. White took his passengers to the west of Ireland, making two approaches and overshoots at the new airport at Knock, County Mayo, to fuel publicity.

On the same day Ryanair also announced it would shortly begin to operate daily flights between Waterford and Gatwick. It developed a small air taxi operation carrying seventy-six passengers on a good day, with many fewer mid-week. But there were frequent problems associated with flying in and out of Waterford. Planes could only land if the cloud base was above 800 feet, which was not always the case. Flights were frequently diverted to Dublin, much to the disgust of the Waterford-bound passengers, and very expensively for Ryanair. The founders had projected their new venture would lose £147,000 but this ultimately proved to be conservative. The service was suspended.

By this time Lonergan had convinced the Ryans that they should be seeking rights to fly between Dublin and Luton. Tony Ryan, who had lobbied Minister Mitchell many times about the establishment of a second national airline, agreed with Lonergan and it was decided that Ryanair would apply to the Department of Transport to fly to Luton.

In May 1986 its request was granted. It was considered to be a brave political decision that effectively allowed the small airline to take on Aer Lingus on its premier route. But the licence for this route was exceptionally prohibitive, ruling that Ryanair could only operate aircraft with no more than forty-four seats on the route.

Aer Lingus, which was carrying thousands of passengers to London, was one of the more successful Irish semi-state companies and there was little political appetite for any initiatives that might jeopardise its position. The Department of Transport on Dublin's Kildare Street was known as the 'Aer Lingus downtown office'. The airline's chief executive, David Kennedy, said he was surprised that the licence to serve the London market was awarded to Ryanair without any kind of tendering process. 'It wasn't like any of the recent processes in telecommunications, for example, where there was a formal application and people were allowed to tender. I thought that was probably not the right way to do it because there would have been other people who would probably have been interested in the Dublin to London route. It was a bit like giving a licence to an electricity supplier just to supply power to the city of Dublin or a postal service. It was picking the most profitable part of the Aer Lingus network.'

Tony Ryan had got what he wanted: a chance to establish a second Irish airline. He immediately set about assembling a team to get it off the ground. Arthur Walls, a mechanical and electrical engineer who had spent twenty years at Aer Lingus and who had been a key member of its management team, was asked to become chairman. Ryan also recruited his former Aer Lingus colleague Derek O'Brien, who became Ryanair's commercial director. Kevin Osborne took on the role of finance director, Tim Shattock and Bluie Gardner were in charge of operations and George White became the chief pilot.

There was much surprise and some resentment when Ryan decided to make his newly arrived personal assistant, Eugene O'Neill, Ryanair's managing director. While Ryan was attracting people with great experience of the airline industry to most of the key positions at the new airline, O'Neill, the man who would spearhead the operation, was a novice to the sector. Ryan's two sons were also installed at Ryanair, Declan as O'Neill's assistant and Cathal as a pilot. Lonergan, who had brought the concept of flying to Luton to Ryanair, left the airline before the licence was granted. Some years later he established Club Air but it closed with heavy financial losses.

The GPA founder had a very specific strategy for the airline, as a low-cost, no-frills outfit. But it soon became obvious to his colleagues that, despite these aspirations, Ryan didn't want his name to be associated with anything cheap. 'Ryanair's weakness in the early days was that it didn't know what it wanted to be,' said one source. 'Tony Ryan said he wanted a low-cost, no-frills airline. He would say, "If people want a cup of tea or coffee, let them pay for it. If they want to buy tickets let them stand." At the same time, though, he was retaining top designers to design desks for the office and insisted on an expensive bound in-flight magazine.'

In 1986 about 800,000 passengers flew on the Dublin to London route every year, typically paying about £200 for a return ticket. It was the most expensive way to travel between the two countries and most people took the boat. In 2003, Aer Lingus' chief executive, Willie Walsh, admitted the airline had been 'ripping off its customers for years' through its fares policy. In the late 1980s, though, it felt no compulsion to offer value for money to its customers.

Aer Lingus was not amused that the Government had allowed a small private airline to set itself up in its back yard. It was determined to clip Ryanair's wings before it got off the ground. 'At one level it was quite helpful to Aer Lingus,' Kennedy remembered. 'You were always looking for change, to get people to do things differently and to cut out unproductive practices. The single best motivator that we had was when there was a Ryanair aircraft sitting out on the ramp outside our window. You were able to say, "Look guys, you mightn't want it or like it, but they're here."'

Ryanair recognised it was going up against a formidable opponent. It couldn't ignore the fact that Aer Lingus aircraft were all painted a patriotic green and bore the names of Irish saints. It was a steadfast carrier with an impressive safety record, and Irish people generally believed they owned part of it. Everyone knew it would be a David-versus-Goliath battle.

Aer Rianta, the state-owned company that owned Dublin Airport and which had originally been part of Aer Lingus, was said to have been indifferent to its newest customer. 'It operated a policy of benign neglect,' one source said. Ryanair found it difficult to get check-in desks. But the company refused to let itself be sidelined, and there was much grandstanding, with the Ryanair crew threatening to bring in orange boxes to construct their own check-in areas until Aer Rianta eventually capitulated. Staff at Ryanair believed that Aer Rianta viewed the new venture as a 'flash in the pan' and wasn't going to annoy Aer Lingus by being too accommodating to its new rival.

Ryanair purchased two BAE 748 aircraft quite cheaply while preparing to launch three daily round trips between Dublin and Luton. It would add additional flights depending on demand and envisaged that its schedule would expand to Cork and Shannon in the future. It planned to carry 80,000 passengers in its first year and began to make the public aware of its existence. 'We had to make noise. We christened Luton as London and ran advertisements saying Ryanair was the only airline with "nothing going for it", to highlight the fact that there were no restrictions attached to our cheap fares,' Derek O'Brien said. 'We needed to make an impression, to show that we were reliable and that we would get them there safely.'

Unusually for the time, Ryanair had no booking restrictions. Customers didn't have to make advance bookings or stay at their destination for a Saturday night, and there were no penalties for cancellation. The airline began to recruit staff and held group interviews to select its crew from the thousands of young Irish people who eagerly applied. The new recruits would work in reservations, check-in and as cabin crew, something the airline believed would enhance customer service. One former employee recalls staff being told that there were only two reasons why they would be dismissed – if they were dishonest or if they were discourteous to a passenger. Another novel departure was that all Ryanair staff were given a shareholding in the airline. On arrival, each employee received 500 shares, valued at £1 each.

A reservations department was established in Dublin's Nassau Street and in the Irish stronghold of Kilburn in London. A queue was hired for the first day to stoke demand. Charlie Clifton, the sixth person to join Ryanair, was working on the reservations desk that day and sold the first ticket, to a little old lady. 'She paid by cheque and shuffled out,' he recalled. 'We nearly mugged her.'

There were no computers. Staff spent their days retrieving files from two carousels, one to record forty-four names for each flight from Dublin to Luton and the other for flights from Luton to Dublin. Passengers had to call to the office to collect their ticket. Pat Carroll headed the London reservations office, which stored its files in boxes. When someone booked a flight, one of the staff would delve into the box and find the flight they wanted and write their name on one of the forty-four spaces, then search for the box with the return flights and do the same. At the end of each day the Dublin office rang through to London to exchange passenger names booked on each flight.

Ryanair's head of public relations, Anne O'Callaghan, was told that the dapper young chief executive Eugene O'Neill was to become the public face of Ryanair and began to prepare for the airline's official launch. O'Neill, known by colleagues as 'Mr Armani', announced that Ryanair would fly passengers between Dublin and Luton for an astonishing £99 – less than half the price charged by Aer Lingus and British Airways. The first flight would take off on 23 May 1986.

Ryanair had started the first price war on the Dublin to London route. Aer Lingus immediately donned its battle gear and began to tinker with its air fares. The airline suddenly realised that it had some leeway to make it cheaper for its customers to fly to London. It informed the Department of Transport that, largely due to a big fall in oil prices, it could reduce its fares to Britain's capital city to £95. The new fare was approved and, just hours before Ryanair's first flight was due to take to the skies, Aer Lingus announced its spoiler fare. The reaction of Ryanair chairman Arthur Walls to the announcement is remembered by many.

'The penny has dropped,' he declared, and slashed Ryanair's introductory fare to £94.99.

At Dublin Airport a piper welcomed passengers as they boarded the small twenty-eight-year-old plane bound for Luton. The Irish national broadcaster, RTE, recorded the debut on television. Its reporter praised Ryanair for its role in cutting the price of air travel to the UK and asked whether further price reductions were on the cards. O'Neill held out the hope that air travel could become even cheaper in the future, saying, 'We have been preparing for this for about eighteen months and everything is set to work very well.' Ryanair basked in the glow of positive publicity, which helped to raise public awareness and encourage bookings.

In Britain Ryanair discovered a powerful marketing ally in the Catholic Church. In the mid-1980s Irish people made few journeys home. They might visit during the summer to see their families; otherwise they tended to return only to attend funerals. Trying to get back to Ireland in a hurry was very expensive, as Aer Lingus would force people who were desperate to travel to pay £200 or £300. Ryanair heard that priests around London were telling their congregations from the pulpits about its cheap flights. News of Ryanair's arrival spread rapidly around the Irish communities and provided a surprise boost for the airline. Within a few months more than 80 per cent of seats on each flight were filled.

The airline used publicity stunts to market itself and showed a flair for producing controversial advertisements. It decided to congratulate Aer Lingus on its fiftieth birthday in an advertisement carried in the Irish national newspapers showing a birthday cake with a slice missing. Aer Lingus, incandescent with rage, plotted retaliation. It was rumoured to have established a committee of nine people to deal with Ryanair. Sources at the airline deny this but admit that senior executives were determined to protect their patch. Reservations staff constantly changed air fares to win passengers from Ryanair. One insider at the airline said the reservations department was like a 'twenty-four-hour dealing room', with prices changing by the hour.

Aer Lingus also stepped up the advertising war and began to warn the public about 'Luton phobia'. In a radio commercial it told listeners: 'Fly to fabulous Luton Airport. Right in the middle of Luton. Cosmopolitan Luton Airport, a stone's throw away from an absolutely fabulous bus stop where you will wait for a bus to take you directly to the train station. Glamorous Luton Station, where you will wait for a train to take you to another train station. Why fly to Luton for more when you can fly to London for less?' It later ran an advertisement to highlight the fact that Ryanair had raised its fares before reverting back to the Aer Lingus official policy, which was never to acknowledge Ryanair's existence. Ryanair was unrepentant. When it advertised its £94.99 fares to Luton it cheekily asked: 'Do you want to pay £100 for breakfast?'

Aer Rianta was initially mildly amused by the new kid on its block. Ryanair staff felt its attitude was, 'Ah sure – they'll learn!' Some remember Walls saying that Ryanair was engaged in a boxing match where the referee owned one of the boxers. To many in Ryanair it seemed like the men in Aer Rianta were all married to Aer Lingus girls; they used to joke that Ryanair employed their granddaughters.

Ryanair's small turbo-prop planes were noisy and cramped and took an hour and a half to fly to Luton compared to the fifty-minute journey to Heathrow with Aer Lingus and British Airways. Cabin crew, bedecked in Ryanair's blue uniforms, served drinks and sold duty-free during the flight. Everyone at Ryanair worked long hours. One former employee said it was like being on a treadmill constantly moving at a frenetic pace. 'Ryanair felt that it owned you. You were hands-on all of the time but there was no direction.'

Reservations staff worked from eight till eight every day including weekends. Cabin crew could work twenty-seven days in a row without a day off. Charlie Clifton said he had often arrived home after working a flight only to be met by a taxi waiting to bring him back to the airport. 'You would see a taxi outside the door and the guy would say, "Are you Charlie Clifton? You're back out again, mate," and you would just get straight back into the taxi again and go out and do more flights. It was great fun. It was fantastic to be involved in something like that. It was and is a great company.'

There were lots of crises. Flights could be suddenly cancelled due to technical problems, leaving angry passengers stranded at the airport. Passengers frequently arrived to check in for a flight only to discover that Ryanair had no record of their booking. The airline had advanced from manually recording passenger details and was now using the British Airways computer reservations programme. Staff had been trained to use the more efficient method, but one former Ryanair customer-service agent explained that the transition to computerisation was problematic. 'You could take bookings all day and forget to close them off. By that evening you would realise that you had booked everyone onto the same flight. There was nothing you could do so you would ignore the booking and worry about it when they turned up at the airport.' In many instances, the airline offered these customers free flights for the inconvenience.

Staff who handled customer grievances were constantly under pressure and won much sympathy from their colleagues. 'It was growing too fast,' one said. 'There was no proper infrastructure and it was constantly taking on more than it could cope with.' 'Everywhere you went you were associated with Ryanair,' said another. 'People would walk up and verbally attack you about problems. As a result you tended to socialise with Ryanair people to protect yourself.'

Their contemporaries at Aer Lingus, who were trade-union members, earned more money and had significantly better working conditions, and some of Ryanair's one hundred staff were being targeted by the unions to seek a better deal. Ryanair executives began to hear that the trade unions representing Aer Lingus staff were lobbying the government to curb Ryanair's growth by denying it any further routes. O'Neill believed that this campaign was unofficially supported by Aer Lingus management. At the same time rumours were beginning to spread about Ryanair's financial stability.

Ryanair was also lobbying the Government to be allowed to introduce bigger aircraft, although the public didn't seem to mind flying on the small planes and were delighted to buy Ryanair's cheap seats. Despite Aer Lingus' opportunistic reductions, the national airline had not changed its overall pricing policy and its booking conditions were as strict as ever; Ryanair's low fares and lack of restrictions had enormous appeal. 'It takes a little bit longer. I go twice a week, it saves a lot of money,' one passenger said. 'I fly Ryanair for the same reason,' said another. 'Because it's cheaper. I just hope it will be more reliable when they get the jets. There are too many conditions with the other airlines. This way we can come and go and can change the dates and there is no problem.' A businessman said he could afford to bring his wife and three children to the UK while he was working there. 'He was able to bring us because he was flying Ryanair,' said his wife. 'With three children we couldn't possibly have gone any other way. It's the price.'

Ryanair had signalled its interest in flying to Knock Airport some months earlier and was now preparing to begin to offer regular flights from County Mayo to Luton. The airport had a controversial history. It was close to the shrine commemorating Our Lady's apparition to three schoolchildren in Knock and attracted thousands of pilgrims. But the West of Ireland, where emigration had become a way of life, was dying. In the late 1970s and early '80s thousands of young people left to find work in the UK or the US as soon as they had finished school or college.

The idea to build a runway between the County Mayo towns of Knock and Charlestown had been hatched in the late 1970s and was first mentioned to the then Taoiseach (prime minister), Charles Haughey, during a lunch with Monsignor James Horan, the shrine's administrator. The Monsignor made no bones about the region's harsh terrain, joking that even the snipe wore wellingtons there. But he believed that if the region had an airport there would be tremendous opportunities to attract pilgrims, tourists and eventually industry to the western counties.

Haughey, who many years later was discovered to have funded his lavish lifestyle through donations from Irish businessmen, steadfastly supported the project in the face of sneers and harsh criticism from the opposition parties and many others. Celtic Air had been granted the licence to operate between Knock and Luton but this had not gone ahead and its licence was withdrawn. Aer Lingus told the Government it would only fly from Knock if the route was subsidised. The airport was branded a white elephant and its detractors laughed at the notion that airlines would take off and land in this 'foggy bog'.

The Government decided to grant the licence to Ryanair. On 1

December 1986 Ryanair landed in Knock and offered cheap fares to Luton. Passengers on the inaugural flight were presented with a specially commissioned tumbler crafted by Galway Crystal. It was a popular service. 'You get home so fast these days it's just like living down the road,' said one Mayoman who was working in London. Others remarked that it was now faster to fly from Mayo to London than it was to get the train from Westport to Dublin. 'It's changed times for us who have to go away,' another man explained.

To some extent the new service did begin to curb emigration from the area. Local men began to commute to London during the week and return home at the weekends for the first time ever. Staff at Ryanair began to notice the steady flow of passengers arriving with toolboxes and other equipment as they headed for work. The airline would later carry passengers from Knock to Birmingham and Manchester.

Tony Ryan had told O'Neill to make Ryanair 'the best airline in Europe'. It had applied to open even more routes. It had boundless ambition and even more crystal tumblers were ordered to celebrate new destinations.

Aer Lingus upped the ante and the following January began to offer cheap services from two other West of Ireland airports, Galway and Sligo, both close to Knock. Suddenly for an extra £10 people living close to those airports could fly to Dublin and connect on to other destinations. O'Neill wanted to complain to the European Commission about Aer Lingus' antics but met resistance from Tony Ryan.

Around this time Ryanair contracted with the organisers of the Eurovision Song Contest to sponsor it in Dublin in conjunction with Airbus Industries. 'Ryanair received a tremendous amount of free publicity throughout the world,' O'Neill explained, 'including having one of the new A320s painted in the Ryanair livery and shown on television to an audience of approximately 60 million viewers.'

Ryanair moved some of its operations to new premises at College Park House and this was where some of Ryanair's crew got their first glimpse of the airline's elusive financial backer. One remembered being told to tidy the desks and alert staff when Ryan's Mercedes pull up outside. 'He came in and walked through to Eugene O'Neill's office without making eye contact with anyone,' the source recalled. 'After about half an hour he left, again avoiding making any contact. I didn't understand that kind of behaviour in a place where people were working so hard for his airline. It didn't go down well.'

It was pretty clear to everyone that, although he had no shareholding in Ryanair, Tony Ryan was actually running the show. On Saturday mornings at 8.30 he would summon the Ryanair executives and board members as well as some of his loyal GPA lieutenants to Kilboy House, to discuss the airline. The group decided that Ryanair should aggressively expand and sanctioned its move into Manchester and the opening of services from Cork and Shannon airports to Luton.

Ryanair was now operating BAC 1^{8}11 aircraft, a type also used by Aer Lingus. The bigger planes were more comfortable and also cut the flying time between Dublin and Luton to forty-seven minutes. Some Ryanair sources remember that a small flight of steps was needed to allow passengers to move from the aircraft to the air-bridge leading into the terminal building. At Dublin Airport, the steps were all owned by Aer Lingus and rented to Aer Rianta. Staff said it was often virtually impossible to get these steps when Ryanair needed to let passengers on and off their flights.

The expansion didn't go according to plan. Ryanair planned to start flying from Cork to Luton in June 1986, but passengers on the inaugural flight shortly found themselves on the tarmac at Dublin Airport. The flight had been re-routed through Dublin because of the British authorities' delay in granting approval for the flight. Ryanair could not fly directly from Cork to Luton and could only continue its journey if it touched down in Dublin en route. The manoeuvre became known as 'touch and go' and was both expensive and inconvenient for the airline and its passengers.

O'Neill accused the British government of using Ryanair as a 'political football', suggesting it was using the issue as a lever over the Irish government to win concessions from a forthcoming EEC Council of Ministers meeting at which European aviation policy would be discussed. The airline decided to abandon its plans to fly between Shannon and Luton.

By the end of its second year Ryanair had carried 322,000 passengers. Its battle with Aer Lingus was taking its toll and the airline's losses rose to almost £3 million. Yet it continued to expand. Ryanair was now poised to fly to Manchester and Birmingham and had applied to open routes from Dublin to Orly Airport in Paris and to Amsterdam. It leased more jets, this time from the Romanian airline, Tarom, which also supplied pilots to fly the Romanian-built Rombac-111 aircraft. The all-white planes carried a large Ryanair logo and were given names that included *Spirit of Ireland*, *Spirit of Tipperary*, *Spirit of Waterford* and *Spirit of Dublin*.

The Dublin to Manchester route was of extreme importance to Aer Lingus, which was looking for the restoration of the 'fifth freedom rights' which would allow it to pick up passengers in other European states and fly them to other destinations. Its presence in Manchester was vital and if these rights were restored Aer Lingus could use the airport as a hub and operate flights to Amsterdam, Zurich, Frankfurt, Brussels and Paris. 'Aer Lingus had had those rights in the 1950s. In 1972 British Airways wanted to develop their British routes and persuaded the government to throw us out,' David Kennedy explained. 'That became one of the big fights for Aer Lingus when the whole question about the liberalisation of air routes throughout Europe started to open up in the 1970s. Our persistent theme was "Don't just say to us that everybody can come in and out of Ireland but that we don't have any rights to serve the big markets."'

Many at Ryanair believed the airline's assault on Manchester was doomed. 'We knew we would be going head-to-head with Aer Lingus. It was suicide,' one said. There was a great fanfare when Ryanair launched a daily service to Manchester on 1 March 1988 for £78. Aer Lingus was charging £204 pounds for the same journey. Ryanair said the fare was an introductory one and would rise to £98 the following month, still much less than its rival charged. But Aer Lingus immediately matched the Ryanair fare and put on three extra daily flights to Manchester. One Ryanair employee said it was like a 'blood bath'. As well as putting on extra flights, Aer Lingus beefed up its presence in the north of England, recruiting more sales representatives and tripling its advertising spend in the Manchester area. Kennedy acknowledged that Aer Lingus put up a tough fight. 'We were not going to move over and make way for them. I know we made life fairly tough for Ryanair at that time because it ran into serious financial difficulties. It had to be refinanced by Tony.'

Ryanair had expected the new Manchester route to make a profit of almost £1 million but Aer Lingus put paid to that. 'It effectively set about trying to limit Ryanair's growth,' explained sources within the airline. 'It had finally dawned on Aer Lingus that people were primarily interested in the price of air fares rather than the service or any feelings of loyalty.'

And so Ryanair's losses swelled. Ryan and the other members of the kitchen cabinet that convened at Kilboy House had agreed in their initial business plan to try to link up with a British airline so they could carry passengers on to European destinations. O'Neill was dispatched to find a suitable airline.

He identified London European Airways, a company in administration whose only assets were the routes it had from Luton to Brussels and Amsterdam and the authorisation in principle it had received from the UK Department of Transport for additional routes from Luton to Paris and Frankfurt. These were potentially very valuable; the London to Paris route is one of the densest in the world. Ryanair purchased London European Airways for £630,000 and Ryan appointed his son Cathal as its executive chairman. It was restructured and relaunched in May 1987. But it was never profitable. It ended up losing about £250,000 a month and eventually cost the Ryan family about £4 million.

By the end of 1988 Ryanair was in a precarious position and the Ryan family's foray into the airline industry was proving very expensive. As the financial pressures mounted O'Neill found himself increasingly at loggerheads with Ryan. O'Neill believed that Aer Lingus had infringed European competition law and abused its dominant position in the way that it responded to Ryanair's expansion. If the Commission upheld such a complaint, Aer Lingus could be fined up to £50 million and Ryanair could recover substantial damages from the company.

O'Neill discussed lodging a complaint with Declan Ryan, Arthur Walls and with the Ryanair board, but he could not persuade them to back him. Some sources suggest O'Neill was being restrained by 'hidden hands'. The Irish government would have frowned on any such commercial threat to Aer Lingus, and O'Neill claimed that at one meeting Walls said its difficulties with Aer Lingus would be resolved through 'political activity'. The chief executive was told to set up a meeting with Aer Lingus through the government. A senior official at the Department of Transport offered to chair a discussion between the two airlines but the meeting never took place. The ongoing problems continued to be aired at the weekends in Tipperary.

Meanwhile, Ryan's new personal assistant was introduced to the Ryanair board members and advisers and quickly became a permanent fixture at those meetings. A young man from Mullingar, he was given an office at the airline's Dublin's headquarters, where the staff wondered what this tall smartly dressed individual was up to. He said, 'I am only Tony Ryan's personal assistant. I have nothing to do with the airline.' His name was Michael O'Leary.

CHAPTER FOUR

Biggles O'Leary

Michael O'Leary didn't make much of an impression on Tony Ryan when they first met. The lanky teenager was part of the gang of school friends invited by Ryan's sons Cathal and Declan to their father's home at weekends and during school holidays. Ryan has been known to joke that the young lad from Mullingar was always the first of the youngsters to rise in the mornings and that he inevitably polished off all of the steak in the fridge. He has told others he doesn't remember O'Leary from that time, adding that Michael would hate to hear that!

Michael was the first of six children, born to Timothy and Gerarda O'Leary on 20 March 1961. The couple came from Kanturk in County Cork but had moved to the midlands town of Mullingar, in County Westmeath, to establish a business and rear their family. His father was an entrepreneur and set up a range of businesses over many years that enjoyed mixed fortunes. 'He used to set up businesses that would be very successful for the first few years and then go bust,' his son explained. 'When we went bust, he would sell the house and when he made money he would buy another house.' At one stage, his father bred rabbits commercially and was a part-owner of a knitwear factory that at its height in the 1970s was one of the town's biggest employers. Michael is said to be particularly close to his mother, who is regarded as the driving force in the family. Her brother, Noel O'Callaghan, ranks amongst Ireland's wealthiest entrepreneurs, with extensive property interests and hotels in Dublin and an interest in breeding racehorses. He is said to have a very close relationship with his nephew.

While the O'Leary family's fortunes ebbed and flowed, they generally enjoyed a very comfortable life and his parents gave their children the best education money could buy. 'We were comfortable,' O'Leary has said. 'The wealth came more from the fact that we had a very good family life. We never went on foreign holidays or anything like that but I never in all my childhood remember ever wanting for anything and certainly not when time came to educate us and there were six children within eight years. By that standard we were very well off and we were very well taken care of.'

He spent his early years at the local school run by the Christian Brothers, where he recalled being forced to sit under the teacher's desk when he failed a spelling test and being kicked by the teacher every time he made a mistake. 'I was only seven years old but I don't think of myself as an abused or battered soul and I certainly got my spelling right the next day.' He added that if he had children and a teacher asked if he could slap one of them he'd say, 'Go right ahead.' From there he went to one of Ireland's oldest and most exclusive schools, Clongowes Wood College, in County Kildare. The fee-paying all-boys' boarding school, which has been described as Ireland's Eton, has educated many distinguished Irishmen, most famously James Joyce. There O'Leary was known as 'Ducksie', a nickname handed out to every pupil who hailed from Mullingar after a boy from that town who had turned-out or 'duck' feet.

Few of his contemporaries remember him as someone they would have expected to become so successful. 'You would never have picked him out in a crowd,' a school colleague said. Another Clongownian remembered him as being very quiet at school. 'He didn't shine in any particularly field of study and didn't show any aptitude for public speaking. He didn't show that much interest in rugby but was fanatical about golf.' O'Leary has said that when he was at school his greatest ambition was to play football for Manchester City. 'I grew up in a big family and you were competitive with your brothers and sisters. I knew I was always ambitious and that I always wanted to do something, not be somebody but to do things. At the Christian Brothers I wanted to be on the hurling team, at Clongowes I wanted to be on the rugby team. I wasn't so I probably came out even more ambitious after that.' His contemporaries were all sons of Ireland's elite. Tony Ryan's three sons, Cathal, Declan and Shane attended the school, and Declan and O'Leary were friends.

After school he worked as a barman at the Greville Arms Hotel in Mullingar. Dublin Tourism director Frank McKee was the manager there and remembered giving O'Leary his first job. 'It was a summer job after he had finished school. It still sticks in my mind that I said to him, "If I were you I would think again about going to college because I think you could have a great future in tourism."' McKee, who still runs into O'Leary, says he hasn't changed. 'He was always confident. I thought when he worked for me that it was evident he was going to be top of the pile. He wasn't a guy who was cut out to be a boring accountant.'

The young barman ignored McKee's advice and went on to Dublin's Trinity College to study for a business degree. He said that business students just wanted to go out and 'rape the world' and that his time at Trinity was about four years of meeting girls and drinking alcohol. 'After four years in Trinity I knew I wanted to go to work. I had had enough of college and didn't want to study anymore. I had a couple of part-time jobs in my second, third and last year in Trinity. I knew that I wanted to make money.'

In 1982 the new graduate turned to accountancy and was accepted as a trainee at one of Ireland's biggest firms, Stokes Kennedy Crowley, now known as KPMG, earning about £3000 a year. He was assigned to work with Gerry McEvoy, a man he describes as a 'brilliant' partner, who specialised in advising major businesses and wealthy clients on their tax affairs.

O'Leary said he knew he wasn't cut out for the accountancy profession after about six days. 'Gerry was very good because he should have thrown me out at that stage. But I would work long hours and I was very good at racking up the time, which in accountancy firms means money.' Instead McEvoy encouraged him to study for the tax exams, which would take about two years to pass. And so he began working on company accounts, working out how much tax they owned and how they could best shield their wealth from the taxman. One colleague at the firm said O'Leary was 'fairly ordinary' but came across as very bright and someone who could get to grips with highly technical aspects of tax law. 'He was impressive when presenting his ideas.' Like the other accountants he wore a suit during his two-and-a-half-year career at the firm, but unlike most of his colleagues he had a burning ambition to become an entrepreneur and set up his own business. One remarked on the speed with which O'Leary volunteered to drop his tax work to join the team being despatched to sort out the mess caused when the large Irish supermarket chain H Williams went into receivership.

By this time O'Leary was preparing to dabble in retailing himself; he purchased a newsagents in the west Dublin suburb of Walkinstown and started investing in property. Some of his peers urged him to think carefully about ditching a potentially lucrative career as a tax adviser. One colleague, Cormac McCarthy, who went on to become chief executive of Ireland's First Active bank, remembered trying to dissuade O'Leary from leaving the firm. He cautioned that he was about to make the 'biggest mistake of his life' and often tells the story against himself.

'I wanted to work for myself because that was the only way to make money in those days. The money was in newsagents, pubs and property,' O'Leary has said. For the next couple of years he did what he described as some 'ducking and diving' buying and selling property. He is coy about how much money he made in those days but when pressed has said it was less than £100,000.

Tony Ryan, who was one of McEvoy's clients, had a range of investments including a substantial farm at his home in County Tipperary and met O'Leary when he arrived to do the farm audit. When Ryan was looking to hire a personal assistant some time later, he thought of the young accountant. He stopped by O'Leary's newsagents one day to ask him to come and work at GPA. O'Leary wasn't interested in working in a big company, but he was restless and looking for a fresh challenge. So he agreed to work for Ryan rather than for GPA. In a mark of his ambition and business acumen, he said he would take the position for a year and would forego a salary in return for five per cent of any profits he generated for his would-be mentor.

'So I started to work for Tony about 1988 and that is how I got into aviation,' he explained. News that O'Leary had signed up as Ryan's personal assistant filtered back to KPMG, where one accountant remembers someone saying, 'Poor Michael....'.

CHAPTER FIVE

Stansted or Bust

Tony and Declan Ryan had returned from the US to London's Heathrow Airport, where they were waiting to catch an Aer Lingus flight to Dublin. The presence of Ryanair's financial backer and one of its directors on Aer Lingus turf hadn't gone unnoticed. As the flight was called father and son moved towards Gate One. A senior Aer Lingus executive was also heading in the same direction. As he moved towards the two men he raised his voice to say, 'Jesus, Ryan, taking an Aer Lingus flight?' A friend of Ryan's recounted that about twenty people were standing around the gate and began to take an interest in what was happening. 'Tony calmly said, "I had to. Ryanair was full."'

The exchange typified the animosity between Ireland's two airlines, and more particularly the deep personal resentment felt towards the former Aer Lingus employee who was now backing a rival airline. Aer Lingus was still a significant shareholder in GPA and business relationships between those two companies tended to be cordial. Indeed, Aer Lingus had rather bizarrely hired a GPA subsidiary company, Transport Analysis Incorporated, to advise the airline on how it should respond to the deregulation of the air transport sector and tackle new competitors.

For all Ryan's bravado, by 1988 Ryanair was a money pit. It quickly swallowed up the millions he was earning in dividends from GPA, and in two years it had racked up losses of more than £7 million and was showing no sign of making a profit. Ryan was losing his patience. 'Tony would be told that something was going to lose money but would forget that and would beat you up when this happened,' said one associate. He decided to put his personal assistant into the airline to keep an eye on its finances and ultimately to stop the cash haemorrhage. Ryan made Michael O'Leary a director of Ryanair and installed him as the family's financial watchdog.

The relationship between chief executive Eugene O'Neill and the rest of the board was deteriorating, and O'Neill was fired in September. He challenged his dismissal in a High Court action that would expose the inner workings of the airline to the public for the first time since its launch. In an affidavit O'Neill said Ryan told him he would 'crush and destroy' him if he took a legal action against Ryanair. 'He told me I would be branded a litigious bastard.' He also claimed that Ryan said that the world was made up of 'fuckers and fuckees and in our relationship you are my fuckee'.

O'Neill took a legal action for wrongful dismissal against Ryanair, accusing the company of reducing the value of his seven per cent shareholding. He also accused Tony Ryan of conspiring to damage him and of controlling the Ryanair board and using his influence to prevent the board lodging a complaint with the EC Competition Commission about the alleged anti-competitive practices of Aer Lingus, all of which Ryan and the airline denied. O'Neill took a separate action against Aer Lingus chief executive David Kennedy and against Transport Analysis Incorporated.

The affidavits claimed that Tony Ryan had spoken to David Kennedy about the possibility of 'carving up' the routes between Ireland and the UK between the two Irish airlines. 'Aer Lingus was to focus on Manchester and Ryanair was to focus on Luton. There were also discussions about starting a joint venture company between Ryanair and Aer Lingus for what Tony Ryan described as "Mickey Mouse" routes.' O'Neill said he took this to mean the routes between Ireland and the UK where Ryanair had established a presence. David Kennedy recalled Tony Ryan initiating a discussion in 1988 about possible cooperation but this was never pursued.

The actions against Kennedy and Transport Analysis were dismissed by the High Court in their entirety. O'Neill appealed the outcome to the Supreme Court but lost. He sued Tony Ryan for breach of contract and Ryanair for wrongful dismissal and breach of contract. Those actions were settled and as part of the agreement O'Neill was to surrender his Ryanair shares. The value of his Ryanair shares remained a sticking point until Ryanair eventually offered to pay his legal costs if he relinquished the shares. He agreed.

O'Leary, who had succeeded O'Neill as Tony Ryan's personal assistant, has publicly acknowledged and paid tribute to Ryanair's first chief executive. 'When I first went to work for Tony, Ryanair was one of the family's largest investments and was run by a quite brilliant guy. Eugene O'Neill had gotten it off the ground, he had great marketing panache, great public relations skills. He gave the airline an awful lot of credibility at a time when the airline was very young and growing very quickly.'

But O'Leary believed Ryanair had lost its way and that its strategy was unclear. 'It had been set up originally to take on Aer Lingus and British Airways on the Dublin to London route and offer low fares but they kind of lost the plot a bit. They were opening up routes all over the place. They were taking on aircraft. There was nobody focusing on costs. I think there was an implicit understanding within the airline: "Look don't worry about the money, the Ryans will kind of pick it up." There was no malfeasance but there was an assumption that there were deep pockets there so they would get the quality right and never mind the costs.' By the time he left the company, O'Neill believed that Ryanair was only a minor enterprise for Tony Ryan and that he ultimately wanted to take over Aer Lingus.

Staff quickly realised that O'Leary was now controlling the purse strings, but few thought he had any designs on Eugene O'Neill's job. Ryan began to trawl his extensive contacts to find a 'safe pair of hands' to run Ryanair, and in 1988 he put Declan in charge in the interim. Ryan's second son was popular with the staff and worked closely with his old schoolfriend O'Leary. Everyone at Ryanair put in long hours as the airline lurched from one crisis to another and it began to take a huge physical toll on them.

The airline had large debts, particularly to Aer Rianta, which owned Dublin Airport, and was coming under increasing pressure to pay its dues. Late one evening, Declan Ryan and O'Leary were wearily sitting in the airline's offices when they heard a truck pull up outside. According to one source, they both believed it was someone from Aer Rianta coming to pull the plug on Ryanair.

The vehicle moved on and the moment passed. They have since told friends that had it been Aer Rianta they would probably have come out with their hands up.

They were both questioning the wisdom of throwing more and more money into Ryanair, particularly as they made fresh requests for cash from Tony Ryan. Every Saturday morning at 8.30 they met with the airline's financial backer at his County Tipperary home. One Saturday the two arrived in the midst of an extensive renovation of Ryan's office. A friend of Ryan's joked that the office looked a bit like a grotto and that a well had been dug into the floor. 'Ryan was known as a hard task-master and the early morning Saturday meetings at Kilboy House were usually fraught. They would probably have needed to change their underwear when they left.' At the end of this meeting someone bravely asked Ryan what the well was for. He replied, 'I am going to put some holy water into it next week for you two!'

Declan's tenure as chief executive in 1988 was short-lived as Ryan had identified a potential new chief executive: P. J. 'PJ' McGoldrick, a pilot who had run his own aircraft leasing and sales company in Stansted in Essex. McGoldrick had been deputy chairman and chief executive of Heavylift Cargo Airlines, was a member of the board of the Cunard Shipping Line and had received an award from the Air Corps for his achievements in aviation management. Originally from County Sligo, McGoldrick had spent most of his career in the UK, but he agreed to commute every week to Dublin to run Ryanair.

When he arrived he found an incredibly hard working but inexperienced staff. He showed up on his first day at 8.30 a.m. to find his staff were already there. 'The next day I showed up at 8 a.m. and over half of the staff were in,' he said in an interview. 'I figured I'd have to arrive at 7.30 if I wanted to beat them in.' He decided his immediate priority was to introduce some management controls. 'It appeared – and I don't mean to criticise anyone personally – that numerous people were making lots of financial decisions. But the accounts department hadn't expanded with all that activity and they were running months and months behind with information. To a great extent the company was flying blind, without the financial information needed to make intelligent decisions.'

It was a young company in every sense, he explained, and in need of direction. 'I initially saw myself coming in and turning things around. Ryanair had traditionally hired younger managers and even had a policy of not employing anyone over thirty. I was an ancient relic by those standards.'

His chief task was to tackle Ryanair's cost base. He drew up restructuring plans that called for job losses and pay cuts, and most importantly a realisation that it could no longer imitate Aer Lingus. Ryanair had started out as a low-cost, no-frills airline, but had never fully adhered to that model. It offered a business-class service and other expensive niceties such as a frequent-fliers programme while charging low fares. All the while the losses soared.

But it had achieved a significant landmark. Since its formation Ryanair had carried close to one million passengers and was intent on celebrating this milestone. McGoldrick saw an opportunity for some good publicity and decided to offer the lucky one-millionth passenger free flights for life. Twenty-one-year-old Jane O'Keeffe, a secretary from Dublin who was working in London, could hardly believe her luck. She heard the good news as she checked in for a flight back to London and was whisked away to meet McGoldrick, who was hosting a champagne reception. He explained that Ryanair wanted to offer her free flights for herself and a friend for life so long as she would step into the media spotlight to accept the prize. A press conference was arranged, a band played, champagne corks popped and McGoldrick swept O'Keeffe off her feet and held her in his arms in front of a Ryanair plane for the television cameras.

Back at Kilboy, however, the kitchen cabinet meetings were becoming more heated. By 1989 the Ryan family had put close to £20 million into Ryanair and the losses continued to swell. For many months the airline had agonised over whether it should focus on growing its business from Luton or from London's proposed new airport at Stansted in Essex. Poor infrastructure meant the commute from Luton into London was arduous, but the airline had also considered the fact that there was a bus service that linked Luton with Kilburn, the heartland of London's Irish community.

The airfield at Stansted had been a United States air force base created for the Marauder bomber squadron in 1942. It had been upgraded as a base for the air force's Strategic Air Command before it was abandoned, leaving a civil airport with one of the longest runways in Europe. In 1979 the British Airports Authority, the company that ran Heathrow and Gatwick Airports, designated it as a future third airport for London.

Its £300 million development was mired in controversy and it was 1986 before the new terminal building, dubbed 'East Anglia's white elephant', was officially opened. Stansted did not yet have a direct rail link into London and the journey from Kilburn to the airport was more cumbersome than that to Luton, but it was obvious that there was huge long-term potential for growth there.

Aer Lingus was the first Irish airline to fly into the airport; it had bought some slots there in 1988 to see how it might develop, and later began to operate some flights there. When Ryanair followed Aer Lingus into Stansted later that year, the latter's retaliation was swift and brutal. Aer Lingus began to slash its airfares on the route and scheduled its flights to leave shortly before Ryanair's. Aer Lingus had by now waged war on Ryanair on every front and was inflicting ever more lethal blows.

The airline was obliged to regularly brief the Department of Transport on its financial position and the picture it painted was getting worse and worse. Rumours about the airline's financial distress circulated around Dublin Airport, unnerving the staff who began to brace themselves for bad news. O'Leary believed the airline had no future. He told Ryan to close Ryanair and began to put the wheels in motion to wind the company up. The board of directors were to be asked to vote on a motion to shut Ryanair, with the loss of six hundred jobs, when they convened for their next general meeting in a couple of weeks time.

But Tony Ryan wasn't convinced that the airline should fail. He sought a meeting with the Minister for Transport, Seamus Brennan. 'I remember a delegation coming to see me,' said Brennan. 'Tony Ryan was in the group, and PJ McGoldrick. They told me Ryanair was going into liquidation and the company would be closed on the following Friday week. The losses were staggering.'

The Minister asked what it would take to save Ryanair. 'I remember at the time thinking that I couldn't give money to Ryanair because there were no funds. This was before the European Union said anything about state aid so I suppose legally the Government could have given them money but we didn't have it. If we had to give money to an airline it would have been to Aer Lingus because we owned it.' The Minister recalled the delegation explaining that Ryanair couldn't get into Heathrow because Aer Lingus had the slots, and that it was being hammered in Stansted. 'It had started flying to Stansted but Aer Lingus was destroying them. They said that if Aer Lingus continued with its massive assault Ryanair would be forced out of Stansted and would be left with Luton which was not profitable on its own.'

The Ryanair delegation had a proposal for him. They believed the airline could only survive if it was given exclusive rights to fly into Stansted. 'In short they told me if Ryanair got a clear run at Stansted for two or three years it would survive,' Brennan explained. 'If I allowed the Aer Lingus attack on them to continue at Stansted they said Ryanair would be crucified and would go out of business. I got the story pretty fast. I saw the significance of it. It would be wrong to say that Tony Ryan didn't convince me that Ryanair should get a crack at Stansted and be given a chance to survive. As the founder and head of Guinness Peat Aviation he would have come with a lot of credibility.' Ryan had also indicated to the Minister that he would invest more money in Ryanair if the Government backed its request. Brennan has a memory of a 'brash' young accountant attending some meetings. 'While everyone was being reasonable he suddenly started banging on the table. He didn't come into focus very clearly for me but I do remember Michael O'Leary being there and I do remember him being cheeky. In fairness I think he was the only one who called a spade a spade even then.'

After the delegation left, Brennan briefed the Department's senior civil servants on the impending closure of Ryanair and its proposed rescue remedy. 'I was advised to be very cautious. I was reminded that on one level, as the owner of Aer Lingus, I should be pleased that Ryanair was going bust, but I can't say for sure the officials advised against helping the airline.'

The Minister said he took wider advice on the sector but that one of the problems at the time was that Aer Lingus was the primary source for the Department in relation to aviation policy. He felt this structure had meant that Ryanair had been given a really tough time. 'The departmental view,' Brennan believed, 'was that Aer Lingus had to be protected. If Ryanair or a new airline wanted to open a new route they applied to the Department. I remember Ryanair's file going out to Aer Lingus to get an opinion on a proposed new route. The file would come back after a couple of weeks of super analysis with all sorts of charts and graphs. It would state that its professional assessment was that the route wasn't warranted as Aer Lingus was already covering it. Officials in the Department would then look at the file for a few days, add a few pages, and then concur with Aer Lingus' analysis and advise the Minister that the route should be turned down.

'That type of thing happened day in day out. I felt it was my job to develop aviation and not just to develop Aer Lingus. I remember one famous meeting in my office. I'm not sure whether it was with trade unions or the board of Aer Lingus but there was a bit of a screaming match. I remember telling them that I was not the Minister for Aer Lingus but the Minister for Transport and that that was an entirely different concept.'

The Minister had been convinced that Ireland should adopt a 'two airlines' policy. He decided to grant Tony Ryan's request to carve up the key routes out of Ireland between Aer Lingus and Ryanair. 'I bought the argument. It was a major turning point during my Ministry. I decided I would take routes from Aer Lingus and give them to Ryanair.'

The proposal was put on the agenda for the next meeting of the Cabinet. 'I went to the Cabinet and told them that assuming they weren't bluffing Ryanair was about to close.' At the meeting he pointed out that the collapse of Ryanair could end up costing the exchequer £18 million if alternative jobs were not found for its staff. He went on to explain that if Ryanair folded there was no possibility of another independent airline being established in Ireland for maybe another twenty or thirty years. He warned that Aer Lingus would fall back on its monopolistic ways, raise airfares and feel less driven to make profits for the state. He also reminded his colleagues that restoring Aer Lingus as the only Irish airline would have dire consequences for the regions. Ryanair's service into smaller airports such as Knock had for the first time brought air travel within easy reach of people living outside of Dublin.

Brennan's forceful argument for the new policy persuaded the Cabinet to back the plan, and in September 1989 the Minister announced it would be immediately implemented. 'I ordered Aer Lingus off the Stansted route and confined it to flying into Gatwick and Heathrow while Ryanair could fly to Stansted and Luton.' He also told Aer Lingus it had to surrender the Liverpool and Munich routes to Ryanair for three years. The national carrier was in turn given exclusive rights to fly to Manchester and Paris, while Ryanair received the rights to offer direct services from Irish regional airports to the UK and mainland Europe.

'When I announced it there was absolute war.' Fourteen years later the Minister, who has returned to that department, believes that if the Cabinet decision had been delayed for a month his proposal would probably have never been endorsed. It met with fierce opposition. 'I hit the Cabinet fairly early before a head of steam had built up. I don't think the Cabinet or myself realised how controversial it would be. I probably convinced them that it would be all right on the night. As we now know it was all right on the night, but I got a very rough ride.'

Aer Lingus was furious. It had invested in Stansted and bitterly resented being thrown off the route by the Government as part of a bail-out package for Ryanair. It said the decision would cost it £50 million as it would have to consider purchasing new planes to service the Dublin-Heathrow route. According to Brennan, Aer Lingus viewed his decision as an act of treason.

The trade unions were also seething. The Federation of Workers Union in Ireland, which represented three thousand workers at Aer Lingus and Aer Rianta, accused the Government of trying to prop up a private company that had failed to compete with a state company. The decision to favour Ryanair was 'a drastic blow to the workers who had facilitated Aer Lingus by agreeing to lower pay scales, increased productivity and changes in work practices', a spokesman raged.

The Minister was interviewed on RTE Radio's flagship programme, *Morning Ireland*, about the decision. He explained that he had held two meetings with what he described as Ryanair's 'major shareholders' but declined to say whether Tony Ryan had been at the meeting. Presenter Cathal MacCoille repeatedly asked if these concessions were being made to Ryanair because Tony

Ryan had given financial support to the Fianna Fail political party, the majority partner in the coalition government. The Minister said the question was 'most unfair', and later that day the Government, incensed by this line of questioning, demanded an apology. RTE's director-general, Vincent Finn, penned a written apology that afternoon. But it proved unsatisfactory and the following Tuesday morning, just after the eight o'clock news, the director-general broadcast a further apology: 'I very much regret that such a question was put to you which carried an implication for which no evidence was provided. The implication was that you, as Minister, could be influenced in any decision by anything other than the relevant issues ... An implication for which no evidence was provided.' The national broadcaster added that no disciplinary action was being considered against MacCoille.

Many media commentators were very surprised that RTE's highest-ranking official would apologise to the Government for having asked a question. *Irish Independent* columnist Conor Cruise O'Brien said that when he heard the famous interview he was quite startled. 'I had not heard any Fianna Fail Minister interviewed on RTE in such an undeferential manner since Charles Haughey became its leader ten years ago. Apparently Fianna Fail was startled too, and intervened to ensure the resumption of the oily flow of deference.

'I heard the question put and pressed and I heard Brennan trying to evade it and sounding pretty desperate about what was going on. It was clear that he didn't want to say "yes" and he couldn't say "no". "Don't know" would hardly do either as Brennan was Director of Elections in the General Election of last June.' Cruise O'Brien said he had formed the distinct impression that Tony Ryan had contributed to the Fianna Fail party fund [which after all is not a criminal offence]. 'If Ryan had not been a contributor it was in Brennan's power to close the whole issue with a simple "no".'

Tony Ryan did not comment on the allegations and the party's headquarters said it never commented on contributions to Fianna Fail. 'Any contributions sought and received are on a confidential basis and we never break that confidentiality,' a spokesman explained. Protestors picketed Brennan's home and constituency office in Dublin. 'The banners were outrageous,' the

Minister recalled. 'The suggestions that I was somehow beholden to Tony Ryan. It was disgraceful stuff. I had no connection in any way with him or his companies. I took the decision purely on national grounds because I believed there should be a second airline that should be supported and that we should give it a chance. I took the view that two airlines would mean more people travelling. I remember newspaper editorials asking what the hell was I at and describing this policy as national sabotage. It was pretty vicious. I don't claim any particular forward vision at the time except a gut feeling that competition was the way forward. Before Ryanair started flying it had cost up to £300 to fly from Dublin to London – in today's money that's about €600. There were no cheaper fares. People couldn't have done business faced with those costs. I knew it would be stupid to let an airline close. I just wanted Aer Lingus to move over a bit. It did save Ryanair and didn't damage Aer Lingus at that time.' Brennan's decision was in line with the first phase of the EC's policy of airline liberalisation.

Aer Rianta had kept a close eye on the manoeuvrings to save Ryanair from bankruptcy. It knew the directors were preparing to wind the company up within days and was preparing to put tugs behind its planes if necessary to collect its debt. Following the Minister's controversial decision to carve up the routes between the two Irish airlines, Aer Rianta gave the airline a break. Some sources suggest Ryanair owed more than £1 million in landing charges and other fees, but the debt was written off. The deals it had with Ryanair at Cork and Shannon were also renegotiated. The sources have also described how Aer Rianta began to provide duty-free products to Ryanair on very generous terms that effectively left the airport operator out of pocket. There are many people at Aer Rianta who remember the significant role it played in saving Ryanair during those dark days. Equally, they know that Ryanair will never acknowledge this.

Meanwhile, Ryanair announced that the Ryan family would invest a further £20 million in the airline to support its development. Part of the funds would also go to a Ryanair subsidiary for investment in tourism-related facilities in Ireland, to be spent in areas near regional airports such as Knock, Galway and Kerry. It also planned to re-engine its own jets and to replace other aircraft it had on lease. PJ McGoldrick said Ryanair was on track to make a small profit that year after a dramatic turnaround. He heaped fulsome praise on the Minister's decision and vehemently denied that any deal had been done with the Department. McGoldrick described the Minister as a 'man of action rather than words' and said that a 'two-airline policy' was a realistic one for Ireland.

Ryanair's reclusive financial backer also publicly praised the Government's broader airline policy. In an interview, Ryan said the new policy was very sensible. 'This policy works well in places like Canada and France. I think the future for Ryanair is for a limited niche airline operating out of Ireland primarily to London.' He also reiterated that he didn't have any beneficial interest in Ryanair. 'I don't own a single share in the company.'

Even with a helping hand from the Government, some staff at Ryanair, and even a few of the cabinet ministers who had backed its rescue request, believed that Ryanair's long-term future was not secure. The airline would still have to put its house in order. O'Leary was still most sceptical about Ryanair's future, believing it would never be successful and should be shut down. He was astonished that his mentor wanted to keep squandering money on it, telling Ryan, 'It will never make money. It will always lose money. It's an airline. Forget it.'

But Tony Ryan disregarded his views and remained doggedly determined to keep Ryanair in business. He told his assistant that instead of trying to close the airline he should apply his mind to drastically cutting costs at Ryanair. Ryan said that he was willing to provide generous financial incentives if O'Leary were to put his back into turning things around.

Those who have known O'Leary for many years have mentioned his incredible toughness, even when he was still quite young, and his lack of emotion in his business dealings. Ryan, who was said to have a 'mean streak' when it came to money, was also renowned for driving a hard bargain and would attach phenomenal targets to any financial incentives offered. The two men began to discuss just how much money O'Leary could expect to earn to make a success of Ryanair. The twenty-eight-year-old had been controlling the airline's finances for almost two years and had an intimate knowledge of the business. He told Ryan it would take some time to stem the losses.

'If I make £2 million will you give me ten per cent?' he inquired. Ryan agreed to these terms, hoping that O'Leary would stop Ryanair losing money. The young accountant then made a further demand: for 25 per cent of any profits above £2 million. Given the airline's staggering losses, Ryan has told friends that O'Leary was pushing at an open door, although many were amazed by what was agreed. They could only conclude that Ryan simply never believed O'Leary could make Ryanair that profitable. Today he would say it was the best deal he has ever done.

And so the terms were agreed in a new contract and O'Leary went in search of his fortune. 'I didn't particularly want a job in the company that I was recommending should be closed down,' O'Leary has said. 'Looking back now it was a very good arrangement from my point of view and from the Ryans' point of view.'

CHAPTER SIX

Cleared for Take-Off

'Ryanair was seen as a bit of a joke. British Airways was almost tittering at this pipsqueak airline flying into a tinpot airport in the middle of nowhere.' So says Terry Morgan, Stansted Airport's managing director, who met Tony Ryan and Michael O'Leary when they arrived in Essex to negotiate a deal for Ryanair.

BAA believed that the airport had huge potential and that its prospects were about to be greatly enhanced by new restrictions to be brought in at Heathrow to tackle the severe congestion there. It had decided to cap the traffic flow at Heathrow by restricting its use to airlines already operating there and forcing new traffic to fly into Gatwick or Stansted. But the plan met fierce opposition from the US airlines flying to Britain and was reversed. The volte-face was announced the day Stansted opened. It was a disaster for the new airport.

Morgan recounted how fifteen or twenty airlines that had signed up to fly there had immediately said they would be transferring to Heathrow. Suddenly the new airport had lost much of its custom. 'We had a dilemma. We needed to try to find airlines to fill up Stansted. I think Tony Ryan and his right-hand man, Michael O'Leary, saw two things. Firstly, that because of their ambitious plans Ryanair would quickly outgrow Luton, which didn't have that much room for expansion. They also saw that the great advantage of Stansted was that it had lots of room to expand, but also that it would have a direct rail link to London and, surprise, surprise, that they could negotiate a good deal here.'

While Ryanair was still a tiny cash-strapped airline Ryan and

O'Leary outlined their very ambitious growth plans to BAA and managed to negotiate very substantially discounted charges to fly into the Essex airport. 'If Ryanair failed it would have been a huge disappointment for the airline and Stansted but it wouldn't have made any difference to us,' Morgan said. 'It was a win-win for us to start working with Ryanair.'

Morgan refused to discuss the specifics of the deal that was first negotiated with the airline that is now Stansted's biggest customer but gave a flavour of the terms. 'I can't give you actual numbers but basically Ryanair was given and still has a deal where it is given a discount off the full tariff mainly related to the volume of traffic that it brings through. The general idea was that we wanted to encourage Ryanair to open up new routes and bring in additional traffic so the tariff was weighted favourably towards opening new routes. If it opened a new route, for the first year of its operation, Ryanair would get a heavily discounted price. As the route matured over time the price went up.' He said the tariffs charged were stepped up over four or five years. 'It has been renegotiated many times over the past fifteen years but the basic structure is more or less the same.'

Its rivals believe Stansted agreed to charge Ryanair £1 per passenger to use the airport, a fraction of the official £6 fee. 'We had an airline that was committed to growing its business, which was great for us. Ryanair had an airport that wasn't charging it too much and had loads of spare capacity. It recognised that it could carve out an empire for itself at the airport and that is what it has done, very successfully.' Stansted's management also got huge pleasure from the fact that Ryanair was such an irritation for British Airways, which had flatly told BAA that it would never fly to Stansted. 'The fact that we had Ryanair basically putting two fingers up to British Airways was an added bonus,' Morgan smiled. 'We gave them a bit of general encouragement because we would never be able to do that ourselves.'

Ryanair's greatest challenge was to make the new routes successful. The Irish government had cleared the pitch at Stansted for Ryanair for the next three years. The airline had negotiated cheap deals at the airports it was using and now turned its attention to acquiring new aircraft so it could carry more passengers to a wider range of destinations. It used jets and pilots leased from the Romanian state airline Tarom on the new routes into Stansted.

Ryanair staff remember these colourful and popular colleagues warmly, and enjoy recounting stories about them. They were very experienced pilots and generally had many more flying hours than the airline's other pilots, but their English tended to be patchy and sometimes their friendly greetings from the cockpit unintentionally unsettled passengers. 'They used to frighten the life out of the passengers by saying things like "Today, we go at Luton!" sounding like they were on a bombing mission,' one Ryanair member of staff laughed. When one flight encountered some technical difficulty forcing the pilot to suddenly abort a landing he attempted to reassure those on board by offering a helpful explanation for the aircraft's sudden ascent: 'The red light she go out. We try again.' Unsurprisingly, the Romanians' flight announcement duties were soon cancelled. This didn't go unnoticed. 'After a while,' remembered one insider, 'you would hear people on the flight saying, "It must be a Romanian pilot today, there was no announcement."'

O'Leary was busy cutting costs at Ryanair and decreed as part of his efforts to put the airline on a sound footing that everyone, including chief executive PJ McGoldrick, had to deal with him on all financial matters. 'This airline has to stand on its own two feet or fail,' McGoldrick told the media. 'The Ryan family has done enough. They've put a lot of money into this company and shouldn't be asked for any more. We should be prepared to tighten our belts and make it work – if we can't we don't really deserve for it to work.'

Its sixty-five pilots, who were the highest-paid employees, found themselves in the front line of the latest cost-cutting drive and fought bitterly with the airline's management for many months. The pilots were given a choice – they could agree to take a £6000 pay cut together with changes in their working conditions, or they could see some of their colleagues lose their jobs. McGoldrick told the pilots that twenty-five would be relocated from Dublin to other bases and that Ryanair would not pay any costs associated with their move. The pilots estimated the transfer could end up costing them up to £800 a month and were outraged. The airline was always hostile to trade unions but had to go to battle with the Irish Airline Pilots' Association (IALPA) which represented forty-eight of its pilots. The union claimed that Ryanair was already paying its pilots rates that were well below the average at other airlines. Senior pilots were earning around £30,000 while their most junior colleagues, the co-pilots flying on the turbo-prop planes, earned just £11,000. In comparison, senior Aer Lingus pilots were receiving salaries of as much as £60,000 a year. 'The pay cuts mean that some pilots will now be on salaries lower than the average industrial wage,' said IALPA president Ted Murphy.

The Romanian pilots had no affiliations with the airline pilots' union. They had been awarded work permits only after the Department of Labour had consulted with IALPA on whether these jobs could be filled by Irish citizens, a legal requirement when employing applicants from outside the European Community. But they got caught in the crossfire in this row over pay and conditions as their Irish colleagues suddenly began to object to the renewal of their work permits. McGoldrick viewed their presence as crucial to the airline's operations and at one point Ryanair threatened to dismiss the pilots waging most resistance to the Romanians. A settlement was eventually accepted, with the pilots agreeing to the controversial new pay arrangements and conditions at a time when Ryanair was in dire financial straits. 'A gun was put to our heads,' one pilot wearily explained at the time. 'It was a case of take it or leave it.'

McGoldrick tried to play down the depth of hostility between the airline and its essential crew members, pointing the finger of blame at IALPA for stirring up much of the unrest. 'Certainly some of the pilots are unhappy but I think the majority of them would not have any interest in pulling the plug on Ryanair.' He suggested the dispute had more to do with IALPA wanting to prevent Ryanair-type pay reforms spreading to Aer Lingus. He believed the union would prefer to see Ryanair close down rather than see its pay regime adopted by the national carrier. 'There is no question that Aer Lingus has used the fact that Ryanair has certain working-condition arrangements as pressure on their own staff to get better terms from them. We are a threat to the working conditions of pilots in Aer Lingus and that is where IALPA's interests lie.'

McGoldrick has said he believed that Ryanair would never have succeeded in implementing the cost-cutting measures over the years if its workforce had been unionised. 'In the UK, where I worked most of my life, the idea of an independent airline was very clear in people's minds. I was never in a union in my life and neither were the people I worked with. Here some people believe that an independent airline is expected to have the same salary structures and conditions as state airlines.' At that time Ryanair had 450 employees and eight aircraft. They had been given a shareholding in the company and had agreed not to join a trade union on the grounds that they would have a measure of influence on how the company was run. A number of brief work stoppages had been staged in the early years at various flash points but had been quickly dealt with. At the same time there were thousands of people who wanted to work for Ryanair. When it advertised to hire fifty cabin crew it received more than six thousand applications from young Irish people. It was viewed as a young and vibrant company in an exciting industry at a time when there was huge unemployment in Ireland. 'The type of person who joined Aer Lingus was different from those who joined Ryanair,' one former employee remarked.

Many staff were rapidly promoted to more senior and supervisory roles at the young airline, something much less common at Aer Lingus. 'If you were any way good at the job you would quickly move up through the ranks,' one explained. McGoldrick liked to highlight the potential for swift career progression at Ryanair. 'We have pilots here flying jets who four years ago were flying turbo-props. We have others who were in operations and became pilots because they had the opportunity within the company. We also have managers who if they were with Aer Lingus would still be in clerical jobs.'

Most people at Ryanair in those years say the place was constantly in crisis. No sooner had the very public wrangling with the pilots ceased than the airline was back in the news again after one of its jets, carrying forty-two passengers, missed the runway at Cork Airport and ploughed into a grassy field before eventually touching down on tarmac. The flight from Luton landed safely thirty yards short of the runway and no one was injured. The airline claimed none of the passengers was aware that it was not a normal landing. 'At no stage was anybody in danger and there was no damage to the aircraft,' a spokesman said. 'The incident became apparent only when mud was discovered on the fuselage.' Ryanair suspended the Romanian pilot and co-pilot pending a full investigation. The airline said the pilot had 10,000 flying hours' experience and 4000 hours in charge of an aircraft and had recently undergone a simulator check organised by the Department of Transport. A spokesman expressed total confidence in these pilots and the aircraft that they were flying.

Fifteen years later, Michael O'Leary would say that Ryanair was much more exposed to a crash when it was using the Romanian planes than at any other time in its history. He admitted that such a disaster at that time would have closed Ryanair. Some who worked at the airline at that time believe O'Leary's comments were unfair. A number, including some who left the airline in less than happy circumstances, stressed that, whatever else was going on at the fledgling carrier, safety was never compromised.

Ryanair's low fares were attracting lots of new customers and the airline had now carried more than two million people between Ireland and the UK. Some of them learned that there was an element of keeping their fingers crossed that things would run smoothly when travelling Ryanair. One man recalled being on a flight into Luton when the emergency exit door fell into a passenger's lap as the plane touched down on the runway. 'What do I do with this?' he yelled. The cabin crew shouted: 'Just shove it back.' A Stansted-bound flight from Galway lost a wheel shortly after take-off and had to make an emergency landing at Dublin. The airport put the emergency services on stand-by and the roads around the airport were closed as the aircraft, carrying forty-five passengers and four crew, circled to burn off fuel before touching down. The young pilot won much praise for having landed the distressed plane safely.

The airline was known to cancel flights if the loads were low and force passengers to wait for later flights. It even diverted flights to other Irish airports to pick up passengers en route to London. Flights into the County Mayo airport could be hampered by fog and passengers would end up in Dublin or Shannon, many miles from their destination. Ryanair staff had to cope with an often frenetic atmosphere and constant demands from the airline's management and customers.

Ryanair had little time for dealing with passenger complaints and simply handed out the number of its public relations company, Wilson Hartnell PR, as a point of contact for them. Brian Bell, the executive who worked on the account, remembers the large number of phone calls they received. 'We got lots of calls from customers whose baggage had been lost, people in wheelchairs who had problems with the airline. I have never known a company to attract so many crises.' Sometimes the volume of calls to WHPR's offices would be so great that they would tie up the switchboard for hours. Frustrated passengers then began to call into radio shows to broadcast their Ryanair horror stories.

O'Leary was making his presence felt at the airline more and more. The staff began to notice his frequent rows with the senior executives and his increasing interest in all aspects of the business. He was also kept busy managing Tony Ryan's other investments. In 1988 Ryan stunned everyone when he spent £35 million to acquire five per cent of Ireland's second biggest bank, Bank of Ireland. The sheer chutzpah of buying that much stock was breathtaking and left everyone, including the bank's directors, wondering whether he was going to launch a takeover bid. Ryan took a seat on the board and O'Leary did much of the behind-the-scenes management of that massive investment, working as a 'fixer' who followed Ryan's endless instructions.

PR executive Brian Bell, who also acted for GPA and the Ryan family, remembers his early encounters with O'Leary. 'He would ring up and say that Tony had a friend in town and could I see if *The Irish Times* might do an interview with him? He was funny and straight to the point.' When Bell began to work with Ryanair, he quickly realised that O'Leary was a powerful force at the airline. 'I walked into their headquarters in College House on Nassau Street in Dublin and met Anne O'Callaghan, who headed Ryanair's media-relations activities, coming out of the office. I said hello and presumed I would be working with her and the marketing people.' She greeted Bell with the words, 'You have just replaced all of us.' That morning O'Leary had made the entire marketing team redundant.

O'Leary had begun to turn up everywhere in Ryanair. He

would throw bags in with the baggage-handlers and work on the check-in desk. He had also made it clear to everyone at Ryanair that he believed customers who were paying cheap air fares had no right to complain when things went wrong. This policy made many of his colleagues uncomfortable but O'Leary was such a domineering figure that few would directly challenge him.

He was said to be a menacing presence at meetings. 'It was like having a Doberman in the room,' one source recalled. 'There were horrendous screaming matches where he would bawl out staff in front of their colleagues. He would tell them they were fuck-all use to him. Within seconds he could turn around and be perfectly charming to a visitor, welcoming them and offering them a cup of coffee.'

Many of the original start-up team had begun to leave, amongst them Christy Ryan, who left following a dispute about his claim to a shareholding in the airline. Some departed after blazing rows with O'Leary. Others said they read the signs and planned their own exit before they were forced to leave. 'I felt the company operated with a US style of management. The idea was to recruit a vibrant start-up team, burn them out, then get rid of them and put in a fresh team,' one former staff member suggested, and others agreed.

O'Leary began to attend the weekly meetings to discuss marketing and public relations and always made a strong contribution. When the company wanted to make an announcement it was McGoldrick or Declan Ryan who would contact Bell. But O'Leary controlled much of what went on at Ryanair. Bell had to talk to O'Leary directly about whether certain journalists should get free flights with Ryanair, a practice that was common amongst airlines as part of their efforts to foster good relations with the media. Bell remembered bringing O'Leary a request from the *Sunday Independent*'s notorious gossip columnist, Terry Keane, who wanted to travel to London to join an onward flight from Heathrow. 'Ryanair flew her free to Stansted and even paid for a taxi to bring her to Heathrow and she thanked us,' said Bell. So O'Leary was apoplectic some weeks later to read a rather bitchy piece by Keane castigating Ryanair for riding roughshod over its pilots. 'He couldn't believe that someone who had been treated so well by the airline could turn around and pen something like that. He wanted the newspaper to apologise.' Bell passed on his client's views to the *Sunday Independent*, and shortly afterwards the 'Keane Edge' column carried a gushing piece about Ireland's newest airline. 'O'Leary was shocked that he could have this impact on journalists,' Bell explained. 'He loathed them. He had nothing but contempt for journalists. His attitude was that they were an evil that had to be turned against itself and used in a certain way.'

Ryanair desperately wanted to generate some positive news, so in March 1991 it rounded up the media to travel to its new UK base at Stansted. O'Leary, who checked the names of those travelling, was incensed that RTE had not sent one of its reporters to cover the story. 'He believed RTE was very much against Ryanair,' one source said. 'He felt it was a case of one semi-state organisation favouring another, namely Aer Lingus.'

Captain Cathal Ryan, the debonair pilot known within Ryanair as 'Captain Gucci' for his dapper appearance, led the charm offensive. Colleagues found Ryan's eldest son arrogant. 'Cathal had the traits of a typical rich kid,' one source complained. One story goes that when a member of the cabin crew was making final checks just ahead of a flight she noticed that the captain's name was missing from the paperwork. She went into the cockpit and asked for his name. Cathal Ryan said, 'It's on the side of the aircraft,' to which the hostess replied, 'So you're the Spirit of Ireland?' He is also remembered for his handling of an incident in the early years when Aer Rianta blocked a Ryanair plane that was due to depart from Dublin airport as part of its efforts to make the airline pay its fuel bill. Ryan is said to have settled the debt with his gold credit card.

Cathal Ryan greeted the twenty-five or so journalists who travelled to Stansted on his family's airline and attempted to repair the airline's battered image. Ryan suggested that the negative publicity it was attracting simply marked the end of 'the period of euphoria' following its establishment in 1986. Drastic cost cutting had been necessary to 'recondition' the airline, he said. 'People realised that the cutbacks were necessary and they have seen the actual results of these changes. We hit our budget for the first four months of 1991. That's a first. And don't forget that 1991 has been the year that the wheels have come off most airlines due to the Gulf crisis. Because we took dramatic action at the tail-end of 1990 we've been able to save the rest of the jobs in the company and can stay ahead of our budget. We may not make an overall profit in 1991 but the loss will be very small and sustainable.'

Ryanair had by now lost £22 million but Cathal Ryan insisted his family was neither upset nor worried about this. 'I want to put the record straight. This is not a loss, it is an investment in the future.' The money involved in developing Ryanair 'would not buy you a new 737–400 series jet', he said, and he expressed optimism that, despite the difficulties being experienced by airlines across the globe, Ryanair's fortunes were improving.

The aviation sector's difficulties began with the spike in oil prices which came at a time when world's major economies, especially the US and Britain, were ailing. The most significant blow was dealt in August 1990 when Iraq invaded Kuwait, heightening tensions in the Gulf region and leading to the first Gulf War in January 1991. Bob Crandall, chairman of AMR, the parent company of American Airlines, calculated that altogether the world's airlines had lost more money following the Gulf War than they managed to make since 1945. Of the world's twenty largest airlines, only British Airways, Cathay, SIA (Singapore Airlines) and Swissair made a profit in each year between 1991 and 1993, with the US airlines suffering most. Passenger numbers were down in every part of the world. Airlines were increasingly closing routes and job losses mounted. In Europe, the flag carriers all turned to the national governments for huge financial subsidies to ensure their survival. Air France received $300 million, Iberia $350 million, Alitalia $400 million and Sabena $1 billion. In Ireland, Ryanair's arch-rival Aer Lingus was also feeling the pain and was extensively restructured in a way that would allow it to qualify for a rescue payment from the Irish government. As the flight headed towards Stansted, Cathal Ryan reminded the media that Ryanair was entirely reliant on private capital and didn't want a penny from the exchequer.

PJ McGoldrick believed that Ryanair had to offer all the ingredients that other airlines offered if it was to survive. Its low and unrestricted fares were easily targeted and beaten by competitors who could play around with multiple tariffs in a bid to put Ryanair out of business. So he introduced a business-class fare, offering its customers more modest frills than those offered by Aer Lingus. 'Our business class is not full of frills, it's just … nice. My reading of Ryanair has always been that it is the airline that gives you a good deal. We aren't going to spend lavish amounts on food. When I travel I want a comfortable seat, a newspaper, a Continental-type breakfast, hot coffee and space to work. And that's what we're offering the businessman. If you want a full breakfast, go to a restaurant.'

McGoldrick was preparing to leave Ryanair. As he departed at the end of 1991, he said the airline was on the threshold of a 'dramatic turnaround' and that despite the trauma endured by Ryanair staff morale was very high. 'I always believed that Stansted would become London airport and that if we got in there early we could get some good slots and facilities.' In the longer term he believed Ryanair would need to have more alliances with other airlines. It had already forged a marketing alliance with Air UK at Stansted to interline traffic and had hoped to extend this to American Airlines. McGoldrick explained that he had never expected to stay long at Ryanair. 'To be honest I don't think I expected to be here as long as I have been,' he said. 'I initially saw myself coming in and turning things around.'

And so another chief executive departed. Once more the kitchen cabinet was convened at Kilboy House and Ryan trawled his expansive list of contacts and potential recruits for inspiration. Ryan asked O'Leary to step into the breach but he refused. Ryan was exasperated with him, telling friends and advisers that he simply 'couldn't get the bugger to do it'. O'Leary explained later that the reason why he wouldn't take the job was because he wouldn't be able to keep Ryan 'out of his hair'.

By now the Ryan family's priorities for Ryanair had altered. Tony Ryan wanted to find a partner to buy into Ryanair to realise some return on their investment. He also had a task in mind for his hard-working assistant. Ryan had closely monitored the success of America's low-cost pioneer, Southwest Airlines, and admired its founder, the legendary Irish American Herb Kelleher, whom he knew personally. He decided it was time to try to learn from Southwest's success and rang its founder. Kelleher remembered the conversation. 'I had known Tony Ryan for some time through GPA. We had never done business with them but I had met Tony through that connection and got to know him fairly well and to like him a lot. He called me and asked me in essence whether I would be willing to sit down and talk to Michael. So I said, "Yes, I would be delighted."'

CHAPTER SEVEN

Herb

A huge crowd had gathered at the Sportatorium, a run-down wrestling ring in Texas, in March 1992. But the event they had come to watch, grandly titled 'Malice in Dallas', was not a bout between hardened professional combatants but an arm-wrestling contest between Southwest Airlines and Stevens Aviation, staged to decide the rights to an advertising slogan.

Stevens, an aviation sales and maintenance company in Greenville, South Carolina, had been using 'Plane Smart' as its slogan for almost a year before Southwest Airlines started trumpeting itself as 'Just Plane Smart'. Stevens Aviation chairman Kurt 'Kurtsey' Herwald decided that a one-on-one arm-wrestling tournament would settle the matter. The winner of two out of three rounds would get the rights to use the slogan, and the loser would donate $5000 to charity. It had been billed as the contest of the decade.

Cheerleaders roused the fans as 'Smokin' Herb Kelleher, then sixty-one, with his right arm in a sling and a cigarette dangling from his lips, strutted to the ring to square up to Herwald. Kelleher's handlers brought a stock of miniature bottles of Wild Turkey bourbon to administer at regular intervals to their champion. The airline chief had allowed a camera crew to record his pre-match training regime, which involved hours of puffing several cigarettes at a time while lifting bottles of his favourite bourbon in the air.

The contenders each won one of the first two rounds. In the final round Kelleher and Herwald's hands gripped, but within ten seconds Stevens Aviation emerged victorious. Kelleher blamed his defeat on a hairline fracture in his wrist, a cold, a stubborn case of athlete's foot and having accidentally over-trained by walking up a flight of stairs. Amid allegations of a fix, Herwald graciously decided to let Southwest continue to use the 'Just Plane Smart' slogan. As Kelleher was carried out of the ring on a stretcher drinking Wild Turkey, he was asked if the whole contest had been a publicity stunt. Seemingly astonished at the question, Kelleher replied, 'Why, I never thought about it in those terms!'

The outrageous, brilliant and ruthlessly competitive founder of Southwest Airlines, known as 'America's funniest flyboy', is regarded as the architect of the most successful business model for low-cost airlines. It is claimed that Southwest Airlines was conceived over drinks at the St Anthony's Club in San Antonio, Texas in 1966. Kelleher, who was practising as a lawyer there, and a client, Rollin King, a Harvard graduate with a pilot's licence, discussed the notion of launching a low-fares airline. By the end of the night the two had sketched a simple route system linking Houston, Dallas and San Antonio on the back of a cocktail napkin. It was an awesome task and one that they both knew would mean all-out commercial war, as the incumbent airlines, Braniff, Texas International and Continental, would do everything to prevent the fledgling carrier from taking off.

And they did. The budding airline chiefs were forced to contest years of bitter court battles before they got airborne. The *Texas Transportation Report* chronicled the skirmishes and told its readers they should grab a ringside seat: 'Don't bother spending your money on a movie or going to see a play or attending a concert. Just come over and watch Herb Kelleher and the lawyers for Braniff and Texas International cut each other into little bits and pieces.'

Kelleher has often recounted his first major victory in the Texas Supreme Court. 'I stayed up all night trying to prepare the case. I wrote my brief and then got a motel room to try to catch a few hours of sleep before going to court. The motel was beside a highway and so noisy that I finally went into the bathroom for some quiet and lay down on the floor. I woke up several hours later and I was completely covered with marks from the tile – you know, I had little squares all over my face. I went into court that way. But then something extraordinary happened. Right after the arguments, the lawyers on the other side came up to me and said, "We're calling our clients and telling them you've won." And sure enough, we had.' Kelleher phoned Lamar Muse, the airline veteran hired as Southwest Airlines' chief executive, to tell him to go ahead with its scheduled inaugural flight no matter what. 'We're going come hell or high water.'

Southwest Airlines took to the skies on 18 June 1971. It had three planes to carry passengers between Dallas, Houston and San Antonio for an incredible fare of $20. Pausing regularly to light a fresh cigarette, Kelleher explained the airline's simple philosophy. 'If you get your passengers to their destinations when they want to get there, on time, at the lowest possible fares, and make darn sure they have a good time doing it, people will fly your airline.' Southwest had made it as cheap to fly as to take the bus to these cities and it attracted passengers immediately. Its competitors met the challenge head on by slashing fares, and a fierce price war ensued. Braniff started offering flights from Houston to Dallas for $13, deliberately undercutting its new competitor in the hope of putting it out of business.

Muse plotted Southwest's retaliation. He came to national media attention by appearing in a newspaper advertisement declaring, 'Nobody's going to shoot Southwest Airlines out of the sky for a lousy $13.' He also announced a promotional offer for Southwest customers – they could fly with Southwest for a fare of $13 or for $26 they could also get a free bottle of Chivas Regal scotch, Crown Royal Canadian whiskey or Smirnoff. Non-drinkers could claim a leather ice bucket. The offer proved very popular – indeed, the take-up was such that Southwest became one of the largest liquor distributors in Texas for a couple of months. Its competitors also waged war on the ground. One battle between Southwest and Braniff became so fierce that Houston's airport authority threatened to throw both airlines out if they didn't call a truce.

'We weren't the Prom Queen for a long time,' Kelleher explained humorously, in a rare interview exclusively for this book. 'The incumbent airlines picked on us so assiduously when we went into business that I think they helped make us successful, because they made it apparent to everybody that we were the underdogs. And what were we trying to bring to the people of

Texas?' he asked incredulously. 'Oh, just lower fares and better service. They picked on us so openly and they were so hostile that their attitudes became part of our public relations campaigns. I would say it probably took fifteen or twenty years before we were not only accepted, grudgingly, but welcomed and sought after.' Kelleher likes to think of Southwest as the 'bar room brawler' of the American aviation industry that set people free to fly.

'Everybody referred to us as the mavericks,' he said. 'When you start out you have to break your way through. People don't just open the door for you and say, "Oh I'd be so pleased to give you my gates" or "I'd be so pleased to have you here." You have to be a bit brash.' But he has always loved a good fight, something he suggests may be partly due to his Irish genes. Both sets of his grandparents immigrated to the United States from the County Cork town of Macroom. 'I have been told there are a lot of businesses there called Kelleher,' he said. 'Also that there were about thirteen bars there for four hundred inhabitants – so that sounded like a likely place for my ancestors to be from.'

Kelleher gradually became more involved in the day-to-day running of Southwest and finally relinquished his law practice to become its chief executive in 1982. By this time Southwest Airlines had twenty-seven planes flying to fourteen cities. It had been steadily making profits and employed 2100 staff who all had a shareholding in the airline. He has modestly said that 'what little' he knows about the airline business was learned from watching Lamar Muse in action. Muse was acknowledged as having been the driving force that ensured that its aircraft ran on time and led its early expansion into out-of-the-way airports. He left some years later following a disagreement with some of the board members and went on to found Muse Air with his son Michael. The airline, which was also based in Dallas, became known as 'Revenge Air' and was eventually bought out by Southwest.

'I really never had any aspirations to be at Southwest Airlines full time but then the board kind of insisted on it,' Kelleher said. 'Then it lasted for twenty-five years, so I guess it's not over yet. When we started our whole approach was that we were going to provide a better service for a lesser fare. We were going to give you better on-time performance than you have ever had. We were going to give you better whiskey that you have ever drunk on an airplane. We were going to expedite your passage through the airport terminal to shorten your total trip time. We were going to give you the most welcoming, warm, delightful people that you have ever seen flying an airline.' Southwest operated on the basis that a competitor with a high cost base couldn't match its low fares and make money. 'Then we said to ourselves, suppose we encounter a carrier that has low costs but lousy service? We beat them on service.'

Southwest was the first airline to brand itself as *the* low-fares airline, and designed a business model that would allow it to provide scheduled flights at a very low cost. It specialised in flying short routes, typically about 400 miles or one hour apart, with great frequency. Passengers could fly with Southwest from one city to another only. They could not book an onward connection to another destination either on another Southwest flight or on another airline. And the airline ferried them to secondary airports that were close to their destinations but cheaper and less congested than those used by the larger airlines. The airline industry had traditionally catered for such short routes by carrying passengers from smaller outlying locations into a hub where they could make onward connections. It was an efficient way to fill a plane but Southwest showed that it was not the most cost-effective way to use an aircraft fleet, because it meant that planes were left sitting on the tarmac for lengthy periods waiting for feeder connections to arrive and for passengers' baggage to be transferred and loaded.

Southwest realised that its aircraft would only make money when they were in the air and that the key to its survival was to squeeze as many flights out of each of its planes every day. Southwest pioneered the twenty-five-minute turn-around. Within that time passengers and their luggage would be unloaded and loaded and the plane would be ready to push back from the gate and head towards the runway. The system's efficiency was assisted by the fact that there were no demarcations between its various staff members and everyone from the pilots to those working on the ground worked as a team to achieve their objective. The airline also only used a single type of aircraft, the Boeing 737, something that facilitated swift servicing and kept crew training costs down.

On board, it offered a simple service. Passengers could only travel economy class and they had no assigned seats, instead selecting their own as they boarded. During the flight they were offered drinks and peanuts rather than meals and were entertained by the cabin crew's zany antics. The airline was based at the run-down Love Field airport close to downtown Dallas and used the concept of love, and everything it might imply, as a marketing theme to endear itself to customers. In the early years the female flight attendants – most of whom had joined the airline after responding to the airline's advertisement for 'Raquel Welch look-alikes' – wore orange hotpants, clinging tops, white belts and white vinyl knee-high boots. They would shortly appear on television in an advertisement, shot from behind and below, that showed them climbing the steps onto an aircraft. Southwest's controversial marketing strategy certainly caught the public's attention and passenger numbers quickly rose.

Everything about the airline was different. As passengers settled into their seats, one of the crew, known as customer service agents, might suddenly jump out of an overhead locker. Safety announcements were frequently enhanced with remarks like, 'There may be fifty ways to leave your lover, but there are only six ways to leave this aircraft.' Airborne passengers might be asked to join in a contest to find who had the most holes in their socks, while one flight attendant offered a $25 Southwest Airlines voucher to anyone carrying a picture of their mother-in-law in their wallet. When a bird flew into an engine, delaying its take-off, the crew divided the two sides of the aircraft into teams and asked them to race each other at passing a roll of toilet paper from the front to the back of the plane, unfurling the paper without tearing it. To explain a delay, one attendant told passengers, 'The machine that beats up your luggage is broken, so we are having to beat them up by hand.' Kelleher will also participate in the in-flight entertainment. On a flight to Houston he got on the microphone and asked passengers to give a round of applause for someone at the front of the plane who was ninety-eight years old that day. 'On your way out, make sure you stop and say "Happy birthday" to the captain,' he guffawed.

For all of the fun and frolics, Southwest has been profitable for twenty-six straight years – even during the recession of the early 1990s that claimed many of its competitors. The airline trades on the New York Stock Exchange and is worth more than $11 billion. It uses 'Luv' as its stock exchange symbol to represent its home base at Love Field, and it also embraced love as a theme for its employee and customer relationships. It is unique in the airline industry for never having laid off staff and historically has had a low level of customer complaints. Its core philosophy is that Southwest Airlines offers the lowest air fares and the highest standard of service.

'No competitor can ever attack us and say, "We are going up against Southwest Airlines because its service is poor,"' Kelleher said. 'Ever since they have kept statistics at the Department of Transportation in the United States, Southwest Airlines has had the fewest complaints per one hundred thousand passengers carried since the very beginning. Now that is an indication of customer satisfaction.'

This formula transformed the small regional airline into the fourth largest domestic US carrier, with 400 Boeing 737 aircraft carrying 64 million passengers a year to 58 cities. It operates 2700 flights every day, has never had a fatal accident, and has the lowest operating cost structure of any US airline.

It grew by targeting cities that were under-served by airlines and where customers were forced to pay high prices to fly. When opening any new route it put on a range of frequent flights at fares typically about one-third or half the price charged by the other carriers to generate large numbers of customers quickly. Initially it had to spend time convincing customers that these were regular fares and not an introductory offer. As it became more successful the airline muscled in on routes dominated by the big carriers, and it braced itself for retaliation. Shortly after United Airlines announced the launch of its low-fares shuttle to compete directly with Southwest, Kelleher sounded a call to arms to all employees in a letter entitled 'Commencement of hostilities'. Staff were photographed in full combat gear and with artillery as they enthusiastically waged war on their new adversary. Southwest advertised its low fares through provocative advertising and Kelleher would act the clown or make outrageous comments to court publicity.

Consultants and academics have spent years studying South-west to discover the secret of its success. In *Hard Landing* (1995), Thomas Petzinger said that no one has ever come up with a better explanation than Robert Baker, the principal operating aide to American Airlines chief Bob Crandall. He concluded that Southwest ran 'on Herb Kelleher's bullshit'.

Howard Putnam, a former Southwest chief executive, told *Fortune* magazine about a meeting with analysts on Wall Street who were highly sceptical about the airline's policy of giving free drinks to passengers. 'We were doing everything differently at Southwest, and analysts were of the mentality that if you don't do it the same way as American and United, it's probably not going to work. This guy was giving me a rough time about giving away the drinks. Finally he said, "How long does it take to fly from Dallas to Houston?" I said, "One hour." He said, "How many free drinks could I get on a flight from Dallas to Houston in an hour?" I said, "Well, the record is seven Jack Daniel's and water, and it's held by the chairman here, Herb." And Herb said, "Seven? I thought I had eight!" He and I used to sit in the back row, he on one aisle and me on the other aisle. He'd just hand his cup around to the galley, and the flight attendant would just put a little more in it. He's pretty funny. For a lawyer.'

Southwest's employees treat him like a cult leader or a pop star rather than a captain of industry. The pilots bought him a Harley Davidson bike and wore T-shirts that said 'Herb's Hogs'. Southwest's dispatchers once stole his car and installed neon running lights on the bottom. When he pulled up to a black-tie event, his car was the only one that had a purple glow. The airline has also issued notices to all employees asking them to 'join together to celebrate Herb's favourite holiday: the repeal of Prohibition'. Kelleher loves the way the employees made fun of him.

It's a company where people work hard and play hard. The sense of fun that permeates the organisation peaks at Halloween when Southwest shuts down its corporate office for the day for a huge party. Each department is given a large budget to create a theme and months of planning go into the occasion. Kelleher has dressed as Roy Orbison, Elvis, a sheik, a medieval knight and a teapot. He still smokes heavily and is famous for drinking into the night. He gives up alcohol for thirty days each year to give his liver an opportunity to recover. 'You know, livers can do that, they can reconstitute themselves,' he has explained. 'A liver is like a salamander's tail – it can grow back.'

In speeches, he'll make fun of himself for having a low IQ and then launch into a sophisticated critique of federal tax law. He once compared Chapter 11 bankruptcy laws to syphilis. He is said to have a patchy memory. He will recall the names of employees he hasn't seen in years, but often forgets where he parked his car. He reads military history and Wordsworth and loves the Blues Brothers.

The airline invests a lot of time in finding the right staff, who have to be touchy-feely extroverts. In fact, it looks for 'mini-Herbs'. It has developed a personality test to rate candidates on a scale of one to five on seven traits: cheerfulness, optimism, decision-making, team spirit, communication, self-confidence and self-starter skills. Prospective employees must achieve a score of more than three to progress to the airline's rigorous people-skills courses at its University for People, in Dallas. This test is used to recruit everyone from pilots to maintenance staff and it is not unusual to interview up to fifty people for one job. In 2002 Southwest received almost 250,000 job applications for over 5000 new posts. It has been included in *Fortune* list of the '100 Best Companies to Work For in America' for three successive years and has one of the lowest rates of staff attrition in the industry. Every Southwest employee's pay cheque says 'from our customers' to remind them where the money comes from. In Southwest employee manuals, the word Customer is always capitalised.

Analysts who have closely studied the Southwest Airlines business model believe that it involves more than pursuing a particular market strategy for its product. In *The Southwest Airlines Way* (2003), Jody Hoffer Gittell, an assistant professor of management at Brandeis University and faculty member of the MIT Global Airline Industry programme, suggested that the kernel of its success is its ability to nurture and sustain strong relationships. 'For Southwest's leaders, taking care of business literally means taking care of relationships. They see these relationships – with their employees, among their employees, and with outside parties – as the foundation of competitive advantage, through good times and bad. They see the quality of these relationships not as a success factor, but as the most essential success factor.

They believe that to develop the company, they must constantly invest in these relationships.'

Kelleher said it has taken a long time to forge strong relationships with airports and officialdom after many years of open warfare with them. 'When people want you all of a sudden it becomes easy to reconcile. They say, "I want you, I adore you." You say, "Fine, I accept that." You can start off with a pretty good common ground for restoring the relationship. Now of course it depends on the individuals involved, the jurisdictions involved. I do understand that, but when people decide they need you it makes it much easier to repair relationships.' Kelleher emphasised that the airline tries to cultivate good relationships with everyone. 'Whether it is airport architects, transportation security administration, whether it is our vendors, we try to cultivate a very good relationship with them and a warm and supportive relationship with them. We don't treat them as adversaries. We say that we are in this boat together.'

Many people have the impression that Southwest's business model is strengthened by the fact that its employees are not unionised. In fact, Southwest Airlines is the most unionised airline in the United States. Several traditional unions represent its employees, including the Transport Workers' Union, the International Association of Machinists and the International Brotherhood of Teamsters, as well as the Southwest Airlines Pilots' Association. 'We are the most heavily unionised airline in the United States and historically have been,' said Kelleher. 'We felt that on some occasions our people were insecure without somebody representing them so in some cases we suggested that they go out and get a union or form one so that they would feel more secure about their job security, their grievances and that sort of thing. There was no reason for them to feel insecure, but in the absence of a trade union it was kind of like when you live in a town where they don't have a doctor. You may never see him, but it gives you a sense of security that there is one there and a sense of insecurity if there isn't.'

The airline has had few labour disputes over the years relative to its competitors. There was a six-day strike with the mechanics in 1980 and Kelleher and his team have signalled that they would be willing to risk another if they believed it was necessary to maintain Southwest's basic commitments. Colleen Barrett told Hoffer Gittell that while Southwest is loving it is also very realistic and very pragmatic. 'We treat people with respect. But we would take a strike if it got down to it – if the demands would hurt all employees. Especially if we simply couldn't concede without hurting all employees by the decision.'

Southwest Airlines staff enjoy a high level of job security and are also well paid. "We are very close to our people,' Kelleher emphasised. 'We have never had a furlough [lay-offs]. We now have eight union contracts where the employees have taken stock options as part of their pay. If you look at compensation as a whole our people are probably the highest paid in the whole American airlines industry. They have taken a risk that compensation, through profit sharing and stock options, is contingent upon the company doing well, which we really appreciate. It's another manifestation that we are all in this together. If we do well, we all do well, and if we don't do well then none of us do well. We really watch out for our people. We share all of their celebrations and any misfortunes that they may encounter, we celebrate their birthdays, their weddings, the birth of their children. We stay in touch with them when they are out sick. It's a very human and personal relationship that we have.'

Kelleher said it had never contemplated treating unions as adversaries, but acknowledged that other airlines that have taken this approach have gone on to be successful. 'You can go one way or the other way. We have chosen to go this way and it has been successful for us. The union leaders are people with responsibilities. We understand the responsibilities they have to discharge to their union membership and they've got political problems just like we've got political problems. If you are sensitive to some of their needs and responsive to some of their needs, it can result in a very healthy constructive sort of synergistic long-term relationship.'

For all its flamboyance Southwest has always managed its finances in a very prudent manner. It has kept its debts low and held large amounts of cash in reserve to withstand the bad times, something which is largely responsible for its success in never having to cut jobs. It protects those reserves by sticking to its policy of gradual steady growth, often flying in the face of the more aggressive expectations of Wall Street analysts and investors. 'In the airline industry you have to be that way because twice a decade you are going to have that type of emergency, you can count on it. It's almost like death and taxes – they are going to happen,' Kelleher explained. 'We have always said that we have to be prepared for those bad times because they are coming. Which means don't get euphoric during the good times, don't get your costs way up, don't over expand and take on too much staff, because the bad times are right around the corner just lurking in that dark alley.'

Kelleher is the acknowledged guru on low-fares airlines and is highly respected by his competitors. Gordon Bethune, the Continental Airlines chief, has described Kelleher as 'the most stalwart competitor in the universe', while adding that he had never met anyone who didn't like him. When he heard that Kelleher was thinking of winding down from Southwest in 2001 he said it was the greatest thing he had ever heard. 'I think every dog marks his own hydrant,' he joked. 'Southwest is definitely Herb. It's going to be a long time before that mark leaves.' The two men used to meet at the industry's annual pilgrimage to the Conquistadores del Cielo aviation club at the A-Bar-A Ranch in Wyoming, which has inspired at least one good tale about Kelleher. 'Herb and I were at the bar,' Bethune recalled, 'but I left him because he wanted to keep drinking. I told him I didn't like him that much and went home at 2 a.m. I think he came in and kissed me at four in the morning. He had to be sure I was tucked in. I was just so flattered that Herb would be concerned about me.' He quickly added that Continental and Southwest were competitors in Texas.

If imitation is the most sincere form of flattery then Southwest has received more than its fair share of adulation. Tony Ryan was one of many people in Europe's aviation industry trying to learn the secret of Southwest's success in the early 1990s. The European Union was moving towards the liberalisation of the airline business across Europe, promising great rewards for airlines that could forge a successful niche. Kelleher recalled that Southwest received lots of requests from various European airlines at the time and welcomed many of them to Texas.

'We had airlines coming from all over Europe to say, "Hey, we are going to be exposed to competition within a very short time – what should we do to be competitive?" They wanted to ask us how we had remained job secure and to be at least relatively successful in bad times as well as good.'

More than a decade later Kelleher still remembers meeting Michael O'Leary. Ryan's young assistant met Kelleher and Colleen Barrett one evening and then spent a few days looking around the airline. 'It was brief but Michael catches on very fast,' Kelleher recalled. 'He doesn't require a lot of time.' Kelleher enjoyed O'Leary's company and has tracked his progress ever since. 'I loved Michael. He's a lively lad. I realised within a very short time that he was a very doughty character and I kind of enjoyed his swashbuckling ways. He has a very forceful personality, very forthright, very outspoken.'

Some of Ryanair's rivals made the same pilgrimage to Dallas around that time. Kelleher declined to name them but seems to have been more impressed by O'Leary than some of his contemporaries. 'We have had all kinds of airlines come to see us but we don't talk about it because we know they don't like us to mention names. We have been thanked publicly by a few who have said, "We came to visit Southwest Airlines and we learned some valuable things and we attribute part of our success to that."' O'Leary's quest for knowledge was very specific and was more focussed on the operational aspects of Southwest than other airlines had been. 'Some came here but not in the same way as Michael. When we talked to Michael he had a number of very significant questions. As an example, some of the rest came to talk to us in terms of finances and that sort of thing. I would say that Michael's inquiries were perhaps more broad ranging with respect to Southwest Airlines than those of some of his competitors. His questioning was very incisive and very pointed. Michael was very curious as to how we did things. Although he was pretty familiar with that he wanted to know why we did them – why we did this this way, why we did that that way, why we didn't have business class, why we didn't have assigned seats, why we didn't serve meals. I could go on and on but he wanted to know what our thinking was – what our strategy was behind the things that we did do and behind the things that we didn't do. He asked magnificent questions with respect to each one.'

Kelleher said that after saying goodbye to O'Leary he told Colleen Barrett: 'That guy is a winner.'

CHAPTER EIGHT

Crash

Michael O'Leary returned from Texas with a blueprint for an efficient airline that he would implement during the first few years of the 1990s. In the meantime GPA, which had spawned Ryanair, was about to hit serious trouble. Its founder, Tony Ryan, by now viewed O'Leary as a kind of fourth son. He was impressed by how quickly and efficiently his assistant executed his tasks and often told friends that O'Leary always 'worked like a beggar'. But the pair never had an easy relationship, and some who know them suggest that O'Leary's greatest achievement was that he managed to work so creatively with Ryan for so long. 'They are very similar in character,' one person explained. 'There are no wallflowers.' O'Leary has paid tribute to his mentor's abilities but admitted to a sometimes strained relationship. 'The guy's a genius. I learnt an awful lot from him. You get few opportunities in life to learn from someone so rich and successful. I get on with him half the time and I fight with him the other half.' Others who know him suspect that O'Leary detested Ryan but managed to conceal his true feelings from his mentor.

Ryan trusted O'Leary to handle delicate business and personal problems, and he was intimately involved in managing the Ryan family's fortunes. 'Tony treated O'Leary with incredible indulgence and gave him a free hand,' said someone who knows the family. 'He would agree something with O'Leary, who would be told to sing dumb until he had told Declan. He could treat his sons with total disdain.' Ryan's gilded sons may well have resented O'Leary's growing role and the increasing level of responsibility their father was bestowing on his assistant. 'Tony would always remark that his sons were not involved in GPA or indeed forefrontally in Ryanair because he always believed that positions should be given to the best people to accomplish them,' said James King, the former GPA executive and a family friend. 'Tony would never have made the mistake of putting his sons into a business unless he thought they were the best.'

O'Leary coped well with his powerful position and kept his feet firmly on the ground. His relationship with Ryan's sons was described as 'bizarre'; there are those who say the young Ryans could at times treat O'Leary like the hired help. 'He seemed to get on well with Declan but loathed Cathal,' one source said. Another recounted an exchange between O'Leary and Cathal Ryan at the Ryanair canteen. O'Leary was sitting with a group of people when Captain Ryan passed through wearing his pilot's uniform. He spotted the group and gave an imperious wave in their direction. 'There goes the Chuck Yeager of Ryanair,' O'Leary declared loudly, likening Ryan to the dashing American hero who was the first pilot to break the sound barrier.

Ryanair was a family business. After leaving school, Ryan's youngest son Shane joined the airline as a sales representative. Tony Ryan's brother, Kell, also worked for the family firm and was based in the UK. The GPA founder has told of his brother calling on a travel agent saying, 'Hello, my name is Mr Ryan. I bet you've never met Mr Lingus.'

By 1991 the other family business, GPA, had grown to become the world's second biggest aircraft leasing company. Its fleet of more than 300 aircraft was bigger than those of British Airways, Lufthansa and Air France and over the next ten years it planned to spend $20 billion on new planes. The sheer scale of its operations was so vast that Ryan and his executives were constantly circling the globe. Ryan was estimated to have flown between 300,000 and 500,000 miles a year or about 20 hours every week. A computer room had been installed at his home in County Tipperary so he could track the company's fleet and his executives. GPA had been acquiring between 8 and 10 per cent of all the new aircraft manufactured by the likes of Boeing and Airbus every year in the late 1980s. It was believed to have negotiated discounts of up to 25 per cent off the list price and was making hundreds of millions of dollars in profits annually from leasing planes to airlines across the globe. A world-class company, it was now gearing up to trade on the international stock markets. The flotation would raise millions of dollars for the company and its shareholders – especially Ryan, who as the main beneficiary stood to make a $300 million fortune.

Colleagues said that Ryan had always had an obsession with having prestigious individuals associated with his businesses. At GPA he had gathered a coterie of the great and the good to serve as directors, including the former British chancellor of the exchequer Nigel Lawson; Sir John Harvey-Jones; former European commissioner Peter Sutherland; and the retired Taoiseach, Garrett FitzGerald. Sutherland had spent much of his four-year term in Brussels targeting the worst examples of protectionism, particularly in the aviation industry, with the aim of promoting competition and liberating Europe's skies. As Competition Commissioner he had ordered dawn raids on airlines and other companies suspected of infringing EC rules, and had done much to create opportunities for new airlines such as Ryanair. Ryan had assiduously courted each of the directors as he believed that having famous names on his board would show international investors that GPA was a substantial company. 'He loved the notion that a train-driver's son from Tipperary could get a former chancellor of the exchequer to serve on the board of his company,' one associate said.

Ryan's phenomenal business achievements and his ambitious plans for GPA featured in the international business press. His social pursuits were also gaining attention. Since separating from his wife, Mairead, Ryan had been linked to a number of women. His liasion with Miranda Iveagh, the divorced wife of Guinness heir the Earl of Iveagh, was frequently mentioned in the gossip columns. Nicknamed 'Jumbo' and now permanently tanned, Ryan had a chauffeur-driven Daimler, a two-bed private jet and homes in Monaco, Mexico City, Ibiza and Hawaii, not to mention a valuable art collection. For a time he served as Ireland's honorary consul to Mexico, and at home he was renowned for throwing lavish parties; he had been known to bring bands from Mexico to entertain his guests. As he once told a reporter, 'I am not a humble man.'

Cathal's romance with the former Miss Ireland, Michelle

Rocca, with whom he had a daughter, also provided fodder for the gossip columns. The High Court was regaled with details of their turbulent relationship when Rocca brought a civil case against Ryan, accusing him of assaulting her at a party at Sheikh Mohammed al Maktoum's Blackhall Stud, in County Kildare in 1992. The morning after the party Tony Ryan rang Rocca to apologise for his son's behaviour and asked her not to involve the police or lawyers, but during a further conversation she threatened to block Cathal's access to their child. Concerned about his granddaughter, Ryan delegated the delicate task of negotiating access with Rocca to O'Leary, who presented her with a document agreeing maintenance terms, which she signed.

When the case came to court, Rocca disputed aspects of this document and O'Leary had to give evidence, exposing in public the nature of his relationship with the Ryan family. Some who witnessed his performance said he gave a good account of himself when cross-examined, but remarked that in the future he would always be seen as 'Tony Ryan's bag man'. O'Leary shrugged off the remarks, saying that he had always been seen as Ryan's bag man. In the event, Cathal Ryan was found to have assaulted Rocca and to have used excessive force. But the jury said Ryan had been acting in defence of his girlfriend of the time and awarded Rocca a quarter of the maximum damages she could have received in a lower court.

O'Leary was also dispatched as Ryan's troubleshooter to tackle Tipperary Enterprises, the EC-backed rural development company that ran into trouble in 1992. The company had been Tony Ryan's brainchild and he served as a director alongside other prominent business figures. Concerns about the administration of EC funds had prompted the Department of Agriculture to send in an inspector to carry out an audit. The Department gave the company a second payment under the scheme but the disquiet continued and in December 1992 its board of directors hired a consultant to audit the business and its account. His report claimed that there was a total lack of management in Tipperary Enterprises and a total misuse of monies paid to it, but concluded that a criminal investigation was not warranted. The Department recovered a significant amount of the money that had been deemed to be misused and the company eventually went into liquidation. O'Leary smartly tidied up this embarrassing problem for his boss.

A year earlier he had also managed Ryan's exit from his loss-making investment in Bank of Ireland. Ryan had decided to call it a day, resigning as a director of the bank and selling his five per cent shareholding. His exit was as startling as his arrival had been. The news sent shockwaves throughout the bank and unnerved its investors. Bank of Ireland was reeling from a disastrous foray into the US market and was exposed to one of the worst property collapses in that economy through its New England subsidiary, First New Hampshire. Investors were puzzled why Ryan had decided to dump the stock at a time when the shares were worth over £1 less than the £1.98 he had originally paid for them. On paper he lost between £5 million and £6 million on this investment, although he would have been able to offset some of that loss against the tax on his dividends from GPA; one source recalled O'Leary explaining that when the tax implications of the transaction were taken into account, Ryan had made money on the deal. Ironically, within a few short months Bank of Ireland's share price began to soar and if Ryan had waited a little longer to sell he would have turned a substantial profit.

But bringing GPA to the stock markets was now Ryan's primary focus. The firm's directors had discussed moving ahead with the share flotation in 1990 when world stock markets had begun to strengthen, but decided to postpone the event for a couple of years, when GPA's need to raise money would be greater. It was a fatal error.

In August 1990, Saddam Hussein invaded Kuwait. His actions heightened tensions in the region and culminated in the Gulf War the following year. These events crippled the global aviation industry, forcing airlines to cancel or reduce their aircraft orders. It was a nightmare for GPA, which had placed one of the largest ever orders for new aircraft that were due for delivery over the next five years. Ryan, a keeper of copious lists, carried details of its ever-expanding fleet in his pocket.

GPA was a highly innovative firm and was constantly breaking new ground with the arrangements and deals it brokered. It was competing not only with other aircraft lessors but also with financial institutions, as it acted as an intermediary between investors, banks, manufacturers and airlines. It made profits by buying aircraft for the lowest price possible and then leasing them out. At the same time it borrowed large amounts of cheap debt to lend out at a higher rate of interest to its customers to fund their leasing agreements. GPA president Maurice Foley was acknowledged as having fostered these impressively complex deals, some of which were said to have been more creative than those offered by many of the large US, Japanese and European banks at that time. The firm was also renowned as a brilliant gatherer of intelligence about all aspects of the aviation business. Its staff were regarded as amongst the most outstanding in the industry and that year the US investment bank Salomon Brothers hailed the company as 'the world's leading aircraft lessor'.

GPA was geared to expand its business aggressively and in 1992 needed to raise funds on the world stock markets to finance the $12 billion-worth of new jets it had ordered. It also had options to purchase another $9 billion-worth of aircraft. Ryan tried to be upbeat in an interview with the *Financial Times* in the months before the flotation to reassure investors about the company's prospects. 'I did not welcome 1991, when we were hit by a series of circumstances we never predicted, like the Gulf War,' he said. 'I told my staff at the time if we can work out of this recession it will be a great way of convincing investors we can manage risks well.'

The flotation, through which GPA hoped to raise $1 billion from investors, was planned for 18 June 1992. It was to be the biggest public flotation in the history of the Irish Stock Exchange. GPA hired the Japanese bank Nomura as its lead adviser to bring the firm to the stock markets, something which was said to have angered Wall Street's blue-blooded bankers Merrill Lynch, Salomon and Goldman Sachs, who had been hired to promote the sale of GPA shares in the US. In the UK Schroders and BZW were wooing investors for GPA. The aircraft leasing company was offering 80 million shares that were to be floated simultaneously on the London and New York stock exchanges. Seven months before the flotation, GPA's advisers incurred Ryan's wrath by valuing the shares at around $20. The GPA founder protested that the price was too low. By the time the shares were being offered to investors in August, though, the stock markets had faltered and the advisers were forced to revise their valuation. It was decided that investors would be offered the shares at a price of between $10 and $12.50 each.

As the flotation grew closer stock markets remained jittery, with investors in the US in particular growing more fearful about the aviation sector. American airlines were fighting yet another fierce price war, racking up $2 billion in losses in the previous two years and on course to report further losses in 1992. There were also rumours that the America West airline, a substantial GPA customer, was close to bankruptcy. Many US investors simply didn't believe that GPA was immune to the vagaries of the US airline business, even though America accounted for just 12 per cent of the Irish company's business.

In Britain too, GPA was proving a hard sell, particularly in the light of huge scepticism about the flotation in certain sections of the media. James King believes such criticism was grossly unfair. 'The British media liked to think we were careless, reckless, swashbuckling people. That wasn't true. We were profitable for seventeen years.' Others at GPA blamed an anti-Irish xenophobia on the part of British institutions, or suggested that, despite the company's reputation for capable management, Ryan's meteoric rise, combined with his 'tycoonery' image, aroused deep suspicion among institutions.

Nonetheless, on the day before the flotation the omens looked promising for GPA. Schroders told Ryan and his executives that the worldwide share offering was fully on target and that demand for GPA shares was so strong that it should be increased from 80 million to 85 million shares to satisfy investors. Nomura reported that there was strong demand for the stock in Tokyo, where investors took 23 million of the 30 million shares offered there – though most of these investors were individuals, with the big Japanese investment houses refusing to subscribe for the shares. In the US Merrill Lynch, Salomon and Goldman Sachs were finding it difficult to attract buyers and the negative sentiment towards GPA filtered across the Atlantic, dissuading investors in London as well.

At the eleventh hour Ryan and his associates learned that investors in the US, the UK and Ireland were interested in taking fewer than 15 million of the 50 million shares offered there. In total, investors had subscribed for less than 50 per cent of the 85 million GPA shares being offered. It was a disaster. Given the noises coming from its advisers, Foley was amazed. 'It fits oddly with the events of the past couple of days,' he said. Last-ditch efforts were made to salvage the flotation, but they proved fruitless and the directors were forced to abort GPA's stock market take-off. At 8.30 a.m. on 18 June Ryan issued a statement that read: 'GPA has been a consistently profitable growth company for seventeen years. It would be unwise to proceed with the offer in circumstances which are adverse to both the company's and shareholders' interests.'

The debacle left GPA in a precarious financial state; it was facing massive legal bills and its unpopularity with the market meant that its value had plunged. It was also a disaster for Ryan and the other shareholders, most of whom had borrowed large amounts of money to subscribe for GPA shares. Ryan had never sold a share in GPA during its seventeen-year history, waiting for the public flotation to unlock his fortune. He now owed Merrill Lynch $37 million he had borrowed against shares and share options. The firm's thirty-five senior executives had borrowed an average of $500,000 each from Dutch bank ABN AMRO to buy shares ahead of the flotation, totalling more than $17 million. GPA's shareholders, including Aer Lingus and Air Canada, prepared to totally write off their investment in the company. Aer Lingus alone lost $45 million as a result of the GPA collapse, sending its finances further into the red.

Banks and major bondholders who were owed millions by GPA began to broker an agreement that would allow them to recover some of their debts. They stressed that they would not be calling for Ryan or other senior executives to resign. 'Their departures would upset the apple cart at this delicate stage of negotiations,' one banker explained to the media. 'Ryan is eventually expected to assume the honorary role of "life president".' Ryan bravely suggested that GPA would return to the stock markets in the future, but few believed that would happen any time soon. Within twelve months GPA was on the verge of bankruptcy and Ryan lost control of the company he had founded when the international conglomerate General Electric, headed by Jack

Welch, bailed out the debt-ridden firm. Welch's management of company takeovers had earned him the nickname 'Neutron Jack', as (like a neutron bomb) he was said to leave the buildings intact but without any people in them. Ryan, incensed at the terms of the deal GPA was forced to negotiate with GE to stave off financial ruin, famously said Welch had 'raped' GPA, to which Welch replied, 'What do you expect when you're walking around with no clothes on?'

Ryan vented his spleen at the US investment banks. Many GPA executives believed that the US bankers never really got behind the flotation. 'You might say that I am arrogant but you should see those arrogant sons of bitches on Wall Street,' he fumed afterwards, in an interview with *The Irish Times*. 'They [the investment bankers] never even replied to letters seeking an explanation. Afterwards there was a terrible temptation on my part in particular for retribution, because I was out of the company. But I felt it was more important in the scheme of things to be calm and to restructure and reposition our people rather than getting into haggling over the causes of GPA going out of business. I would want to be very cold blooded not to still regret what happened. This was a company that had been profitable every year in its existence, an Irish company on the world stage that had been profitable for seventeen years consistently. We continued to pay our bills and paid a $1 billion restructuring charge. The $11 billion of debt was all paid down. None of our lenders lost a cent. It was a sad time and we didn't deserve to go out of business but that's life.'

While Ryan and the GPA executives blamed everyone from the Wall Street bankers to the hostile British press for the company's demise, many commentators suggested that much of the blame lay with Ryan himself and the way he controlled the company. Edward Cahill, a professor of accounting at University College Cork, has examined the financial crisis at GPA and suggested that, while greed and bad luck played their part in the company's demise, corporate arrogance was its Achilles' heel. In *Corporate Financial Crisis in Ireland* (1997) he suggested that the company had simply over-traded. Cahill contended that its executives failed to realise the danger of pursuing an aggressive aircraft purchasing policy when the Gulf War and economically depressed conditions had fundamentally altered the aviation industry. 'Its culture led to an attempt to impose its view on the capital market,' he argued in the book. 'It lost heavily because management seemed to have been blinkered to the economics and psychology of that market. GPA's weakness was that it had insufficient experience of a recession in its business.'

King admitted that mistakes were made, and that the most fundamental failing was GPA's insufficient knowledge of the financial markets. 'Our timing was wrong,' King explained. 'We waited too long to make a public offering. We picked the wrong structure. It was a mistake to pick a Japanese lead bank. No Japanese bank has ever led a global offer and the Americans are going to make sure that they don't. It was a calamity that the company was allowed to go because it was inherently very profitable. The various judgements at the time that our order books were excessive and that our order books going forward were too great were absolute balderdash. Even at the time of the collapse we were still placing more than two new airplanes a week.' King said he still doesn't like to think about those awful days. 'The experience itself was tragic and very disturbing for all of us involved. I admired Tony enormously in the way he handled it. He never complained. I heard him use appalling language about the banks like the rest of us, but he took the blame.'

Ryan's policy of gathering distinguished directors to GPA had proved worthless in the end. King said they didn't help the company in its hour of need. 'When the going got rough, their involvement on other boards and their desire not to have a row with the banks didn't work to our advantage.' In retrospect, King suggested that Ryan's biggest mistake at GPA was that he had never sold a single share of his stake in the company. 'After the whole debacle I remember him saying that he would never make the same mistake again.'

Ryan had suffered a remarkable reversal of fortune. On 18 June 1992 he was worth $300 million; only a few hours later he had debts to the order of $37 million. O'Leary was asked to sort through the financial mess and was sent to negotiate a settlement with Merrill Lynch in relation to Ryan's $37 million loan. And so in 1992 the mighty GPA, the company that had yielded a fortune for Tony Ryan, collapsed, while Ryanair, the airline he had saved from bankruptcy over the previous six years, was now the Ryan family's best hope of restoring their fortunes.

But its future was still far from certain. Ryan realised that he would have to find a partner who would buy some of his sons' shareholding in the airline to claw back some wealth and help to keep Ryanair in business. When friends asked how he was coping with his spectacular loss, he would say, 'I sleep like a baby – I wake up every ten minutes screaming!' He was advised on health grounds to take a holiday, so he went to his home in Ibiza and ran regularly on the beach. 'Someone asked me later how much I had lost. I said, "$300 million and 20lbs."'

O'Leary, who was busily working to earn his bonus at Ryanair, immediately began to search for a way to turn GPA's misfortune to Ryanair's advantage. He reviewed the business relationships that existed between Ryan's two companies and quickly decided that he would use GPA's vulnerability to force it to take back the ATR 425 aircraft Ryanair used on its Galway, Kerry and Waterford routes, which GPA had leased to the company on very expensive terms. At a meeting with some of GPA's distressed executives, O'Leary demanded that they take the ATRs back and refused to pay the £12 million penalty fee they were entitled to charge under the terms of the lease. The GPA executives agreed to take the aircraft back but refused to waive the penalty until O'Leary issued an ultimatum. 'He told them he would park the planes on the runway at Shannon Airport and invite the media to see what Tony Ryan was doing to his own airline,' one source explained. Ryanair managed to get rid of the aircraft; it had to pay around £5 million to GPA but escaped the £12 million penalty, and by the deal also freed itself of about £15 million in debts.

Having got rid of the ATRs, Ryanair announced that it was pulling off the Galway, Kerry and Waterford routes, as part of another restructuring plan that had been drawn up by O'Leary and Ryanair's new chief executive, Conor Hayes. When PJ McGoldrick departed, Ryan and his advisers wanted to find someone who would manage and grow Ryanair, transforming it into a successful and attractive company that an investor might buy into. Ryan asked Patrick Murphy, the chief executive of the Irish Continental ferry group, to join the Ryanair board as executive chairman in the interim. Hayes, an accountant who had trained at Stokes Kennedy Crowley, was returning to Ireland from Saudi Arabia, where he had been chief financial officer of the Almarai food group. In 1991 he signed a three-year contract to work at Ryanair. Despite his refusal to take the top job, O'Leary accepted his first formal executive role at the airline, acting as Hayes' number two with the title of deputy chief executive. Some more cynical observers, believing the cash-strapped airline was close to collapse, viewed the appointments as the Ryans ensuring that they had people in place if Ryanair failed. 'If it hit the wall, they would have clean hands,' one suggested.

Hayes brought a wealth of management experience to the airline, which only had enough cash to stay in business for about two months, and initiated a restructuring plan to tackle its cost base and lose surplus jobs. This time, forty-seven Ryanair staff, including pilots, ground, administrative and cabin crew, would be made redundant, reducing its workforce to five hundred. The airline also began to publicly threaten that it would pull out of Shannon, Cork and Knock airports if the Irish government failed to extend its exclusive rights to fly to Stansted, which were to be reviewed at the end of the year. The drastic cost-cutting measures transformed Ryanair into an airline with one of the lowest cost bases in Europe. It was now also profitable, reporting a £100,000 surplus at the end of 1991 and forecasting that this would treble over the next twelve months.

CHAPTER NINE

O'Leary Air

While GPA plunged into the red, Ryanair's fortunes began to soar upwards. After his visit to America, Michael O'Leary was convinced that Ryanair should now imitate Southwest Airlines, offering low fares, no frills and more frequent flights while maintaining an extremely low cost base. He championed his plan to the Ryan family and the other board members, who agreed to back the transition. 'We decided to follow the kind of low-fares formula that Southwest Airlines had pioneered in the US,' O'Leary said. 'It seemed blindingly obvious that if we couldn't out-service Aer Lingus with better business class and better service, we could certainly offer better fares.'

He worked closely with Ryanair's new chief executive, Conor Hayes, to impose the Southwest Airlines business model at Ryanair. Staff noted that O'Leary was a 'very strong' second in command. While the job cuts and the route closures were public evidence that Ryanair was trimming its costs, its plan to permanently lower its fares was implemented very subtly. It started to offer a £29 fare as a special promotion for one month, with other seats available at £39, £49 and £59, and attracted a large number of bookings. Buoyed by its success, it decided to offer another seat sale the following month.

Aer Lingus began to notice that Ryanair was promoting a new lower fare every month but wasn't overly concerned. 'We were pretty relaxed and viewed this as a one-off promotion,' one Aer Lingus source explained. 'Then the offer kept being extended and the frequency of their flights increased. Then we got very jumpy. Ryanair snuck up on us. We didn't realise it had redefined its strategy. It took a lot of adjusting to.'

Each airline was required to file details of its fares with the Department of Transport and Ryanair began to suspect that its details were being passed on to Aer Lingus. The national carrier had by now started to reduce its fares and was managing to match some of Ryanair's offers. Ryanair decided to make a filing with the Department in the morning and then another in the afternoon with a different fare to cause confusion. It was a vicious skirmish. 'The war on the London route was a commercial disaster for Aer Lingus and cost us at least £10 million,' an Aer Lingus insider admitted. 'The reality was that we misjudged the market. If the price was being reduced we needed to increase our capacity but we didn't do that because we couldn't afford to. We were protecting our market share and holding traffic at Ryanair's expense but we failed to take account of the growth in the market.'

By the third quarter of 1992 Aer Lingus was veering towards a financial crisis. The Dublin to London route, Europe's second busiest after London to Paris, was crucial to its success. If it wasn't making money there the airline's entire profitability was threatened. British Airways despaired of the price war and, after forty-four years of flying between the UK and Ireland, announced its withdrawal, grounding flights from Heathrow to Dublin, Cork and Shannon as well as a service between Birmingham and Dublin. 'They thought it was awful that these Paddies were fighting over price,' one source recalled. 'It had enough and decided it wasn't going to waste its valuable Heathrow slots on ridiculous fares.' British Midland chairman Michael Bishop said BA had 'blinked first', saying this was the first time BA had ever moved off a route as a direct result of competition.

Aer Lingus' financial crisis was a cause for concern for its shareholder, the Irish government, which made efforts to bring the warring airlines together under the International Air Transport Association (IATA) umbrella group, of which Ryanair was then a member. Aer Lingus and Ryanair, as well as Dan Air and British Midland, which also operated on the UK routes out of Ireland, attended the meeting. One source described Hayes' demeanour at that meeting as 'absolutely victorious'. There was a wide-ranging discussion about the price of air fares being charged on the route but IATA failed to broker a truce.

As Aer Lingus's finances worsened the airline imposed its own cutbacks, withdrawing from the Dublin to Gatwick route and raising its fares into Heathrow. Ryanair immediately announced even cheaper fares to London. O'Leary would often join Ryanair's chief executive at meetings with other airlines and some formed an impression that Hayes was increasingly deferring to his deputy. 'Michael O'Leary seemed to be calling the shots,' recalled one airline source. 'We had always given Hayes a lot of the credit for turning Ryanair around, but we were beginning to wonder if O'Leary was responsible behind the scenes.'

The young deputy chief executive studiously avoided the media spotlight, leaving Hayes to present the airline's annual results and speak to journalists. But his growing presence at Ryanair was beginning to be noticed. The company's public relations consultant, Brian Bell, recalled that *Irish Times* reporter John Maher asked, 'Does Michael O'Leary exist?' after he had interviewed Hayes at the airline's headquarters at Dublin airport. 'As we were walking towards the door, Michael was walking down the corridor towards us with his head bowed,' Bell said. 'I couldn't resist and introduced him to Maher. Afterwards he called me in and warned me to never do that again. He said he couldn't stand journalists.'

O'Leary kept a tight grip on the purse strings and his efforts were strengthened by the appointment as financial controller of Howard Millar, an accountant who had worked with Hayes in Saudi Arabia. Millar joined the small management team, which also included chief engineer Brian Taylor and chief pilot Maurice O'Connor. Hayes recruited David O'Brien, who had also worked in the Middle East, to take charge of Ryanair's ground operations and inflight activities, and John Quinlan arrived to take charge of human resources.

The strengthened management team imposed greater financial discipline and sought to put systems and processes in place to make the airline efficient. 'Now Ryanair is known to be brutal to its customers but that wasn't the case then,' one employee said. 'There was no rudeness. The place was very small and there was a very positive atmosphere.' Manuals were drawn up to make sure that Ryanair's ground operations and inflight services were highly professional. They highlighted the need for staff to be friendly and helpful to passengers. 'If we are perceived to be friendly, efficient and professional, we will get the repeat and new business which is vital to our success,' the manual said. 'Ryanair is the "value for money" airline. This means that we do not rely on expensive "perks" or extravagance to create the desired impression. If we are professional and friendly people but are not perceived as such by the passenger, then we have lost the battle.'

The manual also set down the conditions by which passengers could expect to receive compensation or meal vouchers if their journey was disrupted. If a flight was delayed for more than three hours passengers were to be given a snack voucher, entitling them to a beverage, sandwich and biscuit. If the delay was longer than six hours they would also get a meal voucher. The manual emphasised, though, that these forms of compensation were expensive and might not always be necessary to protect the passenger's goodwill. 'Being genuinely concerned for the passenger's plight and offering assistance with practical things, such as phone calls, baggage, queries and directions, will often be valued more highly and save the company a considerable amount of money.'

O'Leary always had the final say over what money was to be spent, insisting that those making the requests proved the outlay to be absolutely necessary. 'It was like it was coming out of his own pocket,' one staff member said. Which of course it was, thanks to his deal with Ryan, which was known only to the Ryan family and the other board members.

By 1992 Ryanair had been turned around and was on a steadier flight path. Now that Ryanair had disposed of the ATR aircraft O'Leary leased in planes from British Airways and Britannia on much more favourable terms. New pay deals negotiated with the crew introduced more performance-related payments. Ryanair's cabin crew started on a salary of £8000, well below the rates offered at Aer Lingus. Under the restructuring plan the airline wanted to slash this by 25 per cent to £6000 and bring in a new commission structure to supplement the crew's earnings. With its new productivity agreement Ryanair said its flight attendants could earn £8 commission for every flight they worked, and that they could request extra flights to earn more money. They were also paid a 10 per cent commission on duty-free sales and told that there would be no pay increases for three years. The staff refused to talk to O'Leary, whom they viewed with suspicion, and would only negotiate with Hayes and other senior managers.

That year Ryanair carried almost 2.5 million passengers and reported a £850,000 profit, although its profits were said to be actually closer to £3.5 million. The airline adopted a very conservative accounting policy and created generous cash reserves for aircraft maintenance, reducing the bottom-line profits. It probably suited the privately owned company to be seen to be struggling financially, as that way it could continue to claim that Aer Rianta's charges were exorbitant. Ryan had also accumulated huge personal debts in the wake of the GPA collapse and creditors would have been closely monitoring his likely income from Ryanair.

O'Leary likes to claim that this reversal of fortunes was not all down to him. 'There wasn't any great foresight on my part. PJ McGoldrick came into Ryanair with a lot of airline expertise, Conor Hayes brought a lot of management expertise. Over two or three years the three of us together did turn the airline around and did put it on the footing it is on today. I get far too much credit for being the turnaround artist.' As its fortunes improved, Ryan wanted to find a partner for the family at Ryanair. Cathal Ryan told the media that Ryanair needed a partner to share the cost of its expansion into Europe. 'We are a small island operator and we will always focus on short-haul routes. To develop routes into Europe would take a long time, certainly to achieve breakeven on those routes. This is why we need a partner.'

Its search for an investor began just as the European Community was opening the skies across its then twelve member states as part of the creation of a single market. Immigration and customs controls between the twelve states were abolished to allow free movement of goods, services and people across Europe from 1 January 1993. The new measures would give airlines unrestricted access to all routes within the EC and also set them free to set their own fares; all constraints in terms of the number of flights and passengers they could carry were abolished. As a further support the Commission introduced competition rules to prevent the bigger airlines from using predatory pricing to keep new airlines out of the market. The EC also tackled the thorny issue of state aid and attached a series of conditions under which governments could provide cash injections.

In Ireland, Aer Lingus' financial crisis continued to worsen and the government ordered a restructuring plan, in line with the new EC regulations, that would allow it to put money into the national airline. Its chairman, the Cork businessman, Bernie Cahill, crafted the rescue plan. He called for swingeing job cuts and proposed to establish a low-cost subsidiary airline, to be called Aer Lingus Express, to capitalise on the growth in passenger numbers in response to cheap air fares. Ryanair vigorously opposed the injection of state aid at its chief rival and lobbied furiously in Brussels.

Around this time Ireland's European Commissioner, Ray MacSharry, was preparing to return to Ireland. Tony Ryan, knowing how useful MacSharry's in-depth knowledge of the European Commission and extensive political contacts could be, wanted to entice him to join Ryanair as its chairman and sent his son Declan to issue the invitation in person. Aer Lingus was also making similar overtures, and sources suggest that Ryan senior bet his son £100 that he wouldn't get MacSharry to take the job. But at a meeting in the Clarence, the Dublin hotel now owned by the Irish rock group U2, Declan persuaded the former commissioner to join the upstart airline ahead of the national flagcarrier. No one is sure if he ever collected on the bet.

Rather than setting up a new low-cost airline from scratch, Cahill began to think about buying Ryanair. Aer Lingus was in search of a bargain and would have derived much pleasure from offering the cash-strapped Ryan family a pittance for the upstart airline that had inflicted so much financial damage on Aer Lingus through its vicious price wars, particularly in the past couple of years.

In May 1993, Cahill and his executives met Hayes and MacSharry to discuss the possible takeover. Over the next six weeks the discussions, which were difficult from the start, became increasingly fraught. Eventually Cahill offered to pay £20 million for Ryanair. 'For the Ryans it was evidence of a recognition that Ryanair had been turned around,' one source close to the family said. 'Once Tony knew someone was offering that kind of money he knew he had an asset.' The Ryanair chairman and chief executive haggled hard and Cahill raised his offer to £25 million, but then Ryan added a twist. He told his negotiators to ask Cahill for £29 million. 'It was a play on Ryanair's £29 fares,' the source said. 'It was a fuck-you to Aer Lingus.' It was also more than Cahill was prepared to pay, and he pulled out of the deal. The Ryan family have told friends that they didn't refuse to sell Ryanair to Aer Lingus but that Cahill just didn't offer them enough money. They felt he had always been on an information-gathering mission for Aer Lingus.

A new Minister for Transport, Brian Cowen, had settled into Kildare Street and quickly got to grips with the bitter rivalry between Ireland's two airlines. Hayes and O'Leary took the initiative to bring him a proposal that identified the potentially huge savings for Ryanair and Aer Lingus if the airlines were to cooperate in certain areas. These included increasing the yield from each passenger by 2.5 per cent, reducing travel agent commissions by 1 per cent and the halving of passenger taxes. Other efficiencies were identified in areas such as fuel, catering costs, aviation insurance and other overheads. Ryanair told the Minister that it would shave close to £5 million off its cost base while Aer Lingus could save more than £75 million. The Minister brought the plan to Cahill's attention but it got short shrift; the Aer Lingus chairman told Cowen he wouldn't deal with 'those two young pups'.

Hayes' three-year contract was coming to an end and he announced that he would leave at the end of 1993. By that time Ryanair had a £12 million cash surplus and was expected to report a £1.5 million profit. Some sources suggest that the actual profit figure was closer to £10 million that year, with the surplus accounted for as maintenance reserves.

By this time O'Leary had become a multi-millionaire, and thanks to his pay deal would have pocketed about £2 million in that year alone. He was now the only candidate to run Ryanair and his appointment as chief executive was announced at the same time as Hayes' departure. A statement detailing the management changes was given to the media, but no photographs of the new airline chief were issued.

The aviation industry is renowned for attracting larger-than-life characters. In the US unconventional chief executive Herb Kelleher had created a new and successful culture within the business world. In Britain, Richard Branson was brawling with British Airways and using high-profile stunts to garner publicity for his Virgin Atlantic airline. The first European aviation chief to do business in jeans and a jumper rather than in a suit, Branson's casual, down-to-earth style was greatly admired and set him apart from other business leaders. O'Leary now began to increasingly model himself on 'Herb', who had made a huge impression on him, although he drew the line at the notion of love-bombing the staff or the customers.

When he first arrived in Ryanair in 1988 O'Leary was a sober-suited accountant who largely kept to himself. As his power grew a forceful personality emerged. Former associates said he created a volatile atmosphere at the airline and instilled fear in the workforce. 'He used his bullying ways to get what he wanted,' said one source. Many blamed O'Leary's tough management style for the high turnover of middle and senior executives over the years.

He was obsessed with Ryanair. 'If you arrived into the office at 6.30 in the morning he would be there, surrounded by half-full paper cups of coffee with cigarette ends in them,' a former colleague said. 'What is more, he would still be there at ten that night.' Some remember him hanging around the office at weekends, where he would sit and read; he was particularly fixated with books on leadership. He had dated a couple of Ryanair staff but was generally regarded as a loner with a fairly humble lifestyle.

Despite his alleged rudeness to senior executives, O'Leary made an effort to be friendly with the rest of the staff. He was on first-name terms with most of Ryanair's five hundred employees, and when he took over the top job he encouraged them to call him 'Michael'. His suits and blazers were left at home and he began to appear in open-necked shirts, rugby shirts and jeans; he is remembered for scampering around the office in his stockinged feet. He dined at the staff canteen and put on his kit on a Thursday evening to play soccer with his colleagues. Some people recall that he seemed to make a special effort to get along with the chief pilot. Every day he would turn up in the baggage hall to throw luggage onto the planes or would hover around the check-in areas doing whatever was needed to get the planes in the air. 'He retains the highest respect for people who do the job, the baggage-handlers, the people on the desk,' a former colleague said shortly after his appointment. 'He may be tough, but he has a genuine fondness for the company and the people who work here.'

The elusive O'Leary was finally captured on camera coming out from a conference in Dublin by RTE, which managed to get an impromptu interview. This was the first time the public would see the young, casually dressed Ryanair chief executive. It was a brief media outing, during which he dismissed suggestions that he was trying to be Ireland's answer to Richard Branson. 'I try desperately not to get into the Branson stuff. This is not O'Leary Air,' he said. O'Leary puzzled business associates. 'At first, you do not know whether to take him seriously,' one said. 'Then you realise that this is for real. This is Michael O'Leary. He is the perfect combination: one of the lads with his employees and arrogant when doing business. When he goes into battle he boots the shit out of anyone or anything that gets in his way.'

O'Leary drove a three-year-old Honda Prelude, owned an apartment in Dublin and had purchased a 200-acre farm and remote country home, Gigginstown House, outside his native Mullingar. In interviews he claimed to live an almost 'hermit-like' existence working long days at Ryanair. At weekends he returned to his farm, putting on his wellingtons to clean out sheds, bail hay, deliver calves and tend to his herd of five hundred Aberdeen Angus cattle. He likes to tell journalists that he was up half the night pulling a calf before heading to Dublin to run the airline. One of his herd was awarded Ireland's 'best bull' title and his photograph is proudly displayed in O'Leary's office at Ryanair. 'All he does is make babies and eat,' he has said. 'That's what I look forward to doing when I retire.' One source at a rival airline quipped that they didn't need agricultural experts to tell them 'that O'Leary had the best bull'.

O'Leary was a hero in his hometown, where he lived a very private life. He could go home for dinner a couple of nights a week and his mother's approval was said to be hugely influential when it came to his serious relationships. 'He's a real mummy's boy and needs his mother's approval for most things, including relationships,' a friend said. 'She thinks most women aren't good enough for her son and has had a stormy relationship with most of his exes.' His sister, Valerie, worked with him for a year at the airline as its head of marketing and would issue statements to the media.

O'Leary's cost-cutting ways at Ryanair became legendary. He banned the use of cover sheets when sending a fax and told cabin crew to buy their own pens. And while he has publicly claimed to champion Ryanair's no-frills policy, others said it was adopted more by accident than design. The catering company that supplied the in-flight drinks and food had been trying to get Ryanair to pay its bill and refused to provide its services until it received a payment. Coincidentally, at the same time, Finches, an Irish drinks company, offered to supply its orange and lemon drinks for free to Ryanair, to promote the brand. The airline demanded that the company also supply the plastic glasses to be served to passengers, and began to sell the drinks on flights for 50p. A fax was sent to travel agents to inform their customers that Ryanair no longer served tea and coffee.

Ryanair later struck a deal with Dunnes Stores to exclusively offer its own-brand St Bernard Cola on flights. The arrangement ran into problems shortly after the deal was done when an executive from the Irish supermarket chain travelling on a Ryanair flight asked the hostess for a St Bernard Cola. The airline still had some stocks of Pepsi on board and the hostess helpfully handed a can to the passenger, telling him it was nicer than the brand he had ordered. The incident led to a dispute between Dunnes Stores and Ryanair, and the deal was unwound.

The European Commission had blocked Aer Lingus' plans to set up Aer Lingus Express, so O'Leary took advantage of the situation to recruit Conor McCarthy, the man Aer Lingus had appointed to run its new subsidiary. McCarthy, an engineer by training, had worked at Aer Lingus for eighteen years and now took charge of Ryanair's flight operations, including maintenance and engineering, ground operations and inflight services. McCarthy said that when O'Leary offered him the position he said he would be leaving Ryanair in a couple of years and the top job would be up for grabs.

Aer Rianta and Aer Lingus quickly came to grips with a fresh ruthlessness and more hardball business style at Ryanair. The state-owned airport authority had never had a warm relationship with the airline, but its new chief executive would prove to be even more demanding than his predecessors. He was always seeking concessions and trying to renegotiate its fees and charges at Dublin, Cork and Shannon airports. 'After O'Leary took control, gratitude played no part in Ryanair's corporate policy,' one source at Aer Rianta explained. 'There was no level of support that would ever satisfy Ryanair. What they demanded would have been putting us in legal peril.'

O'Leary was also haggling with airports in the UK and Scotland, and in 1994 he secured substantial discounts on routes into London's Gatwick Airport and Prestwick Airport, some thirty miles from Glasgow, which described Ryanair's arrival as 'a very welcome moment'. O'Leary liked to insist on secret deals, but Prestwick was so delighted with its new customer that it announced it had waived most of its charges for five years as part of its bid to encourage new airlines to fly into the region. Ryanair said it would sell seats to Prestwick for between £55 and £75 return, compared to the £123 and £187 fares offered by Aer Lingus into Glasgow Airport. It was also preparing to fly to Birmingham and its new chairman, Ray MacSharry, travelled on the inaugural flight on this new route. O'Leary stayed in Dublin and backed out the plane.

Ryanair also returned to Manchester, the scene of its near-fatal brush with Aer Lingus in the late 1980s. Ryanair had abandoned the route hastily, leaving some unpaid bills behind, but while Manchester Airport's experience of Ryanair wasn't good, its executives couldn't ignore the success the small Irish airline had made of the Dublin to Liverpool route. Its marketing development manager, Tim Jeans, decided to go to Dublin to talk to O'Leary. 'All we knew about this small airline was that it had left Manchester owing a large debt, but it was doing some remarkable things with traffic in Liverpool,' Jeans said. 'It took about four months for me to get a meeting with Michael O'Leary. In true Michael style, he set me up with four different people on the way into his office, all of whom told me that Ryanair didn't really need to fly to Manchester.' For all of the bluster, though, Jeans said it was clear that O'Leary wanted to cut a deal. 'In true Ryanair fashion he came over to Manchester and within six days we had agreed a deal and a start date for the route was announced.' The airport quickly realised its new customer was extraordinarily demanding. Ryanair negotiated a discount from

£16 to £1 per passenger on landing and departing fees, the rate it was already paying at Stansted, promising in return that it would bring a quarter of a million passengers to the airport in its first year.

In this case O'Leary was adamant that the deal, which put Ryanair at a huge advantage to Aer Lingus, should remain secret. But Aer Lingus, which was still paying £16 per passenger at Manchester, somehow got wind of it and was incensed. It complained to the airport and eventually got the same deal – a 95 per cent reduction in charges.

Ryanair had many other requirements. 'It wanted slots when there were none available,' said Jeans. 'It wanted facilities when there were none possible but it did absolutely deliver on all of its promises. Even to an airport of Manchester's size an undertaking to bring a quarter of a million passengers wasn't to be sneezed at. It was clear then that the Ryanair model or Ryanair phenomenon was something that made it stand out from the other forty-eight airlines I was dealing with at the time.'

Ryanair was once again competing head-to-head with Aer Lingus on routes from Ireland into UK provincial cities, at a time when the Irish national carrier claimed they were unprofitable. On the fourth floor of the Aer Lingus head office executives would walk around regaling each other with Ryanair's latest trick. 'You would hear people saying things like, "That will definitely destroy them,"' one source recalled. 'We were furious that Ryanair was back on the Birmingham and Manchester routes and couldn't understand how it would make them pay, but they managed them well. We just didn't understand the model.'

O'Leary had plenty of other weapons in his arsenal and wasn't afraid to turn them on Aer Lingus. Twelve days after he was formally installed as chief executive, Ryanair lodged a complaint to the European Commission stating that Aer Lingus was selling fares at below the advertised price in a bid to drive its rival out of business. Ryanair accused Aer Lingus of 'below-cost selling' and of 'seat dumping' and made a specific allegation that in the previous October Aer Lingus had introduced a £69 fare between Dublin and Birmingham as Ryanair had begun to develop the route. It complained this fare was the lowest price ever offered by Aer Lingus and amounted to 'fare dumping' intended to drive

Ryanair off the route. The nub of the complaint was that Aer Lingus was abusing its dominant position to stifle competition. In the late 1980s Ryanair chief executive Eugene O'Neill had wanted to pursue this route but had been blocked by the Ryan family. O'Leary wasn't pulling any punches.

The authorities in Brussels sent four officials to raid the Aer Lingus head office in Dublin to gather evidence of its pricing policy. This was the second time the airline had found itself in trouble with the Commission. A couple of years earlier it had been fined more than half a million pounds for abusing its position on the Dublin to London route following a complaint from British Midland. However. this time it was exonerated from the charges.

The dogfight between the two airlines, particularly on the Dublin to London route, was causing concern amongst pilots. The Irish Airline Pilots' Association's vice president, Jim Duggan, called for the bitter price war to end and warned that safety standards on the route could ultimately be affected. He acknowledged that the travelling public was benefiting from the continuing hostilities but warned that the low prices were not sustainable in the longer term. He said that as airlines sought to use their aircraft more frequently and demanded more time from staff such as pilots, 'safety considerations' were bound to arise, and he called on the regulator to set maximum flight times and minimum rest periods for cabin crew.

A Ryanair senior pilot was suspended after he refused to fly a scheduled flight without being allowed the minimum fourteen-hour rest period agreed in his contract. Captain Henry Murphy had worked at Ryanair since its foundation and had over 10,000 flying hours to his credit without an accident. When he protested about the instruction Ryanair's chief pilot, Maurice O'Connor, phoned to remind him about being on standby and warned him that if he did not take the flight he would be suspended. The pilot refused to back down, and Ryanair suspended him for one week for failing to fly on a specified date, deducting one week's gross pay of £837.74. Murphy brought his grievance to the Employment Appeals Tribunal, where it was established that Ryanair had breached the Payment of Wages Act because it had failed to give their employee written notice about the deduction. It upheld

Murphy's complaint and unanimously ruled that he was entitled to the payment.

Suppliers soon found that, unless they had a watertight contract laying down agreed terms and conditions, supplying Ryanair could end up costing them money. O'Leary was constantly phoning the airline's suppliers to cut costs. One said, 'He was always ringing trying to reduce our fees. You just knew that if he got nowhere with you he would hit someone else.' One company doing business with Ryanair found it was expected to do its work for terms very different from what it had expected. Irish International Advertising resigned as Ryanair's Irish advertising agency less than two months after being appointed, saying that the airline wanted it 'to work for prices that were uneconomic'. The firm had won the account after a competitive pitch for Ryanair's business and agreed the terms on which it would work for the airline. 'They then sent us a contract that did not reflect the agreement,' Larkin explained when it announced it was resigning the account. This in itself was an unusual move, but the agency said it had decided to make its stance public to 'protect its reputation'. A Ryanair spokesman said a British advertising agency which already provided this service for the airline in Britain would do all the Irish media buying in future, and that it had no plans to appoint a new Irish agency. More than one million pounds had been allocated for the company's marketing budget, with about two thirds earmarked to be spent in the UK.

O'Leary had aggressively slashed Ryanair's cost base, while at the same time boosting its revenues by offering more and more cheap flights on routes between Ireland and the UK. The airline claimed to be carrying 35 per cent of all passengers from Dublin to its five UK destinations and 36 per cent of the Dublin to London market. He claimed that Ryanair was making a profit of about £1 per passenger. Industry analysts who monitored the airline's progress closely suggest it may in fact have been making between £15 and £16 per passenger, one of the biggest profit margins ever yielded in the airline industry. Ryanair revelled in playing the underdog and claiming to be strapped for cash, but many observers suspected that the company's finances were in fact in pretty good shape. Ryanair's policy of creating large cash reserves to cover aircraft maintenance reduced its headline profit figures.

As a private company the airline did not have to publish detailed financial information and released only the minimum required under company law. The accounts it lodged for the eighteen months to the end of March 1995 showed that Ryanair had made a £5 million profit. When it floated as a public company, the flotation prospectus restated its profits, disclosing that for the period in question they were actually more than double that figure, at £12 million. O'Leary had become even richer.

The next phase of the Southwest Airlines model Ryanair adopted was to establish a fleet of just one type of aircraft. It began to purchase used Boeing 737–200A aircraft to replace its leased aircraft, which were mainly BAC 1-11 jets. It acquired four 130-seater 737s at a cost of £16 million, one of which came from Transavia, a subsidiary of the Dutch airline, KLM. The aircraft would be rebranded in the Ryanair livery and come into service for the summer of 1995. Ryanair's 'new' aircraft would on average be around eight years old. It planned to pay for them using finance leases, eventually taking ownership of them at the end of these contracts.

Meanwhile O'Leary was unveiling ambitious plans to spread Ryanair's wings over Europe. The young chief executive revealed his strategy at an international aviation conference in London, signalling that the company intended to challenge Aer Lingus and other carriers on continental European routes in the same way it had on the Dublin to London route. 'Continental Europe is a market with over 300 million people, most of whom are now paying outrageously high air fares,' he told delegates. 'I assure you that this is a market that Ryanair cannot ignore, but I cannot reveal our strategy today.' He explained that, rather than stealing Aer Lingus passengers, Ryanair was stimulating two new markets: price-sensitive passengers currently using road, rail and ferry links, and people who would consider travelling if the fare was cheap enough. He also predicted that Europe's newly open skies would soon be crowded with low-cost airlines. 'When the restrictions on airlines are lifted, short-haul, cost-efficient, point-to-point airlines will sprout up throughout Europe,' he declared. 'They will, in a short space of time, change the face of European air travel.'

O'Leary took the opportunity to publicly challenge what he

described as some of the 'structural impediments' to low-cost operators. His chief bugbears were the fees charged to access centralised computer reservation systems and inefficient air traffic control. European legislation set out a standard fee for all users of these reservations systems, which meant that someone booking a cheap fare paid the same tariff as someone reserving an expensive first-class seat. O'Leary's gripe with European air traffic controllers was simple: they were inefficient and they were thwarting his efforts to turn around his planes speedily at airports. 'What hope has any airline in Europe of operating an efficient schedule, with minimum fuel consumption and shorter turnarounds, when at the whim of air traffic control their schedules and costs can be disrupted to an endless degree?' he asked rhetorically.

At the same time O'Leary was building a management team to drive the airline's expansion. In between running Ryanair and addressing conferences, he made a trip to Manchester to meet Tim Jeans, the airport's marketing development manager, with whom he had negotiated the deal a year earlier. He asked Jeans to join Ryanair as director of its commercial team. 'We talked a lot,' Jeans recalled. 'At that time it was singularly the fastest growing airline, even at Manchester, the UK's third largest airport, but it was a relative minnow and wasn't on anyone's radar. It was quite clear to me that Ryanair's business model did mark it out as something quite different. Most people thought that I was clinically insane to leave the UK and move to Ireland,' he added. Jeans would work closely with O'Leary and later return to the UK to build Ryanair's base at Stansted. He remarked that O'Leary is 'at his most persuasive' when a relationship was in its infancy, recalling that the chief executive mentioned that he would only be hanging around Ryanair for a few years and then his job would be up for grabs.

In 1995 the airline also went on a recruitment drive, hiring 108 pilots and cabin crew to bring the total staff to 600. Chairman Ray MacSharry said the airline was pursuing a 'carefully planned' strategy and was one of the few European airlines making a profit. 'Without the assistance of any state funds or European aid, Ryanair today employs 600 Irish people,' he said. 'Through Ryanair's own investment and continued hard work, the airline will carry 2.3 million passengers this year.'

While O'Leary might have wanted to keep his mentor at arms' length, Tony Ryan had other plans. He was now completely focused on Ryanair, or, more precisely, focused on finding a partner to buy some of his sons' shareholding in the up-and-coming airline. Such was his commitment that, for the first time in Ryanair's ten-year existence, Ryan decided to emerge from the backroom and formally join the airline's board of directors. In February 1995 Ryanair announced his arrival and his intention to take over as non-executive chairman when Ray MacSharry's term lapsed at the end of the year. A spokesman told the media that Ryan would be attending just four board meetings each year and that most of his time would be spent abroad on GE business. 'He will be spending very little time in Ireland and has no intention of taking any shareholding,' the spokesman added.

In a statement, Ryan said he welcomed the 'opportunity of working with the board and staff as well as my family'. He noted the exciting opportunities that Ryanair was planning to pursue over the next couple of years. The airline also welcomed James Osborne, the former managing partner at A&L Goodbody, one of Dublin's leading law practices, as a director. MacSharry would remain on the board together with Ryan's two sons, Declan and Cathal, and another former chairman, Arthur Walls.

Over at Aer Lingus, the announcement that Ryan was joining the Ryanair board was greeted with great guffaws. One executive joked that the appointment was akin to a couple who had been covertly cohabiting for ten years announcing that they were getting married.

CHAPTER TEN

Peanuts

M ichael O'Leary was frustrated. It was November 1995, and Ryanair was planning its inaugural flight between Stansted and Prestwick Airport, west of Glasgow. Since the airline had announced its £59 return fare, which included free rail travel from any station in Scotland, thousands of people had rung to book the cheap seats. But its rivals had conspired to ground the flight, and it now looked like the airline chief might have to cancel any further bookings. 'In what other business do you not only have to tell your competitors what you plan to do before you do it, but have to ask them if they have any objections?' he asked wearily.

As a foreign airline, Ryanair had to set up a separate company in Britain, Ryanair UK, which had to apply for an airline operators' certificate to get airborne. This would take ten to fifteen weeks. In the interim Ryanair had arranged for GB Airways to lease one of its Boeing 737s to operate the service. It was the use of an Irish-registered plane on an internal UK route that prompted the first objection from rival carriers, who insisted that Ryanair operate a British-registered aircraft on the route. Ryanair's chief in Stansted, Tim Jeans, quickly searched for a replacement. At such short notice he could only find a smaller 1–11 jet, which was disastrous. It would mean that Ryanair would have to leave at least one passenger behind on the inaugural flight and that many who had enthusiastically booked seats on the new service would have to be turned away.

Then British Midland, and Air UK, which were both operating Scotland to London services, and British World Airways, objected to a non-UK airline operating an internal service at all.

Although the restrictions were due to be removed throughout Europe in two years, the airlines made it clear that they wouldn't tolerate any relaxation of the rules ahead of schedule. British Midland also threatened to sue Ryanair for its 'misleading' advertising, which said it flew to Glasgow rather than Prestwick. The management at Prestwick, which stood to gain enormously from Ryanair's custom, put pressure on the UK Ministry of Transport to let the service go ahead, and the airline was granted a last-minute special dispensation. After days of fraught negotiations and crisis management Ryanair was ready to fly to Scotland. By now, though, it had another competitor on its tail.

Stelios Haji-Ioannou, a twenty-eight-year-old Greek shipping tycoon, had spent two years travelling around the US, studying Southwest Airlines and its fellow low-cost operator ValuJet in Atlanta, Georgia. Just as Herb Kelleher had impressed O'Leary, Stelios (as he became known) claimed to have a friend and mentor in ValuJet chairman Robert Priddy. 'He was kind enough to let me understand how the whole concept works,' he said. 'We ring each other up and swap ideas. I understand the concept and believe there is a tremendous opportunity to make it work in Europe. If I don't do it now someone else will.'

Stelios established a base at a prefab at Luton airport and with two Boeing 737s was ready to launch his new airline, named easy-Jet. The carrier would fly between Luton and Glasgow Airport, charging passengers £29 each way. For the first two weeks, he pledged that all 130 seats on each of the three daily flights in each direction would be available at £29. After that, some seats would be available on every flight at this low rate on a first-come, first-served basis, and once they were all booked single fares of £39, £49 and £59 would come into play. He guaranteed that 100,000 seats a year would be available at the lowest price, and promised that in two weeks easyJet would offer the same fare to Edinburgh. 'Scotland is a huge market already – it will only take a small percentage rise in travellers to enable us to fill our aircraft. The market will respond to lower air fares.' He said that he didn't want to steal customers from other airlines but intended to create a market by encouraging people to fly rather than take a coach or train to Scotland. With such low fares, he said flying would become an impulse decision, 'instead of buying, say, a pair of jeans'.

The young Stelios had deep pockets. Three years earlier he had started a shipping line, Stelmar Tankers, which had a fleet worth more than $150 million. His father owned one of the world's biggest tanker fleets, and the family chipped in some of the £5 million used to start easyJet, the minimum required by the Civil Aviation Authority. Sources close to his company suggested the family had set strict stop-loss targets in terms of the time and money they would invest in the new venture. 'In essence, if the business isn't working in six months the plug is pulled,' the source said.

Stelios admitted that he was a novice when it came to the airline industry but believed he could make it work. 'Look, I know nothing about running an airline and I don't think I can do it any better than other airlines, so we subcontract that to someone else who can do it very well,' he explained. 'I will be concentrating on the marketing. The strategy calls for someone to start from scratch. You cannot convert a normal airline into a discount operator, because you have to bear costs like dealing with labour relations, you have the reliance on travel agents, and the costs of the big airline's computer systems. We have bought our own proprietary booking system from the US and passengers will book directly with us over the phone. We eliminate the middleman. So all I have to do is promote my phone number.'

The airline was the first to totally exclude travel agents to save money. Customers phoning easyJet's sales centre in Luton were told there could be no cancellations, alterations or refunds on tickets. The airline would not assign seat numbers when passengers checked in, leaving them to choose their own on board, and during the forty-minute direct flights to Glasgow and Edinburgh they would have to pay for drinks and snacks. In two weeks easyJet claimed it had sold 11,000 seats – enough to fill one hundred planes – and it launched an attack on Ryanair to generate some publicity. It placed an advertisement in the UK papers headed 'AYR MILES' to highlight the fact that easyJet flew to Glasgow International and not to Ayrshire's Prestwick Airport. The Irish airline raised no objections, but easyJet did offend Air Miles, the British Airway subsidiary company, whose lawyers dispatched a letter saying that the airline's use of 'Ayr Miles' was a phonetic infringement of its copyright.

Stelios managed to ruffle quite a few feathers, and it wasn't long before newspapers in London began to receive anonymous calls to alert them to an explosion on board one of his father's oil tankers which killed five employees while Stelios was working for the company four years earlier. The court case in Italy following the explosion on the *Haven* was still outstanding. The Greek airline chief said he was 'extremely sorry about it. It was a lesson well learned from many points of view and has made me determined to run only the safest of operations'.

About 33,000 people made the journey between London and Scotland every week and could now choose to fly with British Midland, British Airways, Air UK, Ryanair or easyJet. The airlines had collectively added close to 10,000 additional seats every week and were embroiled in a vicious price war to fill these flights. British Midland, the second-biggest carrier on the route, offered a £58 return ticket for some flights from Glasgow and Edinburgh to London. Air UK followed suit with the same fare. British Airways' lowest fare was £74 and it said it had 'no plans' to match the new prices but was watching developments. BA chairman Sir Colin Marshall said, 'We welcome new, low-fare competition if it helps to expand the market overall.'

As the only foreign carrier on the route, Ryanair wasn't allowed to sell more than half the available seats to Scotland until its operating certificate had been granted. It was offering 240,000 seats a year at £59 return, but to qualify for the cheapest ticket travellers had to spend a Saturday night or two other nights in London. In a bid to attract more business it decided to match easyJet's cheapest fare of £29 each way, and also pledged that every seat would be available at this price without restrictions. 'We saw other airlines matching our fares but with all kinds of length-of-stay and capacity controls,' Tim Jeans said. 'Passengers were still confused so we decided to establish this price on every single seat on every flight.' Stelios said he was 'flattered' that Ryanair had decided to imitate easyJet's fare structure. 'I don't think we need to do anything. Our service is still very competitive,' he added.

Jeans now admits that Ryanair found the London to Prestwick route very tricky and almost abandoned it. O'Leary demanded that any new route would have to break even in a very short period, and he was beginning to despair of its assault on Scotland. "Some airlines enter a new route and aim to make a profit in three years,' he claimed. 'We will not enter a route if we cannot break even in three hours and grow the market by at least one hundred per cent.' Jeans said they decided to add more flights to try to stimulate greater demand as a last-ditch effort to make the route work. 'It was very slow and we very nearly pulled off it. We felt that we had too little frequency and decided to give it one last go. We increased the number of flights, and to our surprise it worked.'

Every Monday morning Jeans, who directed the commercial team and was responsible for sales and marketing and for developing the base at Stansted, would take the first Ryanair flight to Dublin to attend the airline's weekly management meetings. One person suggested that Ryanair doesn't have a senior management team but one that 'recognises the Führer'. Staff who have been on the receiving end of one of the chief executive's ferocious verbal assaults – known within Ryanair as O'Leary 'hate beams' – are left shattered. When problems are raised he will simply bark at the person bearing the bad news to 'fix it'. One of the Ryanair crew said you always had to be careful about what you said to O'Leary. 'If you raised a problem, there had better be a problem and you had better have a start, middle and solution to that issue. You didn't start something and expect him to fix it.'

His five lieutenants came in the direct line of fire every Monday morning. The meetings would start at 8.30 sharp and, just like Tony Ryan at GPA, O'Leary would spend an hour goading Jeans, Howard Millar, Brian Taylor, Maurice O'Connor and Conor McCarthy to achieve the most stretching targets possible over the following days. 'Nobody missed them. There would be five or six of us. People would be savaged,' Jeans recalled. They came to be known as the 'spin the bottle' meetings, with O'Leary randomly selecting his victim. Those who managed to escape would sigh with relief, one source said. 'If you argued your point you would get your head kicked in. It was bizarre. He would be personally insulting and would be roaring and shouting. He was very frustrated because he could always see the full picture and was impatient when this wasn't obvious to others. Nine out of ten times he was right.' One person suggested that O'Leary, a consummate workaholic, felt that as they had had the weekend off they needed a 'kick up the backside' to get back to work on Monday. 'He would view a weekend off as being lazy,' the source explained.

O'Leary's aggressive management style increasingly began to rub off on others. 'More and more people began to get impatient, and shout and roar at staff when really they shouldn't,' one employee remarked. The management team was organised around making Ryanair an efficient airline, making sure that flights arrived and departed on time. 'He was trying to run an on-time, efficient organisation. That was his number one priority. That never altered,' said Jeans. O'Leary would send Jeans and Bernard Berger, who was in charge of route development, to negotiate deals with new airports. 'He would of course issue instructions on what we were to look for and get and wouldn't spare us when we returned with less than that,' Jeans recalled. 'His language would be at its most choice on those occasions. But when push came to shove though he was prepared to come out and back you up, do the publicity for the launch. This was a good example of where the team played to their individual strengths. We were very focused.'

'Once he trusts you, you can do what you want. The biggest sin in Ryanair is to do nothing. If you did something wrong you would get a bollocking, but if you did it again, God help you!' Conor McCarthy said that if your head was on the line at one of the Monday morning meetings you could expect to get no support from the others. 'If you jumped in to help someone else O'Leary would tell you to mind your own business. He wouldn't like it.'

One source said that the chief executive was a great motivator, although his behaviour could be appalling. 'He is aggressive, a bully and worse but he has a great ability to motivate people. The longer people stay the more cynical they get. People have a huge ability to take their medicine. He gets a lot out of people. He leads. His attitude is that if you won't do your job then he will do it.' It was a small and lean organisation and there was little office politicking played out at the upper echelons, mainly because it was clear that no one was going to get O'Leary's job. 'Loyalty is the most important thing as far as Michael is concerned,' the source added. 'He is a control freak.'

Staff were encouraged to come up with ideas to make Ryanair more efficient. O'Leary himself was always full of ideas and was never afraid to try them. One person remarked that he didn't have great listening skills. 'He would have a view and would stick to it. It would take a lot to talk him out of something. He was usually right, though, which could be very frustrating.' O'Leary would say that Ryanair's strategy was to simply run an airline in the way that people wanted. 'Our strategy is low fares, high capacity at busy times, flexible tickets,' he said. 'There are only three layers of management. No secrets. No dogma. No unions. I drive buses at the airport, check in passengers, load bags and get a good kicking when I play for the baggage-handlers' football team. The only thing I will not do is fly aircraft.'

Some staff said there had been much more fun before O'Leary arrived at Ryanair and that some of the early start-up team had been as good at managing the crew as the young chief executive. 'Derek O'Brien was as good a motivator as Michael O'Leary. Eugene O'Neill was good at giving people a role to do,' one explained. Another suggested that people who joined Ryanair in the 1980s 'joined a dream' while those who joined in the 1990s 'joined an airline'.

O'Leary had his own interpretation of the Southwest Airlines business model. He enthusiastically embraced the low-fares element but ignored its fundamental concern and courtesy for its customers. 'His attitude to passengers was that as they were paying so little they should just put up with problems,' one source explained. 'If things fell apart his view was, "Look, you got a cheap ticket, we are not going to put you up in a hotel."' This approach was not supported by all of his colleagues but few challenged him directly.

Many staff had stayed and some enjoyed rapid career progression, moving onto senior management posts or training as pilots. Most of the departures had been from amongst those dealing with customers, whether on the check-in desks or as cabin crew, where the airline's uncompromising attitude to its customers created huge pressure. 'Sometimes people came in and decided after a year that they just couldn't hack the pace,' one employee said.

Tony Ryan, now Ryanair's chairman, was growing frustrated. He had been searching for a partner to bring new investment to the airline for more than four years and Ryanair still needed huge capital investment to stay in business. It was a difficult time for an airline to try to raise money, even to buy aircraft, as many banks lacked the sophistication to understand and support its needs. Ryanair had managed to strike a deal on eleven Boeing 737 aircraft that were all ten years old and had to put down $20m from its own coffers as a one-third deposit on the finance lease. The rest was to be paid off over the next five years with bank loans from New York, leaving the airline with fairly modest cash reserves.

Ryanair, with its advisers, had devised what they considered to be a clever and attractive deal that would give a new investor a shareholding in the Irish airline. Just as Ryanair had talked about selling out to its most bitter enemy, Aer Lingus, some years earlier, this time it was prepared to strike a deal with its most arrogant adversary, British Airways. The British flag carrier had begun to recognise the success of the so-called 'peanut' airlines like Southwest Airlines, Ryanair and easyJet, and had drawn up tentative plans to start its own no-frills subsidiary. It had been steadily expanding its position in the British domestic market over the past three years and had signed up regional airlines such as Manx Airlines, Rayair, City Flyer Express and Brymon as franchise-style partners. These airlines used the BA Express name and could sell their flights as part of the BA network, which helped them to piggyback on the larger company's worldwide marketing and distribution services. BA was beginning to acknowledge publicly that the low-cost airlines were a force to be reckoned with, although its chairman, Sir Colin Marshall, suggested they were not stealing its customers: 'In terms of the low-cost carriers, it is obviously competition and it would be foolish to deny that, but they are offering a totally different service and operating in a totally different market.'

Tony Ryan believed that given BA's stated interest in the low-cost phenomenon it would certainly consider a proposition from Ryanair. The Irish airline claimed to have the lowest cost base of any airline in Europe and was on track to carry 3 million passengers between Ireland and the UK each year. But no one was underestimating the scale of the task involved in dealing with the high and mighty British flag carrier. Ryan's son Declan was sent to London with Michael O'Leary to bring the deal to BA. Their abrasive, no-nonsense style was in marked contrast to the more reserved and conceited demeanour of their would-be partners, making the discussions between the two airlines extremely awkward right from the outset. Over the weeks and months that followed the already poor relationship steadily worsened. 'BA was very bureaucratic and extremely arrogant,' one source said. 'It wanted to test the Ryanair executives.'

The Ryan family wanted to sell 25 per cent of Ryanair to BA – according to airline analysts, a stake worth around £10 million. But BA wanted to control Ryanair. There were suggestions that BA's first priority was for Ryanair to take on its red, white and blue livery and flight codes and to become part of its BA Express franchise network. This had been a successful formula for the airline, allowing BA to offer passengers services under its own name while actually using a much lower-cost operator to fly them.

The British carrier had a very clear idea about what it wanted from Ryanair. 'BA was looking for a 49 per cent shareholding with an option, that they didn't want to pay for, to eventually take full control of the airline,' one source believed. 'They wanted to get involved and then to screw it and take it out.' The Ryan family dearly wanted to cut this deal, though, and believed that they came close to agreement. One Ryanair source suggested that there were faults on both sides and that what was on the table was ultimately a good deal for BA and the Irish airline. 'Management on both sides had different philosophies. BA should have done the deal with Ryanair,' the source said. O'Leary was fully behind the proposal and stood to make some money from the deal. But the talks fell through. BA has said the discussions ended after Ryanair raised the price, while others suggest the deal unravelled because the structure would not have allowed the Ryan family to realise enough of a cash windfall. It was a huge disappointment for the Ryans and for O'Leary. 'The Ryans viewed the collapse of the discussions with BA as a total failure,' the source said. 'Today, they would still suggest they were lucky to survive after that time.' British Airways later talked to easyJet but the discussions came to nothing and the following year it started its own low-cost venture, Go.

Tony Ryan remained determined to find a partner for the family at Ryanair and trawled his extensive contacts. Right across Europe entrepreneurs were monitoring the battling peanut airlines and weighing up the opportunities to start new carriers to take to Europe's open skies. More than a hundred new airlines went into business around this time, although the casualty rate was extremely high: in 1994 alone, fifty-seven new airlines opened for business, of which thirty-seven closed within two years.

Richard Branson, who had founded the Virgin music, entertainment and transport group, was now toying with entering the fray. His Virgin Atlantic airline began to look at Euro Belgian Airlines, a charter-flight business that had just launched a subsidiary, EBA Express, offering low-price daily scheduled flights from Brussels to Rome, Barcelona, Madrid, Milan and Vienna. Branson wanted to restructure the business, modelling it on the US Continental Airlines' low-fares subsidiary, Continental Lite. He had assembled a group of investors to join him, including fifty-five-year-old former civil-rights lawyer David Bonderman.

The previous summer, Bonderman had joined up with Branson in the £300 million takeover of the MGM Cinema chain now known as Virgin Cinemas. Bonderman was known as the 'Buyout King'. He specialised in searching for high-yielding investments and generally backed businesses that other investors wouldn't touch. One US commentator summed him up by saying, 'When others zigged, Bonderman zagged.' He was one of the founding partners of the Texas Pacific Group, which bought into distressed companies in the US and was increasingly casting around for opportunities in Europe. One of his associates explained that TPG liked companies that required turning around or were complex. Regarded as a highly skilled and tough negotiator, the group was known to spend a long time courting deals it was really hungry for.

Bonderman, who had been part of the legal team that oversaw the re-organisation of Braniff Airlines, the first major US carrier to go broke, had gone on to work for the legendary Texas billionaire Robert Bass before founding TPG. He is described as a 'quirky' character with a wide range of interests. He was a rock and roll fan with a 500-strong record collection, all committed to memory, and was renowned for his 'blow-out parties' at his Washington home. When he started out as a lawyer he had worked for free to help to save New York Grand Central Station, one of America's finest Beaux Art buildings, from demolition. He had a degree in Russian studies, had studied Islamic law in Egypt and Tunis and travelled extensively. Associates, who call him 'Bondo', knew him as an entertaining character who didn't take himself too seriously. He had gained notoriety in the US for spearheading two of the most dramatic corporate turnarounds of the ailing Continental and America West airlines. Bankers on Wall Street were enthralled by his success, and he was spoken of as a corporate wizard who 'glowed in the dark'.

The Virgin group, together with Bonderman and other private investors, were preparing to buy 80 per cent of EuroBelgian Airlines from City Hotels for £43 million. Branson had poached Jonathan Ornstein, the former chief executive of the US Continental Express airline, to head the venture. The Ryans, who remained convinced that the deal they put to BA was a winner, contacted Ornstein to discuss a potential investment. Meanwhile Bonderman was frustrated with aspects of the proposed investment with Branson. He travelled to Ireland to thank the executives who had worked with him during the restructuring of America West, one of GPA's biggest customers, and when he met executives from GPA, now part of the General Electric group, for dinner in Dublin, he spoke about his difficulties. By the end of the night, it had been suggested that Bonderman should talk to Tony Ryan about getting involved in Ryanair.

The discussion was relayed to Ryan, who decided to travel to New York with the aim of renewing his acquaintance with Bonderman and enticing him to invest in Ryanair. Ryan brought the deal they had crafted for BA to Bonderman and over three months his associates modified what was on the table, refining the details to a high point of sophistication. When it looked like he was close to buying into Ryanair, Bonderman dropped out of Branson's consortium. Before signing the agreement he flew to Dublin to meet O'Leary's lieutenants.

The top management team, assembled at the Ryan family's salubrious offices on Dublin's Merrion Square, were surprised to see that Wall Street's golden boy was wearing slippers with his suit. They made a presentation to him, during which each explained their roles and answered specific questions about the airline's operations. It was Ryanair's final effort to impress Bonderman to come on board, and it worked. Shortly afterwards he concluded a deal with the Ryan family. They were delighted to have found someone they could do business with. 'He is a good down-to-earth person and he has a very good team around him,' one source explained. 'It was a very clever deal for both sides. It was the structure that was clever.'

The deal, arranged in August 1996, was based on bringing Ryanair to trade on the international stock markets, and it would prove to be very lucrative for the Ryans for Bonderman and for O'Leary. The staff who joined the airline in 1986 had each been given 500 Ryanair shares. But in the late 1980s the Ryan family offered to buy the shares back for around £200 to each member of staff, in a transaction explained as a 'tidying-up' exercise. One staff member fought hard to hold onto his shares but was eventually browbeaten into submission. The airline was owned, through a company called Ryanair Limited, by a trust set up by Tony Ryan, whose beneficiaries were Declan, Cathal and Shane Ryan. The company now possessed substantial cash reserves, but its structure meant that Ryan was unable to access this money directly.

In a complex series of transactions, the Ryans, Bonderman and O'Leary established a new company, Ryanair Holdings, that bought the airline from the family for £56.7 million. In return, the existing company, Ryanair Limited, made a £27.7 million interest-free loan to Ryanair Holdings, which was paid directly to the Ryan family, while Bonderman and his investors lent another £24 million to the new company to top up the cash payment to the Ryans. But the sweetest part of the transaction was that together the Ryans, Bonderman and O'Leary paid the remaining sum, just £5 million in cash, to take control of Ryanair, an airline they had valued at nearly £57 million.

The Ryans chipped in £3.1 million of their new-found wealth to purchase a 62 per cent shareholding in Ryanair Holdings, the new company that owned the airline. Bonderman, through a company called Irish Air, paid just £1 million to buy a 20 per cent shareholding in the same company while O'Leary bought the remaining 18 per cent of Ryanair for a mere £900,000. The 'Buyout King' and his new partners had instantly made a more than ten-fold return on their investment, while the Ryans had walked away with nearly £50 million in cash and could look forward to much more in the next eighteen months. And this was only the start.

The Ryans believed that in David Bonderman they had found the 'perfect partner', according to sources, and Tony Ryan was delighted to announce his arrival. He said the new shareholders would bring financial and airline industry expertise that would allow Ryanair to grow. He also mentioned that Ryanair might seek a stock-market flotation to raise the funds it needed to acquire new aircraft to speed up its expansion into Europe, and added that Bonderman's arrival wouldn't herald any changes to the airline's management team. Bonderman said he saw great opportunities for the airline; as his spokesman announced, 'He sees that the European airline industry is at a turning point, which offers real opportunities for a company like Ryanair.'

CHAPTER ELEVEN

Floating on Air

I t was a remarkable reversal of fortune for Tony Ryan and his family. Having seen a $300 million fortune slip from his grasp three years earlier he was in the mood to celebrate, and planned a lavish party to mark his sixtieth birthday. Over a hundred friends and family, including his new partner, the international fashion designer Louise Kennedy, were invited to La Mamounia in Marrakesh, Winston Churchill's favourite hotel. They travelled on a Ryanair plane from Dublin during which the airline's no-frills policy was stood down: those boarding the flight were handed a fez and treated to champagne and Turkish delight while a Moroccan belly dancer writhed through the aisles. Everyone raved about the festivities.

Ryanair's ten other aircraft were busy flying to fourteen destinations, with the airline expecting to carry 3 million passengers that year. Ryanair's shareholders – the Ryan family, David Bonderman's consortium and Michael O'Leary – were planning to grow the airline by a very ambitious 25 per cent a year. Their top priority was to expand into continental Europe. With the new investors on board, the airline found it easier to raise money from banks to acquire more aircraft, and it purchased six Boeing 737 aircraft from Lufthansa. Now all Ryanair had to do was negotiate a deal with Aer Rianta on the charges to be applied to its new European routes. But the talks quickly descended into a public slanging match, and in 1996 Ryanair's very public battle with Aer Rianta began.

O'Leary's abhorrence of the media continued. The young chief executive allowed Ryan to take the spotlight for much of the debate and would only emerge to grab the headlines on specific issues, afterwards beating a hasty retreat to his bunker at Dublin Airport for months on end. Ryanair claimed that Aer Rianta's charges were more expensive than the other airports it was serving. Indeed, Ryan's frustration was such that he decided he would build a competing airport at the military airport at Baldonnel in the south Dublin region. The project was to be managed and funded separately from Ryanair and Ryan promised to organise the £50 million investment required. When outlining his proposal, Ryan explained that he would ideally like to buy the original terminal building at Dublin Airport, which housed Aer Rianta's offices, but knew this would never be a runner. 'I think that making a formal offer to Aer Rianta for anything is a waste of the typist's time,' he explained.

Ryanair's chairman began to lobby politicians and to talk publicly about his new venture, announcing that Ryanair would soon offer flights for £80 to Europe from the new airport. 'Dublin Airport is the most expensive airport we operate into,' he claimed. 'We know how much money we pay Aer Rianta every year and it makes eminent sense for us to do it on our own.' Ryan said that a 'privately owned farming stock company from Tipperary' couldn't afford to subsidise the travelling public.

O'Leary met some politicians with Ryan when the project was being presented, although he seemed opposed to the building of a second airport. 'He would raise his eyes up to heaven and discreetly mention that none of Ryanair's money would be used at Baldonnel,' one source said. As the concept was further advanced, O'Leary publicly distanced the airline from Ryan's plans and wrote to the Irish newspapers stating that Ryanair had 'no plans, no interest and no intention of moving to Baldonnel'. He added that the airline had submitted its own growth proposals to the Irish Government, which involved the development of a second and competing terminal at Dublin Airport instead. 'It is important that the Ryan family's plans for Baldonnel do not cloud this debate,' O'Leary wrote. 'Baldonnel is not and does not form any part of Ryanair's growth plans.' It was a very public rebuke for Ryan, particularly harsh for coming from his protégé and former personal assistant.

Tensions between the two men were running high at this time, with Ryan's once-loyal lieutenant now leading the charge to oust him from Ryanair. The airline's board of directors, which included Bonderman and two of his associates, Richard Shifter and Geoffrey Shaw, was focused on bringing Ryanair to trade on the international stock markets. A committee comprising O'Leary, Declan Ryan, Shaw, Shifter and director James Osborne was formed and given total authority to determine and control all issues relating to the flotation.

Going to the stock markets was a bold move, particularly for the Ryan family after their previous experience with GPA. Everyone was nervous and there was a determination that the problems that beset GPA would not haunt Ryanair. Some of the directors, particularly O'Leary, were concerned that Tony Ryan's association with GPA's collapse could scupper their plans to attract investors to Ryanair. When Bonderman had bought into Continental Airlines he had become chairman and was visibly associated with the airline's turnaround. The committee driving the flotation wanted investors to view his arrival at Ryanair in the same way: they wanted Bonderman to take over as chairman and began to pressurise Tony Ryan to give the role up. O'Leary was far more ruthless. He believed his mentor should leave the Ryanair board altogether and relinquish all ties with the airline that bore his name. 'He felt the airline's credibility would be damaged by the failure of GPA,' one source said. 'I thought Michael was being very cheeky.'

Deeply wounded by the suggestion that he was a liability to Ryanair, Ryan put up fierce resistance. One person close to the company recalled there was a 'big battle' to wrest the chairman's role from Tony to give it to Bonderman. Ryan turned to close friends for advice. Former GPA director James King remembered drinking several bottles of good wine while discussing the problem. 'I think it was a very sore thing for Tony. I remember he was told: "Tony, you can't be chairman. There is going to be an IPO [an initial public offer of shares on the stock market]. You have egg all over your face from GPA. You have to step aside."' King believed Ryan's pride was injured, but said he agreed to do what was required. 'He had the courage to take it on the chin and stood aside.'

Ryan resigned as chairman, making way for Bonderman, just three months after the American investor has arrived at Ryanair.

But he refused to bow to O'Leary's demand that he should step down from the board. When the new chairman's appointment was announced O'Leary said this had never been a condition of the deal struck with Bonderman. 'Dr Tony Ryan indicated some time ago that he wanted to step down as chairman in the medium term,' he explained, using the honorary title Ryan had received from Trinity College Dublin.

The Government failed to back Ryan's proposal for Baldonnel and instead sanctioned a £95 million investment by Aer Rianta at Dublin Airport to cope with the extra capacity. Disappointed with the decision, Ryan said Ryanair would shelve its expansion out of Ireland and consider moving its entire operational base from Dublin to Stansted. 'The new service between London and Glasgow is perhaps a template for the airline's future development,' he warned. Competitors dismissed these words as a classic diversionary tactic, designed to take attention away from the fact that the airline was finding it uneconomical to offer £49 fares to London. But some politicians took the threat seriously. Mary Harney, the leader of the Progressive Democrats opposition party, accused the Government of creating a 'hostile' environment for private businesses. 'It would be no surprise if Ryanair decided to concentrate its expansion elsewhere,' she said. 'Every effort is being made to protect the State.'

O'Leary chimed into the debate to drive home the message that Ryanair was a consumer's champion whose only aim was to offer low fares. He claimed that Stansted Airport had agreed to charge Ryanair £1 per passenger on new European routes such as Paris, Brussels and Amsterdam. 'While Aer Rianta may seem competitive on published rates, this is not the case in reality,' O'Leary argued. Ryanair said that the landing and departure charge it paid at Dublin Airport was almost twice that charged at the next most expensive airport in Britain – and ten times as expensive as the cheapest. Ryanair had negotiated such good deals in the UK that two airports didn't impose any charges on the airline at all. 'They get revenue from items such as car-parking, duty free and customer services,' O'Leary claimed. Of the airports that did charge fees, he said that Glasgow's Prestwick Airport was the lowest, while Bristol and Teesside airports had welcomed the carrier warmly and encouraged its expansion there, and another eighteen were courting Ryanair. The airline submitted proposals to the Irish Department of Transport to operate new European routes but stipulated this would only be possible if Aer Rianta lowered its landing charges.

The airline had enjoyed remarkable success on the Ireland and UK routes, largely due to the huge numbers of friends and relatives who had begun to visit each other regularly now that airfares had become cheap. Before Ryanair's arrival fewer than one million people flew between Dublin and London each year. By 1996 this number had more than trebled, and over half of these passengers flew with Ryanair. But the airline needed to open European routes if the company was to be marketed as a diversified scheduled airline rather than a low-fares commuter linking Ireland and the UK. It wanted to build a series of routes out of Dublin to the main European cities and then to manage a similar expansion out of Stansted.

Ryanair was now ready to test the next part of Southwest Airline's successful business model in Europe. The low-cost pioneer had shown that it was possible to attract millions of passengers to fly to out-of-town airports close to major US cities by offering cheap fares. Ryanair just had to find suitable airports in Europe, and that task fell to Bernard Berger. 'He was always going to places you couldn't pronounce,' said Conor McCarthy. 'He oozed with demographics and would look at the traffic patterns for building up airports. In the end we went to the airports where we could get the cheapest deals.'

O'Leary researched airports close to France and Belgium's capital cities and dispatched his lieutenants to talk to their owners. They identified the tiny Beauvais Airport, 60km north of Paris in Picardy, as the most promising link to the French capital. The Chamber of Commerce and Industry of Oise that owned Beauvais airport was delighted to do business with Ryanair. In Belgium, Charleroi Airport, 46km south of Brussels in the Walloon region, also had potential. Owned by the Walloon regional government, Charleroi would only really get busy when staff had to cope with the arrival of a flight diverted from another airport. Indeed, such was its tranquillity that when the Ryanair team arrived they noticed there were sheep lazily grazing around the runway. Charleroi, which had once been a thriving mining town, was an unemployment black spot. When a new airline offered to bring millions of passengers into the region the Walloon government readily agreed to Ryanair's terms.

And so O'Leary announced that Ryanair would begin to fly from Dublin to Paris and Brussels on 1 May 1997 for just £79 return – almost £100 cheaper than Aer Lingus. There would be six daily flights to the French capital and four to Brussels, he said, declaring, 'This is a great day for the consumer.' Ryanair promised that at least 70 per cent of the capacity, or some 950 seats a day, would be sold at £79 or £99. A special coach would meet each flight to ferry passengers to the city centre for an extra £5, and local taxis had agreed to charge a flat rate for Ryanair passengers.

Travel agents said the announcement was excellent news for customers in Ireland, France and Belgium, but warned that numbers travelling would need to double to sustain the current capacity. 'At the moment there are four flights to Paris a day, three Aer Lingus and one Air France,' said Neil Horgan, managing director of Abbey Travel. 'Ryanair is putting on three more. In the short term at least that is overcapacity.'

O'Leary was unconcerned about the travel agents' view on Ryanair's push into Europe but was getting more and more irritated by the commissions that the airline was forced to pay for their services. He was viciously cutting costs at the airline to swell its profits and impress potential investors, and he saw the potential for saving millions of pounds by restructuring its reservation systems to encourage more people to book their tickets directly with the airline, steadily squeezing out the travel agents.

About 75 per cent of Ryanair's seats were sold by travel agents, who booked them through the British Airways Booking System and others such as Galileo and Worldspan. Ryanair was charged for participating in these reservation networks and had to pay a transaction fee based on the number of journeys booked through these systems, as well as a 9 per cent commission to the travel agents for every ticket sold. The remainder of Ryanair's tickets were sold directly, to customers phoning the airline's reservations centres in Dublin and London. This was a far cheaper system for Ryanair, and to capitalise on it the airline established a new company, Ryanair Direct, which centralised the reservations operations and allowed callers from the UK to book tickets for the price of a local call. It expected to employ up to 200 staff in this business and was awarded employment grants and other assistance from the Irish Government's development agency, Forbairt – £9000 for every full-time permanent job created, up to a maximum of £1.8 million, and a further £400,000 towards the cost of its new Dublin offices. As part of the grant aid agreement, Ryanair gave Forbairt an option to purchase 5 per cent of Ryanair Direct which could be cancelled in lieu of a cash payment.

O'Leary appointed Caroline Green, who had huge experience of computerised reservation systems, to run the new company. The airline recruited a hundred staff to man the phones and planned to process 4 million customers a year in this way. The new direct reservations systems had the capacity to handle 10 million calls annually, and staff were incentivised to win new business by cold-calling groups of customers who had previously used Ryanair. The company also planned to undertake contract telemarketing work for other companies.

But the majority of the airline's tickets were still sold through travel agents. In the UK these included Thomas Cook, Going Places and A.T. Mays, and when Ryanair expanded into Europe it would be relying on major travel agents in Scandinavia, France and Belgium to market and sell its fares to new passengers. O'Leary wanted to continue to do business with the travel agents but was determined to reduce the costs involved. He said that the 9 per cent commission, the rate recommended for international flights by the International Air Travel Association, was too high and proposed it be reduced to 7.5 per cent, a move that would save the airline about £1.3 million a year. He argued flights between the UK and Ireland should be considered as domestic and stressed that the company needed to keep costs down to maintain its low fares.

The travel agents were outraged, and feared that Ryanair could inspire other operators whose business was much more valuable to do the same. Travel agency associations in Ireland, England and Scotland threatened to boycott the airline, a move that had potentially devastating consequences for Ryanair, particularly at a time when it was preparing to come to the stock

markets. 'It could comfortably lose 20 to 25 per cent of its business, and that's the difference between profit and loss,' predicted
Tony Hughes, chairman of the Guild of Business Travel Agents.
Willie Stewart, an executive member of Scotway, a consortium of
120 Scottish travel agencies, suggested the boycott could be lethal.
'If all the agents who say they'll stop selling Ryanair to leisure
passengers do it, it could ground them.'

Undaunted, O'Leary accused the travel agents of living in the
past, when air fares were high. There was never a bad time to
reduce costs and air fares, he said. 'I don't anticipate any effects
on sales. Where would 25 per cent of the traffic go? If a passenger
goes to A.T. Mays or Lunn Poly and asks for a £59 flight from
Prestwick to Dublin, will they tell them they have to buy a dearer
flight with someone else?' When agents such as Thomas Cook
had refused to take part in a recent Ryanair £29 flights promotion, they had simply seen customers go to other agencies.

Ryanair held private discussions with trade bodies, which
only resulted in both sides trading insults in public. Ryanair
accused the Irish Travel Agents' Association of 'double standards'
and of having privately suggested adding £5 to fares as a way
round the dispute. 'We told them to go to hell,' O'Leary said.
ITAA chief executive Brendan Moran dismissed the claims as
mischievous: 'We never said it. That's ludicrous. Confrontation
seems to be the language Ryanair understands.' The smaller travel
agents, which had been the backbone of Ryanair's success, said
they felt 'kicked in the teeth'.

The Irish Competition Authority received a complaint that
the travel agents' adoption of a uniform level of commission and
its threatened boycott was anti-competitive, and launched an
investigation. It warned the travel agents their campaign against
Ryanair was indeed anti-competitive and that the organisers
could face immediate court action. The travel agents suspected
Ryanair of making the complaint but the airline denied any
involvement. The UK Office of Fair Trading received an anonymous complaint and was prompted to assess the boycott, and the
European Commission also fired a shot across the travel agents'
bows. 'It's all getting a bit hairy-chested. It's unfortunate,' said
one travel-agency representative. These powerful interventions
stopped the boycott and handed a victory to O'Leary. Over the

next twelve months Ryanair reduced its commissions from 9 per cent to 7.5 per cent, as they had planned.

O'Leary's colleagues on the flotation committee were meanwhile busy preparing Ryanair's stock-market debut. They had hired one of the world's most prestigious firms, Morgan Stanley, to manage the share issue. Bonderman had forged close links with the firm over the years and potential investors were impressed that Morgan Stanley was to underwrite the share offering. Credit Suisse First Boston and Robinson-Humphrey joined as underwriters and in Ireland Ryanair appointed Bank of Ireland's corporate-finance division and the country's largest stockbroking firm, Davy, as advisers.

Ryanair's new chairman opened doors for the airline; the world's major investment houses were all prepared to meet the company that Bonderman had aligned himself to. Ryanair sold itself as 'the Southwest of Europe', and O'Leary and his team showed how they had adopted Southwest Airlines' successful business model and made it work in Europe, pointing to Bonderman's investment in the company as proof of its tremendous potential. 'What David brought was, "Hey you guys, I have found it [the Southwest of Europe]. I got a piece of it,"' said a Ryanair source. Some of these investors still bore the scars of GPA, though, and the airline told US investment bankers that 'overcoming the Ryan "taint"' was one of Ryanair's key hurdles along the path to flotation. Documents presented to the bankers referred to the 'overhang of Ryan family ownership position' and 'prior negative GPA experience'. Because of GPA's crash landing in London, Ryanair decided to list the share on stock exchanges only in Ireland and the US. Publicly it suggested it was avoiding the London market because of a 'lack of understanding' in the City of its low-cost, no-frills philosophy, but it was forced to admit that the 'hangover' from GPA made other markets more attractive. It optimistically said that a successful float would 'rekindle' interest in the Irish airline in London.

In the weeks before the flotation, O'Leary and the Ryanair team travelled across the US and Europe trying to woo investors. As they went from one institution to the next they kept bumping into another Irish company, Esat Digifone, founded by Denis O'Brien, that was also heading for the stock market. It was the first time that O'Leary met O'Brien, the young entrepreneur who had also started his career as Ryan's personal assistant.

The move to the stock markets catapulted the media-loathing chief executive into the public eye. O'Leary began to give interviews in the media to help to build the airline's profile and impress potential investors. He joked with journalists about his more public persona. 'You're probably wondering why we're suddenly talking to everybody for the first time in ten years. When this is finished we'll probably disappear for another ten years.' Ryanair was coming to the stock markets to raise between £100 million and £120 million through the sale of 54 million shares. The shares were due to be listed on the Dublin and New York stock markets on 29 May 1997 at the beginning of its busiest season and the flotation was expected to value Ryanair at about £300 million. Its timing was good. The US airline industry had undergone a remarkable turnaround, with the likes of Delta, United and American all showing good profit margins for almost two years. The Dow Jones Transportation Index, where they were listed, was trading near an all-time high, having risen by as much as 20 per cent on the previous year. There was a tremendous appetite for new offerings, with particular interest in turnaround companies and foreign stocks.

It was now that Ryanair revealed, through its flotation document, that it was much more profitable than it had previously declared. It explained the extra £7 million profits as a result of a new accounting policy that changed the way it accounted for the depreciation and maintenance of its aircraft. The figures just confirmed what many of Ryanair's competitors had suspected for many years: that despite always wearing a poor mouth, the airline was one of the most profitable in Europe.

Its almost 700 staff, who had endured pay cuts and far fewer benefits than their equivalents at other airlines, were horrified to learn of the extraordinarily generous executive bonus scheme through which multi-million pound payments had been doled out to O'Leary and to Cathal and Declan Ryan. The lucrative deal O'Leary had cut with Tony Ryan when the airline had been on the brink of bankruptcy in 1989 had since been extended to Ryan's two elder sons, leaving the three men entitled to pocket 50 per cent of the annual profits. Details of the scheme, which had been introduced in 1993, were first disclosed in documents prepared for investors ahead of the flotation. In 1995, when the airline was said to be making profits of £5 million, O'Leary and the two elder Ryan sons shared a £5 million bonus, which was more than 25 per cent of the airline's £16 million wage bill. The following year, the bonus payments rose to £8.9 million, or almost half of Ryanair's £20 million wage costs. By 1997 O'Leary was the only executive director and was paid a £9.8 million bonus – more than 40 per cent of the £24 million Ryanair paid to its staff that year. By the time Ryanair was ready to become a public company, its thirty-two-year old chief executive was already fantastically rich. In the previous three years he had taken bonus payments worth £17 million, and in addition now owned 18 per cent of the airline.

When the media began to question these payments Ryanair explained that they were the result of the arrangements put in place many years earlier when the company was losing money, and would end after the flotation. 'Nobody thought then that profits would grow so rapidly,' a source said. 'But it would be impossible to bring in outside investors with this scheme in place so it was terminated.' O'Leary had drawn up a new three-year contract by which he would be paid £198,000 a year plus bonuses of up to 50 per cent of his annual salary. The airline also took out a 'key man' insurance policy on O'Leary, though it warned investors that the £5 million it could collect in the event of his untimely demise 'may not adequately compensate' for the loss of his services to Ryanair.

The airline admitted to investors that the disclosure of its true profits and its executives' generous rewards could trigger pay claims from its staff. In 1997 Ryanair's total staff costs were well below those of other airlines. It had just recently concluded a five-year pay deal with its pilots, to be reviewed only 'in exceptional circumstances', that provided for a 3 per cent annual increase in their base salary, but also contained provisions for a 17 per cent to 61 per cent rise in the payments to be awarded based on the number of flights they worked. The company told investors that 'a variety of factors, including, but not limited to, the company's recent profitability and disclosure of the level of executive director bonuses, may make it more difficult to maintain its current base salary levels and current employee compensation agreements'.

Ryanair said it could offer no assurances to investors that it would be able to maintain its low pay levels for any extended period of time, or that its employee compensation agreements might not have to be modified in the future. It also mentioned the fact that its main base, Dublin Airport, was 'highly unionised' as an investment risk factor. 'Ryanair is unable to predict whether any of its employees will elect in the future to require formal binding negotiations through a collective bargaining unit. If Ryanair's employees were to opt for such negotiations, Ryanair's flexibility in dealing with its employees would be restricted, which could result in a material increase in its operating costs,' the document stated.

Ryanair's staff were aggrieved by the figures disclosed, and the baggage-handlers in particular were feeling hard done by. In return for dealing directly with its staff on pay negotiations rather than through trade unions, the airline had assured the workforce that they would enjoy higher pay than their unionised contemporaries. But the baggage-handlers had just learned that, following negotiations with SIPTU, Servisair, which also had operations at Dublin Airport, had sanctioned a pay rise for its ground handling staff that brought their average earnings to £16,000 a year, compared to £13,500 at Ryanair. They were raging.

O'Leary, who was travelling abroad leading the Ryanair investor roadshow, heard of the growing discontent through regular phone calls to the Dublin headquarters. Conor McCarthy was in the front line trying to contain the swelling pressure. Everyone knew that a strike could derail the flotation. 'Everyone was afraid of another GPA,' one source said. 'The baggage-handlers could see an opportunity to screw things up. They wanted money now. O'Leary could read what was going on. He told his lieutenants they were doing a great job and to keep control of it until he came back.'

SIPTU, the trade union that represented most workers at Dublin airport, seized on disclosure of the bonuses paid to the executives to criticise the pay and conditions at Ryanair, as part of a campaign to win members at the airline. Its negotiator, Paul O'Sullivan, described the bonus payments as 'extraordinary' given that pay rates at Ryanair started at just £3 an hour and that staff didn't receive extra pay for working shifts or on Sundays or bank holidays. He said that if O'Leary's final bonus of nearly £10 million had been shared between its staff, they would have received about £14,000 each. 'Ryanair has pleaded the poor mouth but the fat cats at the top creamed off the money that could have been used to pay the workforce a decent wage,' O'Sullivan told the media. 'Bad conditions don't apply to pay alone. Regarding staff, Ryanair operates like a revolving door. There is little or no job security and a climate of fear operates.'

McCarthy dismissed O'Sullivan's claims, saying that Ryanair cabin crew were paid a basic hourly rate of £3.60 but that with flight-related pay and commissions on duty-free sales they earned an average of £18,000 annually. He said the ground handling staff were paid £7.80 an hour, which included a 10 per cent productivity element, and rejected SIPTU's 'revolving door' claims, saying the airline's staff numbers had been growing strongly over the previous three years.

McCarthy met the disgruntled group. He told them that Ryanair was prepared to match the new Servisair rates and that this would be agreed when O'Leary returned to Dublin. 'We needed to agree how it would be paid and didn't want to be seen to be dancing to SIPTU's tune,' he said. 'O'Leary was genuinely concerned about what was happening.' The baggage-handlers demanded a meeting with O'Leary as soon as he touched down in Dublin. The jetlagged and weary chief executive went directly from his New York flight to the meeting and managed to concede just enough ground to keep them on side. It was agreed that Ryanair would give the baggage-handlers a pay increase one year ahead of the next scheduled review. O'Leary also gave a commitment that the airline would pay them more than its competitors and promised to review overtime rates. Details of what was agreed were recorded in an internal memo and the baggage-handlers accepted the deal. As part of the flotation, it was agreed that all of Ryanair's 698 staff would share a £1.9 million bonus payment, and the airline also agreed to set aside 5 per cent (the staff had wanted 10 per cent) of Ryanair's shares as part of an employee share-option scheme.

O'Leary's colleagues were very impressed with his handling of this potentially disastrous situation. 'He has that great ability to think clearly even when he was looking over the edge of the cliff,' said one source. 'He was amazing. He fixed it.' According to McCarthy, O'Leary expressed his appreciation for his efforts in containing the potentially devastating problem in a handwritten note.

O'Leary's lieutenants, McCarthy, Howard Millar, Tim Jeans, Brian Taylor, Maurice O'Connor, and Michael Cawley, an accountant who had joined Ryanair three months earlier as its chief financial officer, were also discontent. They felt short-changed by the 100,000 share options they were each being offered, equal to about £1.4 million in total. The £17 million O'Leary had taken out of the company in the three previous years really rankled with them. 'There was a bit of jealousy about what Michael had been paid,' one employee explained. 'Some felt that they had worked hard too and that it had been a tough grind and that they should have gotten more.'

Cawley felt so undervalued that he refused to come into work one day in protest at what was on the table. Millar, the longest-serving lieutenant, vented his spleen when the team gathered with O'Leary to discuss the flotation. The airline chief was incensed by their attitude. 'He told them they could all fuck off and said if they weren't happy they could take the high road,' said one Ryanair source. 'His attitude was that they should be grateful that they were getting more than anyone else in the airline. He also pointed out that none of them yet had anything in writing to confirm their share options. He was really pissed off with them.' Just before the flotation, O'Leary elevated Charlie Clifton, the fifth person recruited by Ryanair and now head of ground operations and in-flight services, to the top management team to share in the lucrative share options on offer.

Ryanair's dealings with potential investors had been far less troublesome, and in the days before the shares came to trade on the Dublin stock exchange and on New York's NASDAQ index, the share offering was heavily oversubscribed. The shares were to be offered at a price of £1.95. On 29 May 1997 Ryanair's biggest shareholders, the Ryan family, would reduce their stake in Ryanair from 62 per cent to 35.5 per cent, and stood to gain more than £40 million. Their remaining shareholding in the airline was worth another £100 million. Bonderman and his investors and O'Leary did not reduce their shareholdings but their stakes did fall as a result of the number of new shares that were issued for the flotation. Bonderman's shareholding declined from 19.9 per cent to 15.7 per cent and was worth more than £48 million. O'Leary's shareholding, diluted from 18 per cent to 14 per cent, was valued at close to £44 million. The majority of Ryanair's staff subscribed for shares to the value of £2.2 million, paying the offer price of £1.95 each.

The omens for this flotation appeared very good. The day before the stock-market launch Ryanair shares were changing hands on the unofficial 'grey' market for up to £2.50 each, some 30 per cent above the offer price. A big screen was installed at Ryanair's Dublin headquarters so that staff could monitor the performance of their shares. When the Dublin stock market opened for business that morning Ryanair shares soared strongly ahead, shooting up to £3.15 by the close of business that evening. At that price Ryanair's stock-market value had swelled from £300 million to £500 million. The Ryan family's shareholding was worth £164 million. O'Leary's stake had risen to £71 million and Bonderman's to £73 million.

As the shares began to surge the Ryanair staff at its Dublin head office whooped with delight. By the end of the session their investments has almost doubled in value, and many had made an instant profit of between £5000 and £10,000. 'It was the price of a new car or a deposit on a flat. There was a fantastic atmosphere,' Jeans recalled. 'Of all the days in Ryanair, that was the greatest.'

CHAPTER TWELVE

Strike

Terry Morgan, Stansted Airport's chief executive, had struck up a good relationship with Michael O'Leary and the Ryan family, and they exchanged hospitality during the Ireland and England rugby matches. 'It's been going on for about ten or fifteen years,' Morgan said, as he recalled one weekend he spent as O'Leary's guest. 'About the second or third time I went to Dublin Michael very kindly offered for myself and my wife to stay at his apartment. We had a particularly heavy evening of drinking with the Ryan brothers, Cathal and Declan, and with Michael. It was very late when we ended up at his apartment. Everybody was feeling a little bit delicate and went to bed. We were in bed for no more than a couple of hours when we were awoken at about eight in the morning with someone knocking on the door. Michael came into the bedroom with a tray with toast and stuff for breakfast and said he had to go.' Morgan said he told them to let themselves out of the apartment and drop the keys through the letterbox. 'We were due to fly out with Ryanair that morning and got to the airport at about ten o'clock. And as we were getting onto the plane we spotted our host, Michael O'Leary, loading bags onto a Ryanair flight. I thought that was dedication. It was a busy weekend for them and he was there at the frontline keeping things going.'

O'Leary, like Herb Kelleher, likes people to know that from time to time he puts his back into loading and unloading the bags on Ryanair flights alongside the airline's baggage-handling crew. He enjoys being known as 'one of the lads', the casually dressed chief executive who mucks in and takes on any task to ease the day-to-day operations at Ryanair, cheerfully humping the bags while sharing wisecracks with the crew.

However, O'Leary's relationship with the Ryanair ground staff has not always been as happy as this image suggests. Unlike Kelleher, he has also stridden down to the baggage hall to taunt, threaten and humiliate these same colleagues, notably during the dark days when they dared to contemplate joining a trade union. Ryanair's role model, Southwest Airlines, is the most heavily unionised airline in the US and Kelleher and his team encourage all workers to be part of a union, believing that the company-union relationship has contributed fundamentally to the airline's enduring success. Ryanair had a different philosophy.

It had always been a demanding employer. By this time Aer Lingus' 5000 employees enjoyed far better working conditions than the almost 900 at Ryanair. They were paid more money and had good holiday and shift arrangements, much of which had been brokered by the trade unions that represented the majority of workers. Some of the Ryanair crew had made informal approaches to the various unions that had a presence at Dublin Airport in the company's early days, but it was not until the early 1990s that the first real skirmish took place, when the Amalgamated Engineering and Electrical Union (AEEU) sought to represent eight craft workers complaining about low pay and served a strike notice on the airline. That strike was averted after Ryanair senior management contacted each of the workers at their homes over the weekend to persuade them to abandon the industrial action threatened for Monday morning. They all reported for work and the strike was abandoned.

Over the years various staff tried to establish from trade unions such as SIPTU what type of entitlements they should be seeking from Ryanair, which was now a highly profitable airline. 'They were paid a lot less than the staff at Aer Lingus. By and large the company wasn't paying people proper holiday pay, never mind the basic rates,' said the union's former official at Dublin Airport, Paul O'Sullivan, who said he had been approached by various Ryanair staff.

The promised increase in the baggage-handlers' wages, sanctioned by O'Leary at the last minute ahead of the Ryanair stockmarket flotation, had materialised. But it had left some of them still earning less than their colleagues at Servisair, something that

Ryanair had promised in writing would not be the case. 'When the workers started to look at what they got, they discovered, yes they got a pay rise, but it didn't bring them up to Servisair. They were very sore over that,' O'Sullivan recalled. 'Every time they met O'Leary he would always deny that a promise had been made in any form of document. He wouldn't accept any type of documentation as evidence.'

In December 1997 fifty baggage-handlers decided that the only way to resolve this impasse was for SIPTU to represent them and negotiate on their behalf with Ryanair. The trade union wrote to Ryanair to seek a meeting. 'Prior to sending that letter I was well aware of Ryanair's track record. I knew the company was not going to turn around and start talking with SIPTU.' O'Sullivan said the union's executive at Dublin's Liberty Hall knew that once it sought to represent these workers it was likely to end up in a dispute with Ryanair. It endorsed the sending of the letter and began to plan an effective strategy to manoeuvre O'Leary and his executives towards negotiations with a trade union. 'We knew that we would have to affect Ryanair's operations if we were ever to get O'Leary to talk,' O'Sullivan explained. SIPTU also had to avoid triggering a situation where Ryanair would 'lock out' the baggage-handlers, effectively dismissing them.

Ryanair ignored the letter. So the trade union decided to stage a series of one-hour stoppages, beginning on 9 January 1998, whereby the baggage-handlers would leave their posts for short periods and cause some limited disruption. Meanwhile O'Sullivan continued to write to Ryanair seeking a meeting. Each time Ryanair replied curtly that it 'would continue its policy of communicating directly with employees on industrial relations matters', while O'Leary rubbished the workers' claims about low pay in the media. On 5 January a notice was posted at the Ryanair headquarters stating that Ryanair ground handling agents were earning more than £2000 a year more than their equivalents in Aer Lingus. Signed by O'Leary, it said that employees would continue to enjoy good conditions 'for as long as they deal directly with us'.

Ryanair's intransigence on the trade-union issue was increasingly causing consternation, not only amongst the top echelons of the union movement but also in the Irish government. The latter had recently brokered an agreement – Partnership 2000 – with the Irish Congress of Trade Unions, the umbrella organisation for the 750,000-strong movement, in order to moderate pay claims in the Irish economy. The politicians were worried that refusals by high-profile companies to recognise unions could undermine the agreement.

On the eve of the first work stoppage, Ryanair's operations manager Conor McCarthy wrote to O'Sullivan outlining once again Ryanair's refusal to negotiate with SIPTU: 'Neither we nor any of our people require the help or intervention of SIPTU, the Aer Lingus union, in any of our dealings, and we will continue to deal directly with each other and, as a result, our people will continue to do better.'

On Friday 9 January, the day of the threatened strike, O'Leary arrived at the airport before the baggage-handlers' first shift began at 6 a.m., still not sure whether they would down tools. When it became clear that the stoppages were going to happen, some thought he looked physically ill. 'That was the first time I saw him nearly shit himself,' one source said. 'Personnel issues were not his best point. It scares the life out of him. He felt the situation was out of his control. Someone else had targeted his style and there was nothing he could do.'

Others said he hid the stress remarkably well as he walked down to meet the seventeen baggage-handlers due to start their shift that morning. For the next hour he tried a variety of colourful language, threats and promises in an attempt to prevent the stoppage. (Later that day one of the baggage-handlers expressed shock as the language and abuse they had been subjected to. 'Even his tone was bad for a chief executive,' he told a reporter.) Amongst other things he offered to pay them for the full day, even if they stopped work, provided they stayed on the premises and did not go down to the union office.

But the group wasn't swayed, and they staged their series of one-hour stoppages in the morning and afternoon as planned. During that time O'Leary, Howard Millar and McCarthy became baggage-handlers. The airline said a number of other staff had 'volunteered' to help with the loading and unloading of passengers' bags. It said none were being paid but would be given time off in lieu.

Ryanair played down the impact of the industrial action and insisted to the media that no flights had been cancelled. SIPTU officials and some baggage-handlers began to check Ryanair's timetable of flights to discover that in fact there had been cancellations, but none had been displayed on the passenger information monitors around the airport. O'Sullivan got his hands on a memo that had been circulated to Aer Rianta detailing the flights that had to be cancelled. 'It was given to me on condition that I would not disclose its contents,' he explained. 'One thing I do regret was that I had that document in my hand yet at the same time Ryanair was telling journalists that no flights had been cancelled. I maintained the confidence of the person who gave me that document all of the way through and I probably shouldn't have.'

O'Leary continued to meet the baggage-handlers as they turned up for work the next day and the day after to try to avert any further stoppages, but he was unable to deter them. The company issued a statement thanking the '97 per cent' of its staff who were helping to ensure that the airline's operations continued as normal throughout the busy weekend. But the situation was becoming critical. By this stage, the cost-conscious airline was prepared to pay top crisis-management fees and instructed its public-relations firm, Murray Consultants, to assemble a response team to regurgitate its non-union stance to the media. This team continued to deny that any flights had been cancelled as a result of the dispute.

In the war of words that erupted over the next two weeks Ryanair claimed that 95 per cent of its staff were operating normally, while SIPTU insisted that 134 flights listed in the airline's winter schedule had not operated during the stoppage periods. The number of people participating in the dispute became a hotly debated issue. O'Sullivan claimed that O'Leary was consistently wrong about the number of people engaged in the dispute. 'He kept saying that there were less than twenty when in fact it was fifty. To disprove that we brought everyone involved in the dispute into the Dail Eireann [the Irish Parliament] for a photo call. It was only after that happened that he stopped making that claim,' O'Sullivan said. 'I found it amazing that journalists then realised that the company was wrong but it didn't seem to dent

Ryanair's credibility in relation to the other claims it was making.'

Ryanair was also incensed with the media, and berated journalists for peddling SIPTU's cause. McCarthy believed the trade union's stance in relation to Ryanair was indefensible, as the trade unions had never attempted to seek union recognition at the growing number of US multinational companies that had become major employers in Ireland. 'SIPTU and the other unions had allowed Intel and others to operate without trade unions,' he argued. 'But because Ryanair was a local company and based at Dublin airport it had to be unionised. SIPTU had a pretty selfish agenda.'

And all the while the stoppages continued. They were sporadic and had begun to lengthen to two and three hours on some days but the baggage-handlers always returned to work. When they arrived back O'Leary would frequently be waiting to vent his spleen at them. One, who was from Ballymun, the nearby working-class Dublin suburb, found himself in O'Leary's firing line as he led the return to the baggage hall. As work resumed, one source recalled O'Leary began shouting at him: 'Why would I be talking to some scumbag like you from Ballymun? What do you know about anything?' The young baggage-handler was totally unfazed by the chief executive's outburst and is remembered for his curt response. 'I may not have gone to any posh school like you,' he replied, 'but if I did I wouldn't let anybody call me Ducksie [O'Leary's nickname at Clongowes Wood].'

O'Leary and his team were continuously offering inducements for the baggage-handlers to abandon the dispute. Some took them and went back to work. O'Leary told others that he would close Ryanair before he would negotiate with a trade union, and he refused to respond to the Labour Court which had offered to intervene. The number of protesters had shrunk from over fifty to about thirty-nine, which strengthened Ryanair's tough stance against trade-union recognition and allowed the company to say that 97 per cent of its staff wanted to remain non-unionised. But while the numbers were dwindling, many of Ryanair's other staff were closely monitoring developments. Cabin crew were paid basic rates of just over £100 a week and largely relied on duty-free sales on board to boost their earnings, typically to around £15,000 a year. As duty-free sales would be abolished in 1999 these employees were anxious to enter fresh pay negotiations with Ryanair themselves.

SIPTU's officials called on the Taoiseach, Bertie Ahern, and his deputy, Mary Harney, to introduce emergency legislation dealing with Ryanair's refusal to respond to the Labour Court. They warned the Government that the Ryanair dispute was at the forefront of a 'make or break' battle that could lead to the collapse of the new social partnership agreement. McCarthy felt the politicians wanted Ryanair to take the blame for the stand-off. 'They had a problem if SIPTU was made to look like a laughing stock,' he suggested.

A few days later, O'Leary spoke at a conference in New York where he told investors that Ryanair had made a 'tremendous start' to 1998 and planned to carry 5 million passengers that year. In the three months to the end of December 1997 he said the airline's profits had swelled from £3 million to £8.1 million, bringing the total amount earned in the first three quarters of its financial year to £32 million. Meanwhile European transport workers were beginning to distribute leaflets in support of the baggage-handlers to passengers boarding the Ryanair shuttle bus from Charleroi to Brussels. The Federation of Transport Workers Union's general secretary, Hugues de Villele, said that airline workers throughout Europe were 'horrified' by the way Ryanair treated its workers.

The Labour Party leader, Ruairi Quinn, called for a Garda investigation into claims that many of the workers were being kept under surveillance by private investigators – claims the company's public-relations response team said were 'totally untrue'. The Garda authorities later confirmed that it had investigated one complaint and concluded that the individual concerned was indeed under surveillance, but as this was not a criminal offence nothing could be done. When the protesters gathered for meetings, various individuals would conspicuously watch the proceedings.

The Government was desperately trying to keep a lid on the simmering Ryanair dispute and to ensure that its outcome did not have major ramifications for the US-owned multinationals that operated a staunch non-union policy. Some politicians pointed out that the Ryanair case was not directly comparable with the multinational sector since the latter generally paid its employees 'above the odds', in stark contrast to the Irish airline.

Towards the end of February Ryanair delivered a letter to the home of each of the protesters, telling them they had two choices: either report for work as normal – and give Ryanair an undertaking that they would cease their industrial action – or effectively dismiss themselves. The striking workers decided they would return to work on Friday 6 March, but they would not agree to end their protest. Aware that things might turn nasty, they asked SIPTU's representative to accompany them to work that day. At first the workers were refused entry by the airport police – as instructed in a memo from Ryanair – but after representations from SIPTU the police let them through and provided a discreet escort for their journey to the Ryanair section, where they assembled in the break room.

O'Leary's response was to take the matter to the courts. Later that morning he obtained a High Court injunction preventing SIPTU members from interfering with the airline's operations. 'O'Leary subsequently claimed the workers were abusive to colleagues working in the baggage hall as they entered that morning but I certainly didn't hear any of it,' O'Sullivan said. 'They had been warned not to behave in that manner and not to give any excuses to Ryanair to have them ejected. None of the airport police made reference to any abusive behaviour in their official reports.'

The stand-off lasted until late morning, when the airline informed the airport police that the group in the break room were trespassing and that they wanted them removed from the premises. 'They were effectively being locked out,' O'Sullivan explained. 'They left and went back to the union office and decided to mount a picket within the airport perimeters to familiarise the other workers with their plight. The picket was very orderly, very peaceful and anybody who was from a company other than Ryanair was told that it was specific to Ryanair and that there was no instruction from the union not to pass the picket. There would be no recrimination for those who passed.'

The thirty-nine picketing workers took up their position at the inner perimeter of the airport. By midday workers who would normally enter the perimeter to operate catering services or make oil deliveries were refusing to pass the picket. The situation was posing problems for Aer Rianta. The airport authority did not allow any form of protest within the airport complex and had always stipulated that any picketing must move to the outside perimeter – the main passenger entrances to Dublin Airport.

In hindsight Aer Rianta might have been wiser to turn a blind eye. As requested, the protesting Ryanair baggage-handlers complied with the airport authority's bylaw and moved away from the inner perimeter, instead beginning a very public protest at the three entrances to the airport. Businesses and workers at the main terminal building grew increasingly uncomfortable about passing the picket and in the late afternoon the airport's cleaners led a walk-out to support the Ryanair employees, throwing the airport into chaos. After brewing for thirteen weeks, the strike had finally spiralled out of control.

The next morning, Saturday, more than 2000 SIPTU members, including airport police and workers at Aer Lingus, refused to pass the pickets. Taxis and buses wouldn't bring passengers beyond the main airport entrances and there were desperate scenes as passengers, many with young children, struggled with their luggage to walk the mile to the departure area. Aer Lingus and British Midland had begun to cancel flights because of the lack of crew but Ryanair was still in business, the only airline operating its scheduled flights in and out of the airport that morning. As its crew arrived in their distinctive blue uniforms they were jostled and jeered at. Some arrived for work in tears. 'Our cabin crew got awful abuse trying to get through to work,' McCarthy said. 'Then later on staff from Aer Lingus and other airlines marched around our aircraft to stop them taking off. It was total anarchy. A Garda superintendent refused to move the protesters and was telling us to keep away from our planes. He threatened to take me into custody.'

At about one o'clock Aer Rianta's emergency fire services left their posts and everything ground to a halt. Aer Lingus and other airlines immediately stopped checking passengers through, cancelling sixty flights. Ryanair staff continued to deal with passengers but were eventually forced to concede at 2 p.m. that there would be delays. It was not until shortly before 5 p.m. that the ten thousand people waiting to travel out from Dublin airport finally heard a British Midland announcement telling its passengers the airport was closed and realised that they were grounded. Five minutes later Aer Rianta confirmed the shutdown.

The result was utter mayhem. There were no security personnel at the terminal building. 'You could walk right through the building and out onto the runway without being stopped,' one official told journalists. Garda officers arrived later to man the entrances while a skeleton airline staff worked furiously to divert flights to Belfast, Shannon and Cork. Luggage was piled all over the terminal and passengers were distraught. It was an unmitigated disaster for the airport.

O'Sullivan appeared on RTE's main six o'clock news bulletin to talk about the all-out strike. The report also included many angry, weary and upset passengers whose travel plans had gone up in smoke. 'I didn't see the report but spoke to a good friend of mine who was not involved in the trade union movement to ask him how he thought things were going,' O'Sullivan recalled. 'He said, "You were doing great until the six o'clock news, which was full of chaos at Dublin Airport. There were clips of families, children crying and people talking about their ruined holidays. It is going to turn against you very quickly," he warned.'

Wanting to ensure that SIPTU's position came across clearly, O'Sullivan decided he should prepare to do another piece for the nine o'clock news and rang RTE to make the arrangements. He told the station that he would have something new to say for the next bulletin. 'I borrowed the shirt, tie and jacket from one of my colleagues. I wanted to make it all look different. I sat down to prepare what I was going to say. I was trying to remember what were the key phrases that Gerry Adams [the Sinn Féin leader] uses at times of strife. So I did a piece live for the 9 p.m. news where I spoke about "moving the process forward".' O'Sullivan was pleased at his performance and felt the union had managed to win back the public's support for its stance. 'When it was over, the reporter said to me, "That sounded awfully like Adams-speak." I said, "Yes, I reckoned if the most popular politician in Ireland after thirty years of murder and mayhem in Northern Ireland could use that language then it was good enough to use in the context of the closure of Dublin Airport."'

Ryanair had assembled its own war council but McCarthy

said they felt like they were 'wrestling with a 300lb gorilla' and were being unfairly represented in the media. 'There was a view that we were beating up on different guys and screwing with their lives,' McCarthy said. 'Nothing could have been further from the truth. I felt we got a very raw deal from the Irish media during the strike.' One source said Ryanair's war council was completely at sea. 'We had no clear direction. We would sit around thinking of things to say but this was pointless. SIPTU was such a sharp operator. It was like *Apocalypse Now*.'

Ireland's most senior politicians had been trying to broker a truce between SIPTU and Ryanair since the walk-out began, but O'Leary refused to back down. Ahern and Harney, a personal friend of O'Leary's, and their advisers tried to persuade him to cooperate with an independent inquiry team, but he flatly refused to talk to the politicians or to acknowledge their efforts at conciliation. One source expressed amazement at O'Leary's total disrespect for the Taoiseach's efforts to resolve the impasse. Ahern retaliated by publicly criticising O'Leary's pursuit of 'tooth and claw capitalism' and the deadlock continued.

The Government was furious about the situation at the airport, particularly as the closure happened just as the Taoiseach and other politicians were out canvassing in that area of North Dublin, where a by-election would be held in four days' time. The politicians and their advisers were in contact with Jim Milton, the director of Ryanair's public-relations firm Murray Consultants, who in turn was trying to persuade O'Leary to engage in talks. O'Leary eventually agreed to talk to Harney's press adviser, Martin Territt, but refused to go to government buildings for a meeting. However, as the pressure grew he was persuaded to participate in a telephone conversation that would also include SIPTU boss Des Geraghty, with Ahern and Harney acting as intermediaries. Labour Affairs Minister Tom Kitt conducted negotiations with Geraghty. The situation was described as tense. 'There were some fairly robust exchanges and O'Leary was told to come to his senses and to come to government buildings for a meeting,' said one person close to the negotiations. 'He was told that he could avoid the television cameras by sneaking in a side entrance. The Government just wanted to get the airport open so that we didn't look like a banana republic.'

By Sunday morning, O'Leary had decided to cede some ground to get the airport re-opened. Some of his lieutenants wanted to hold the line but O'Leary said it would be impossible for Ryanair's staff to tolerate the level of abuse from the picket line as they arrived and departed from work. 'We can't ask them to keep doing it,' he explained. And so he phoned Ahern. 'Bertie threw everyone out of the room and spoke to him. There was a shouting match and the airport opened,' one source recalled.

The Government put forward proposals designed to deal with the immediate problems but there was nothing to address the substantive issue of union recognition. A tribunal of inquiry was established to look into all elements of the dispute and the workers agreed to return to their posts. And so Ryanair, which had now parked its aircraft at the back of its hangar and away from the protestors, ordered that three planes should be pushed and taxied and readied for take-off.

The report found that Ryanair baggage-handlers were paid more than £5000 a year less than British Midland handlers, more than £2100 below Aer Lingus and more than £1300 below Servisair. Ryanair disputed this and said that the comparative pay rates, undertaken by the Irish Productivity Centre, contained 'manifest errors'. The airline subsequently took a judicial review of the report's findings, but the challenge was rejected by the High Court. However, the inquiry did yield a solution for tackling difficulties that could arise at Irish companies that failed to recognise trade unions. New legislation was adopted that would allow a trade union to refer such disputes to the Labour Court, which was empowered to deliver a binding outcome.

O'Sullivan said that in hindsight the inquiry itself was a neutered exercise, as the team had no power to make recommendations. O'Sullivan thought that the Ryanair workers should have returned to the picket at that stage and demanded that the inquiry team be empowered to make recommendations, but admitted that would have been difficult to achieve. 'At that stage I don't think there was any appetite in the airport or at senior level in the trade-union movement for that,' he said. 'They just wanted to see it go away and there was a lot of political pressure for that to happen.' He claimed that if the report's finding had been implemented Ryanair would have faced a back-pay bill of over

£295,000 to bring its baggage-handlers' pay in line with Aer Lingus.

O'Leary has acknowledged that the dispute was a public relations disaster for Ryanair, but argued that this wasn't the airline's fault. 'I think though everybody would say that was the media's fault,' he told RTE. 'I think the media in Ireland at that time has an awful lot to answer for. The unions, with Aer Rianta, had ruled Dublin Airport and Aer Lingus for years. We stood out like a sore thumb – an oasis of efficiency with a different way of doing things. They saw the terms and conditions of their members being threatened by what we were doing. It was a public relations disaster. The media refused to see that there were 900 employees and 871 of them worked normally through work stoppages and ultimately on the weekend where other unions in other companies closed Dublin Airport. Nobody wanted to represent the side of 871 of our people. If you worked for Ryanair during that period every time you opened a newspaper you would read, "Oh Ryanair mistreated the workers". At one stage they were saying that we were paying peanuts and getting monkeys to work for us. People would find themselves in pubs and nightclubs at the weekends and all of a sudden they were ashamed to say that they worked for Ryanair. It was a very difficult time.'

O'Leary said that Ryanair's practices reflected how US firms worked with their employees. 'Employees do better as a result because they will always hold over you that if you don't beat what the unions are getting for their people then we will get a union. So you are in a competitive environment all of the time.' Ryanair's board of directors backed the airline's tough stance against the union and David Bonderman described the airport closure as appalling. 'It was quite unbelievable. The notion that you would let the airport be shut down because you let the police and the firemen go out in sympathy with thirty-two baggage-handlers is something that would never happen in the US. No government agency would tolerate those services being part of the same union as baggage-handlers. But what happened here in the first place would not have happened in the US because thirty-two people out of nearly one thousand employees wanting to join a union and causing the dispute would not be tolerated.'

Bonderman said the strikers were 'a small group of malcontents' and claimed that Ryanair was not opposed to trade unions. 'Ryanair is not anti-union in any respect. The substantive position it took was the right one, agreed by the board, but we should have been better at explaining why and where. Michael is a great chief executive. Michael is as good as it gets. But his strong point is not public relations. He simply doesn't care what people say about him. But while the substance of our argument was right, we let the union side make the headlines.'

Some board members and some of his management team thought O'Leary's total antipathy towards the Taoiseach was wrong and would set the airline back in the long run. 'The stuff with Bertie was very bad,' one said. 'O'Leary will suffer for that for a long time yet.'

The thirty-seven-year-old Ryanair chief was still spoiling for a fight with the unions, though, and claimed on national radio that SIPTU's president, Des Geraghty, travelled regularly with the airline: 'It is breathtaking that Des Geraghty, or "D. Geraghty", has flown six times with Ryanair in the past six months.' Geraghty demanded that O'Leary immediately retract the 'misrepresentative claim' and threatened to seek an apology in the courts if necessary, saying, 'He is well aware the person in question is not me.'

O'Leary's appetite for revenge was insatiable and he enthusiastically continued the public spat. 'If Mr Geraghty was not flying on Ryanair, were the hard-earned dues of union members being frittered away on higher fares for SIPTU bigwigs?' he demanded. 'Did Mr Geraghty get a special deal on Aer Lingus and travel with the other fat cats in business class?'

Geraghty rose to the bait and counterattacked, saying, 'I don't travel with fat cats, skinny cats or any other cats. Actually, I usually take my car and the ferry when I go on holiday. I would normally travel economy class and I travel with Aer Lingus because that's where our members work.'

CHAPTER THIRTEEN

Conquering Europe

H erb Kelleher enjoyed reading about Europe's low-cost airlines as they sought to emulate Southwest Airlines' success across the Atlantic. In many ways, he believed, Southwest's accomplishments had made their challenge even greater, as the world's major airlines now recognised the scale of the threat. 'Southwest Airlines was able to fly under the radar of the mega-carriers for a while because they said, "Oh, Southwest is small, an intra-state carrier flying only within the state of Texas,"' Keller believed. 'Then we gradually got bigger. It was almost a stealth operation, like we were F117 stealth fighters. But because of Southwest Airlines everybody would know what the low-cost airlines were up to from the very beginning. They would be focusing on them and they would be trying to stifle them from the very outset because they knew about us. Southwest was kind of a toxin, kind of a warning, and as a corollary to that I believed that it was perhaps incumbent on these airlines to expand faster than we did.'

Europe was also very different as a territory to be conquered from the US, something that Kelleher believed presented even greater obstacles for the ambitious upstarts. 'It was much more difficult because you were dealing with so many different airports, so many different nationalities and cultures, separate air traffic control systems. I think it was a harder job in a sense because you had so much disparity and diversity, in the people with whom you are dealing and with how they approached their business and what they are sensitive to. It was tough.'

But Michael O'Leary was still spoiling for a fight. Ryanair had revolutionised flying between Britain and Ireland. The airline had adopted a simple formula for success: 'pile 'em high, sell 'em cheap', which had worked so well for supermarkets and other retailers. Ryanair had proved that it could be successful in Ireland and the UK, but the real prize was to conquer Europe. 'I had a strong feeling that the ethnic connection would work, and at the right price Irish people would visit each other more regularly,' a Ryanair source explained. 'We knew that making the low-cost, no-frills concept work in Europe was going to be much more difficult.' Securing a slice of that market would mean taking on Europe's aviation giants: British Airways, Air France, Lufthansa, SAS and Alitalia. It was a daunting task. Tim Jeans, who was now based in Stansted with instructions to advance into Europe, admitted there was huge trepidation about the airline's next move. 'That was the $64 million question, but O'Leary had an absolute conviction that it would work,' he said.

Just weeks after the bitter dispute at Dublin airport in 1998 O'Leary called his troops to battle again. 'In three or five years time, there will be one or two large, low-cost carriers in Europe. Ryanair will be one,' he vowed. 'The question is: will there be another one?' David Bonderman and the airline's other directors had staunchly backed O'Leary's battle against SIPTU during those difficult weeks, although many were embarrassed by the way he had treated the Taoiseach. 'With hindsight everything could have been done better,' one source close to the company said. 'It didn't reflect badly in terms of the business but issues between different parties might be better if it hadn't gone so badly.'

During the strike it was business as usual as far as Bonderman and Tony Ryan were concerned. During those highly charged months they had begun negotiations with the world's two biggest airline manufacturers, the US Boeing group and the European consortium Airbus, about purchasing new aircraft to support the airline's ambitions to conquer continental Europe. 'We had the two best heads in the aviation business negotiating with the manufacturers,' one source close to the company explained. 'Through Tony's experience at GPA and David Bonderman's at Continental we were able to make them both think they were so close to a deal. They were never biased and did not have any loyalty to any manufacturer.'

Ryanair wanted to more than double its fleet of twenty-one Boeing 737 aircraft, which were now more than fifteen years old, and engineered a Dutch auction between Airbus and Boeing to strike a bargain. The airline said it would place firm orders for twenty-five Boeing 737-800 or Airbus A320 planes worth about £800 million, and buy options over another twenty, worth another £650 million. By 1998 Ryanair's annual profits had risen by 19 per cent to almost £40 million, and its successful stockmarket flotation had shown that it could easily raise more funds from investors. Yet to the manufacturers Ryanair was a relative unknown, and they rigorously examined its business model before putting their terms on the table. Boeing set up a computer simulation of Ryanair's system to check for flaws that could potentially damage the company's creditworthiness in the future. This involved stress-testing the airline to see how it might weather a drop in demand, movements in exchange rates or fluctuations in the price of aviation fuel. Talking about the exercise in an interview, Boeing's director of sales in the UK and Ireland, Eric Hild, said the company couldn't find a single three months during which Ryanair would not be profitable. 'The lowest we could do was break even,' he explained. 'It is probably the most robust model we have encountered.' Boeing was ready to do business with Ryanair, and Airbus, the dominant supplier of aircraft in Europe, was equally enthusiastic.

As the negotiations moved into the crunch phase, Bonderman flew to Dublin to conclude the deal. At the Ryan family's Dublin offices, Bonderman and Tony Ryan played one manufacturer off against each other, with Boeing emerging victorious. The airline refused to disclose the level of discount it had secured from Boeing but didn't deny suggestions that the new aircraft had been secured at a 30 per cent reduction from the official list price. The deal was sweetened by the fact that Ryanair could finance part of the transaction through attractively priced loans from the US official export credit agency, the Export-Import Bank, set up to assist in financing US goods exported to international markets. The contract, to purchase twenty-five Boeing 737-800 series jets that could carry 189 passengers, was signed in March 1998, and the airline also took options over twenty more aircraft in the future. Ryanair paid Boeing a £27 million deposit for the aircraft, which were to be delivered at a rate of five a year from the following March. It raised £50 million from investors and got a twelve-year loan from the Export-Import Bank at an interest rate of about 5 per cent. The airline said it would reassess whether it would exercise its options over the remaining aircraft in 2001 and indicated that then it would also consider opportunities to source cheaper secondhand aircraft.

Announcing the deal, O'Leary said the new aircraft would allow Ryanair to launch more new routes and make low fares more widely available to Europe's travelling public. 'It's not just twenty-five aircraft. These will be the first of one hundred,' he declared. 'This new fleet of aircraft will allow Ryanair to compete head-on and beat any low-fare competition from Europe's major airlines.' SIPTU welcomed the announcement, saying pointedly, 'If they can afford this kind of expansion, they can afford to have decent pay and working conditions for the baggage-handlers.'

The airline had just recruited its thousandth employee and predicted that when its expanded fleet was fully operational it would employ over 1100 staff, many of them based in the UK. Trade unions noted that Ryanair's continuing growth and planned expansion could have an impact on its industrial relations structures. Under the European Works Council directive, any company with over 1000 employees and at least one 150 people employed in another EU member-state was required to hold elections to a company-wide works council. If trade-union members were elected to a works council, or if works-council members sought the assistance of trade-union officials, the company could not object.

While the trade unions were still smarting from their tussle with Ryanair, the public was enthusiastically booking cheap flights promoted in massive seat sales. The airline offered a groundbreaking deal by which two people could travel from Dublin to London and on all of its internal UK routes for £79 return. In the following months, more two for one offers were promoted, with Ryanair advertising fares of £99 return from Dublin to its European destinations, Paris Beauvais and Brussels Charleroi. Customers quickly learned that these prices were not available during peak periods such as the October bank holiday weekend, and some complained to the advertising standards authorities in the UK and Ireland. Ryanair explained that the seats for the bank holiday had been filled instantly, and that seats were still available for other dates covered by the offer; the complaint was not upheld.

Ryanair also offered a million seats from Stansted to its European destinations at fares as low as £16.99. O'Leary unveiled the massive offer in a promotional banner that had been draped outside the British Airways flight shop in Piccadilly in London. 'We're doing this deal now to re-emphasise Ryanair's position as Europe's low-fares carrier,' he explained.

Ryanair was now also flying from Stansted airport to Scandinavia. It promoted a £99 return fare to Sweden's capital city, Stockholm, less than half the price charged by the Swedish carrier SAS on that route. For this Ryanair would fly its passengers to Skavsta airport, 100km south of Stockholm. Tim Jeans said that this didn't get much publicity at first. 'The British press were indifferent to Ryanair,' he recalled. 'I think about two journalists turned up for the launch.' Ryanair was warmly received in Skavsta, though, where Swedish people were delighted to be offered such cheap fares to London. 'We found strength in Stockholm,' Jeans said. 'It was a turning point. We knew we had something that European consumers would buy into.' Six months later the airline expanded to Norway, offering £99 return fares from Stansted to Oslo – or rather to Torp Airport, some 110km away. 'Michael had an absolute conviction that it would work,' Jeans said. 'He believed that we had found a formula and just had to make it work but it was a measured expansion. One of Michael's great abilities was to play the long game. He was ultra cautious. You got the impression that he was probably holding back the board in terms of expansion.'

Michael Cawley, Bernard Berger and Jeans were meanwhile scouring France and Italy for airports that would offer Ryanair the cheapest deals to fly there. 'Airports were easier to deal with at the start,' Jeans explained. 'We were offering something that nobody else was. The French Chambers of Commerce welcomed Ryanair with open arms. The deals were not that hard to cut in the beginning. Pisa Airport had rather sporadic charter traffic; it wasn't difficult to do a deal to bring scheduled fights there.' Cawley, the chief financial officer, conceded in interviews that

Ryanair had earned a tough reputation in its dealing with airports but pointed out that the sheer numbers of Europe's secondary airports and the airline's measured growth policy meant it could safely reject approaches and cherry-pick its destinations. 'Every airport says we're bastards to deal with but they will always recommend us to somebody else,' he said. 'We go to airports and say we will deliver on what we promise to deliver, which is passenger numbers. If the fare is right, people will fly.'

By the end of 1998 Ryanair had opened new routes from Stansted to Toulouse in France (or at least to Carcassone, some 91km away), to Pisa and to Treviso Airport, twenty miles from Venice. It had also launched a flight from Glasgow's Prestwick Airport to Beauvais. With new aircraft due to arrive in the coming months, the pressure was on to launch even more new routes 'We got really lucky. We were ahead of the others, with the exception of easyJet,' Jeans said. The Greek shipping venture was Ryanair's main rival, although it didn't compete on the same routes. EasyJet operated flights from Luton to Amsterdam, Barcelona and Nice and, unlike the Irish carrier, flew passengers directly to the main airports in those cities. British Airways was also now finally ready to enter the low-cost battle for Europe and in 1998 announced the launch of new airline Go, headed by the American former management consultant Barbara Cassani.

Go's arrival upset Stelios, who immediately issued a High Court writ against BA, claiming the airline would be abusing its dominant market position when Go opened for business at Stansted. He alleged that Go was part of BA's plan to eliminate other low-cost carriers and then to raise fares again, which he said was in breach of the European Commission's competition rules. 'It's a question of seeking to ensure Go competes on an equal basis and does not attempt to abuse BA's dominant market position,' he explained. Cassani rubbished the claims, insisting that 'every bill' for the airline would fall on her desk: 'We've made it very clear that the BA board wants us to break into profit in our third year of operations. No way will we be throwing money into the market just to gain a foothold.' EasyJet lost its High Court challenge.

Debonair, also based at Luton Airport, opened flights to Munich, Dusseldorf, Rome and Barcelona starting at £39 one-way.

Ryanair and Debonair both accused BA of seeking to use Go to drive them out of the market. Debonair's founder, Franco Mancassola, said: 'It is like putting a ten-year-old kid in the ring with Mike Tyson. BA, and Go as a result, have everything – money, planes, slots and gates. Then you have some of the kids, like Debonair, who are smart enough to survive a couple of rounds with Tyson. Then, when they go back to the playground, they pass Go. And Go is again Mike Tyson, dressed as a kid.' Debonair had most to fear from Go's arrival as it put on flights from Stansted to Rome, one of Debonair's key routes, as well as to Milan and Copenhagen, for £100, including airport taxes – less than a third of the price charged by BA on some routes. British Midland, which had stayed out of the low-fares fray, said that Go's arrival would spark another round of price cuts amongst those carriers and predicted that the next price war would yield at least one casualty. The airline's chairman, Sir Michael Bishop, believed that Debonair, which was making heavy losses, was the most likely victim.

Richard Branson's consortium had now also finalised their deal in Belgium and established a new Brussels-based low-cost operation, Virgin Express, while the Dutch airline KLM had begun to muscle in on British routes through its KLM UK operations, much to the annoyance of BA. O'Leary predicted that most of the new carriers would disappear, speculating that Go would ultimately be absorbed back into BA and that Virgin Express would become part of Belgium's national airline, Sabena. 'The one that I can't predict is Stelios,' he said. Stelios, it seemed, was the only rival O'Leary rated.

While Ryanair was busily spreading its wings from Stansted, its chief was also turning his guns on Aer Rianta, publicly blasting the Irish airport operator for its expensive charges and its refusal to negotiate. The airline claimed it wanted to operate flights from Dublin to Germany, Italy, Sweden, Norway and the south of France at fares of £70, but that it had cancelled these plans because Aer Rianta would not agree to offer it reduced charges on these new routes. Such was O'Leary's frustration with the regime at Dublin Airport that he began to speak again about the airline's desire to build a second terminal there, which would not be under the control of Aer Rianta. This plan had first been mooted in 1996 but hadn't been seriously considered by the Government. By now a new minister had taken charge of the transport portfolio. Few envied Mary O'Rourke, a seasoned politician who had previously served as a minister for education, her task in dealing with the feuding factions at Dublin airport.

The row had been simmering in the months ahead of the abolition of duty-free sales across the European Union, which had been scheduled for 1997 but then postponed until June 1999. In light of the new arrangements Aer Rianta, which earned substantial income from this source, had proposed to increase its charges over the next seven years to offset the shortfall. Ryanair was once again claiming that Dublin was the most expensive of the twenty-six European airports it used. Aer Rianta wearily denied the claim, and insisted that Ryanair had never intended to launch the routes from Dublin and was simply using its charges as an excuse to start new routes from the UK. One source recalled O'Leary sitting in the Aer Rianta boardroom telling the executives that if they didn't give Ryanair what it wanted he would get it 'over their dead bodies'. The source added 'and he has been working hard to achieve that ever since'. Aer Rianta believed its relationship with Ryanair had turned sour the minute it stopped doing what O'Leary wanted. 'It is not necessarily all about the money now,' the source believed. 'It has become personal.'

Staff at Ryanair's headquarters would hear O'Leary say that he was going to meet the 'jackasses' or 'wankers' at Aer Rianta as he headed out the door to a meeting at their Dublin offices. 'Effectively O'Leary would end up hosting the meeting and everyone would shut up. One of his tactics was when everyone would sit down with a cup of coffee he would walk around and might stand behind the person he was negotiating with and talk to the back of their head in a bid to unsettle them,' one source recalled. 'When this didn't work he would sit down and rant calling them "fucking wankers" or worse.'

Aer Rianta took up the cudgels to rubbish O'Leary's accusation of high charges and furiously issued retaliatory press statements to Irish media organisations. At the same time Ryanair's public-relations advisers, Murray Consultants, badgered journalists to carry the airline's every utterance and O'Leary blasted off letters of complaint to various newspaper editors when he felt its side of the argument wasn't being given sufficient coverage. Frustrated, Aer Rianta revealed that it had given its most demanding customer nearly £32 million in rebates in the previous four years, forgoing landing fees and passenger load fees when the airline reached agreed growth levels. 'It annoyed the hell out of us to have Michael O'Leary going on about our high charges when Ryanair was getting rebates on that scale,' a spokesman said.

At one point Tony Ryan attempted to broker a truce between the two foes, arranging for himself and O'Leary to have lunch with the Aer Rianta chairman, Noel Hanlon. They ate in Aer Rianta's executive dining room and O'Leary even dressed up to look smart for the occasion, according to one source. By the end of the meal it had been agreed that O'Leary would return for a meeting with Hanlon and that they would attempt to resolve their differences. Shortly afterwards Hanlon once again hosted lunch and invited O'Leary as his guest. This time, though, the pair were arguing almost as soon as they had begun their starters. O'Leary later told associates that he had stood up, cursed at Hanlon and walked towards the door.

And the war continued. Ryanair threatened to withdraw from Dublin Airport by Christmas 1998 if Aer Rianta didn't reduce its charges. O'Leary issued the threat at the airline's annual general meeting and went on to explain to shareholders that it was seeking its own low-cost base in Dublin by operating its own terminal as part of a new extension of the Pier D area of Dublin Airport. Ryanair told Minister O'Rourke that it would build the terminal for £20 million. 'The quid pro quo is that we promise to open new low-fare routes to Europe,' O'Leary suggested. Ryanair's development was in European traffic, he said, adding that this could also be managed from Britain. The airline was 'indifferent' if no deal was struck in Dublin. 'If it is not done by Christmas, we will be gone,' he warned. 'The Government has to make up its mind what it wants to do.'

Richard Branson quickly let it be known that Virgin Express would be delighted to replace Ryanair if it pulled out of Dublin. The airline would be 'waiting in the wings', a spokesman said. 'If you pull out of Dublin we'll step in. I've no wish to undermine Ryanair or put them in a negative position, but if they really did pull out we'll step in. It's a very competitive market today.'

Ryanair's spokeswoman, Ethel Power, said the airline wasn't worried by Virgin's threat to poach its market in Ireland. 'We are not threatened at all. I don't mean to belittle Virgin but they are a much smaller operation. They would only be able to handle one tenth of the business that we do here in Dublin. We would be extremely surprised if they could take over our operation. We have over one hundred flights a day flying out of the capital.' That week Aer Rianta, which was still in talks with Ryanair on the issue, was named as the third cheapest of fifty European airports in an independent study. Its spokesman said, 'Basically Ryanair is getting very cheap deals in airports in Europe which are on the outskirts of cities in Europe. They can't expect to get in for nothing with an airport attached to a capital city.'

Some days earlier, the *Financial Times* had reported O'Leary saying that Ryanair would cease to expand its services at Stansted Airport if the British Airports Authority increased landing charges to compensate for loss of earnings from duty-free sales. Terry Morgan, Stansted's chief executive, said the growth in its duty-free sales revenues as a result of Ryanair's expansion had been part of the reason why it had been able to offer the airline an attractive deal there, and the airport had made it clear to O'Leary that the terms would have to be revisited when duty free was abolished. 'He frequently slags off BAA but we see that bluster as part of the negotiations,' Morgan said. 'We had signalled that that event would have to coincide with a review of their deal. The deal is still essentially the same but the quantum was changed to reflect the loss of duty-free revenues. But in terms of the profitability for them and for us it is still a good relationship.'

Morgan described O'Leary as very focused when in negotiations. 'Michael is incredibly flexible and fleet of foot,' he said. 'And while I think he has a pretty clear idea about what he wants to achieve overall he is not averse to saying, "Well, if you want to charge me that in that area then we will look for something else in this area." He and BAA tend to look at the whole picture rather than getting hung up on the specific elements of it. He is very aggressive and very demanding as a customer but then again he has proven that that is a very successful business model to run. There is no point in me complaining that we have an aggressive and demanding customer because we make it work for him and us. He would probably say that I am avaricious.' All aspects of the many relationships between BAA and Ryanair would be considered as part of any negotiations. 'Ryanair has to pay for check-in desks, landing fees, office accommodation – there are a whole series of transactions,' Morgan explained. BAA had been shocked by Ryanair's growth in the previous three years and recognised its potential to become a dominant force in Europe. 'There is a perception that easyJet was the first low-cost airline. But it wasn't. EasyJet came to see us way after Ryanair had established its business. At the end of the day they were quite good for each other.'

Morgan said that Ryanair was initially seen as the 'odd man out' or the 'maverick'. 'Michael plays on that a lot and I think a lot of the brand is based on that image. In a way the maverick image worked and I think it did help to establish its identity in the early years. It also suffered the downside, though, as it labelled Ryanair as a sort of niche player.' Morgan thought that the arrival of other low-cost airlines gave credibility to this type of airline. 'Instead of being a maverick Ryanair became part of the credible low-cost model.'

Though Ryanair was able to conclude a favourable deal at Stansted it was failing to make any progress in Dublin, and it wasn't long before O'Leary was again regurgitating his well-rehearsed insults at Aer Rianta. When he spoke at an investment conference O'Leary pledged that Ryanair would 'fight anybody, anytime, anywhere about costs'. The building of a second terminal, known within Ryanair as 'T2', was another raging battle and O'Leary appeared before a parliamentary committee to explain his proposal. One committee member, the Labour Party's Emmett Stagg, rejected the plan on the basis that it would amount to a 'massive state subsidy' for Ryanair. 'What we have really is a sweetheart deal proposal where the taxpayer would be asked to subsidise Ryanair to the extent of £140 million. How does it make sense for Aer Rianta or any airport authority to give him free land to build a pier?' he asked. O'Leary angrily rejected the suggestion that he was seeking a state subsidy and said he was not looking for exclusive use of the proposed terminal.

Fine Gael Senator Shane Ross also challenged O'Leary, citing cases taken against Ryanair by the advertising standards authorities in Ireland and in Britain. 'Not just with the UK Advertising

Standards Authority, your record with the Irish Advertising Standards Authority is deplorable and does you no credit. How can I believe you?' he asked. 'This is a matter on which those who have a great deal of time and goodwill for you find it very difficult to defend you.' O'Leary responded that eleven of thirteen complaints in Britain the previous year had related to Ryanair stating in its advertising that it flew from London, not mentioning that the airport involved was actually Stansted. He said that Go and easyJet, which also used Stansted, had followed the same advertising strategy without being reprimanded, and said that Ryanair would be challenging the Advertising Standards Authority in the High Court in London on this basis.

Aer Rianta chairman Noel Hanlon, who also met the committee, accused Ryanair of telling 'blatant lies'. O'Leary was incensed and wrote to the committee chairman, Sean Doherty, asking that Hanlon's allegations be 'properly corrected' and the damage to Ryanair's reputation redressed. The committee replied to O'Leary, saying that it believed the matter was between Ryanair and Aer Rianta.

But the Tanaiste (deputy prime minister) Mary Harney voiced public support for O'Leary's plan and was joined by the Irish Hotels' Federation. And O'Leary sought a meeting with Mary O'Rourke, the minister who could order Aer Rianta to hand over the land at Dublin Airport for the second terminal. She agreed, but cautioned that the media should not read anything into such a meeting. 'Aer Rianta is doing a good job,' she added, 'It hasn't raised its landing charges in a decade. That is some feat.'

But Aer Rianta was about to apply to the Minister to be allowed to raise its charges, justifying the increase on the findings of a report it commissioned from accountants Pricewaterhouse-Coopers that found its fees were among the lowest in Europe. The report strongly contested many of the points made by Ryanair during the most recent debate and said Ryanair's suggestion that increases in airport charges would reduce the number of airlines offering services at the airports 'has been greatly exaggerated'. The report claimed Ryanair was unlikely to move the core of its operations out of Dublin Airport because its Irish routes were 'more profitable than its new continental routes'.

Ryanair dismissed the report as 'irrelevant'. O'Leary's truculent style failed to make any impression on Mary O'Rourke, the minister whose support could have swung the decision Ryanair's way. She signalled that she would not fight on Ryanair's behalf for a second terminal.

In 1999 Ryanair expected to carry 6 million passengers, with just over 20 per cent of its customers flying to and from Ireland. At Stansted, the centre of its European operations, another competitor was about to open for business. KLM, which had been operating domestic flights from the Essex airport, was creating a new low-cost airline, Buzz, which also had lofty aspirations about winning European territories. Ryanair immediately added four additional flights per day to its Stansted schedule to coincide with the Buzz launch. This would mean that every Monday morning between 7 and 7.15 eleven Ryanair flights would depart from the airport. 'Aer Rianta lost out on that expansion by default because it was so dogged about not reducing passenger charges,' Jeans said. 'Stansted wasn't Ryanair's first choice but Aer Rianta was so intransigent.' All the while O'Leary bombarded Hanlon with letters that would describe the Aer Rianta chairman's previous reply as 'rubbish' and suggest that his memory was 'somewhat jaded' in relation to other issues. O'Leary wanted Aer Rianta to reduce airport charges to about £1 per passenger instead of the current £9.20. In return, he again promised to provide new scheduled services from Ireland to European destinations. Hanlon said his promises were based on 'dubious tourism projections' and claimed that Ryanair had previously failed to deliver on the number of new passengers it promised to carry on new routes from Dublin. For all the hostilities, though, O'Leary showed a benevolent side at Christmas, splashing out on a festive hamper for Hanlon; according to the Aer Rianta chairman, it contained enough food and drink 'for a small village'.

Ryanair wasn't finding the going any easier in Britain. British Airways fired off salvos at the low-fares carriers by promoting one million free seats to a range of European destinations. Ryanair immediately announced new cheap fares starting from as little as £16.99 and accused British Airways of being an industry mafia figure. O'Leary said the BA deal was 'limp-wristed' and a 'con job' because it was littered with small print that restricted availability. 'If BA wants a fares war, they have come to the right place,' he warned. 'We have the financial clout to be able to do this. We do not operate the same way as BA. There is no con.'

He insisted that Ryanair could afford to sell seats at these rates and not lose money, declaring that Ryanair's prices undercut the fares being offered by easyJet, Virgin Express, Debonair and Go and warning that some of these airlines would be driven out of business. Sources from other airlines were quoted in the British media speaking disparagingly about Ryanair, with one suggesting the airline's cheap fares would largely appeal to 'gangs of lager louts' who would cause mayhem in European cities. O'Leary retaliated saying Ryanair carried 'very upmarket' passengers on its European flights. 'We call them the Chianti louts heading to villas in Tuscany and the South of France. We expect the Chianti louts, the lager louts and anybody who just wants a stunningly low fare to buy tickets. We declared that we were going to smash the BA monopoly of high fares on short-haul European routes; that we have clearly done.'

CHAPTER FOURTEEN

No Frills

'We don't fall over ourselves if they say, "My granny fell ill." What part of no refund don't you understand? You are not getting a refund so fuck off.' This was Michael O'Leary's reply when asked about how Ryanair deals with customers seeking a refund on their tickets, their most common complaint. Telling customers to 'fuck off' is a long way from most companies' policies, and a far cry from the days when Ryanair staff were trained to be polite and helpful to the travelling public. O'Leary used these tactics to fend off complaints and keep costs down, and at the same time argued that the airline was delivering a high level of service to its millions of customers.

'Our customer service is about the most well-defined in the world,' he has said. 'We guarantee to give you the lowest airfare. You get a safe flight. You get a normally on-time flight. That's the package. We don't and won't give you anything more on top of that. We care for our customers in the most fundamental way possible: we don't screw them every time we fly them. I have no time for certain large airlines that say they care and then screw you for six or seven hundred quid almost every time you fly.'

Reluctantly, the travelling public began to understand just what Ryanair meant when it said it offered no frills. Essentially, they could buy a cheap ticket that would take them from one airport to another. If they wanted a drink or a snack, or a wheelchair to take them to the departure gate, they had to pay for it. The airline took no responsibility for delayed or cancelled flights and if for any reason passengers had to cancel their journey, they should not expect to have the fare refunded. In media interviews O'Leary made his policy quite clear: 'If a plane is cancelled will we put you up in a hotel overnight? Absolutely not. If a plane is delayed, will we give you a voucher for a restaurant? Absolutely not.'

Ryanair's millionth passenger, Jane O'Keeffe, was also about to have a bruising encounter with the airline's customer services. Over the nine years since she had first won the free flights for life she had taken about three or four flights a year, and always rang the airline a couple of weeks in advance to make the arrangements. She had married and moved from London back to Dublin, and was now planning to travel with her husband to visit family in Scotland for the October bank holiday weekend. On 15 October 1997 O'Keeffe booked two seats on Ryanair's flight to Glasgow's Prestwick Airport. To her surprise, the airline failed to forward a booking number to confirm the arrangements, and when she inquired about her tickets the airline denied that she had made a booking. A few days before the holiday weekend O'Keeffe attempted to sort out the tickets again, only to be told there were no seats available on the flight. During several frustrating phone calls Ryanair staff quizzed her about the free flights arrangements, inquiring whether she had anything in writing to prove her entitlement. She was eventually put through to Tim Jeans, who explained that as she didn't have a written contract with the airline it had decided to change the arrangement. Instead of unlimited free flights for life, it was now restricting the number of free flights she could take, and asked her to participate in some extra publicity.

Unhappy with the proposed new condition, O'Keeffe rang Michael O'Leary himself. The result was an unpleasant and distressing conversation during which O'Leary shouted, 'Who do you think you are, ringing up demanding flights?' O'Keeffe claimed that she asked him not to 'bully' her and said she had found it difficult to make herself heard during their conversation. She pointed out that she had clippings of newspaper features about her prize and video footage of Ryanair's former chief executive, PJ McGoldrick, presenting it to her. When she told O'Leary she felt she was being very badly treated, he allegedly replied: 'That's your problem. You're not to phone anyone in Ryanair again.' He told her to send in the tape and said that he would look at it.

O'Keeffe felt understandably aggrieved. Convinced the airline could not arbitrarily renege on the prize it had so publicly awarded her, she hired a lawyer and took a legal action against the airline, seeking £360,000 in damages from Ryanair for negligence, misrepresentation and loss of expectation.

It took five years for the case to be heard in the Irish High Court, where the airline vigorously defended its behaviour. Ryanair claimed O'Keeffe had no enforceable contract in law and contended that what she had received in 1988 was simply a gift bestowed on her by the company. O'Leary also rejected O'Keeffe's claims that he had been abusive and hostile towards her during their phone conversation. The airline did attempt to settle her claim during the hearing but she rejected the proposal on the basis that she did not trust Ryanair.

Justice Peter Kelly found in her favour, stating that Ryanair had breached its contract with her when it started to restrict the offer. He also took a dim view of O'Leary's behaviour, saying that the Ryanair chief executive had been 'hostile and aggressive' when the winner contacted the airline to complain. He noted O'Keeffe's 'modest' use of her prize and determined that despite the lack of documents the arrangement had worked well until 1997. 'I found the plaintiff a more persuasive witness than Mr O'Leary and I therefore find as a fact that the version of events given by the plaintiff is what occurred,' Justice Kelly said. 'I reject Mr O'Leary's assertion that he was not hostile or aggressive or bullying towards the plaintiff. I find that he was.' He added that he was 'satisfied that an enforceable contract' had been made between the airline and O'Keeffe and that it had reneged on its promise. The judge ruled that Ryanair should pay €67,500 in damages to O'Keeffe and pay her legal costs, estimated at €200,000. After the verdict O'Keeffe said she felt Ryanair had treated her shabbily: 'I was very, very upset by the telephone call [to Mr Michael O'Leary] and I was vindicated.' Reporters asked O'Keeffe whether she would fly with Ryanair again. 'I anticipated being asked that question,' she replied, laughing, 'and I'd say, "subject to availability".'

The court case had not cast the chief executive and the airline in a particularly good light, but O'Leary obviously believed that there was no such thing as bad publicity. Many of his colleagues thought it was stupid to have pursued O'Keeffe through the courts. 'There was no talking to him,' one complained. 'You could only talk him out of some such action if you could show him a way of going down with all guns blazing.' O'Leary feigned a degree of contrition when questioned about the case by a shareholder at the company's annual general meeting. He apologised about how the episode had unfolded and said it had decided to fight the case because O'Keeffe was looking for €400,000 in compensation. 'I would regret that we put the girl herself through four days of court which was no great fun. It distracted us for three or four days, we had bad publicity for a few days and now I'm characterised as hating women and all the rest of it. But four hundred grand is four hundred grand.'

While it didn't appeal the verdict, Ryanair took its time paying the €67,000 in damages to O'Keeffe, who subsequently applied to the High Court to have Ryanair put into liquidation unless it settled its debt. The airline's commercial director, Michael Cawley, said the petition was completely unnecessary and explained that the payment had been delayed while the airline confirmed whether it had to pay tax to the Irish Revenue Commissioners on that amount. 'We are happy to pay it and we said at the time we were very happy to pay it,' he said. O'Leary claimed the case would send a message to the legal profession that Ryanair would never be 'held to ransom' on any issue. It also sent a clear message to customers that they had better be prepared to engage in full-scale warfare if they wanted to pursue complaints against the Irish airline.

Forcing the disabled to pay up to €25 for the use of a wheelchair was one of Ryanair's most controversial policies, and one that drew the ire of equality agencies and disability action groups. The wheelchairs were owned by airport authorities who charged for their use, but other airlines were happy to absorb this cost. Ryanair, alone even amongst the low-cost airlines, refused to do so. The chairwoman of the Disability Authority in Ireland, Angela Kerins, suggested that while Ryanair was intent on attracting millions of new passengers, this did not include the 30 million disabled tourists who travelled within Europe. 'Maybe the airline is not looking at the advantages of having these tourists in its flights,' she said. The airline trenchantly defended its position in the face of growing criticism for its treatment of the disabled, stating that its policy was part of its low-cost business model.

It was difficult for disabled people to board a Ryanair flight regardless of whether they were forced to pay for a wheelchair or not. One of its more visible cost-saving measures was dispensing with the airbridges that took passengers directly from the departure gate onto the aircraft. Ryanair passengers had to walk out onto the tarmac and climb the steps when they wanted to board or leave a flight. The airline claimed it had a quota of 'four or five' wheelchair passengers per flight. A spokeswoman said this was based on European Union guidelines. Its only consideration was safety, she explained.

Stories about the problems Ryanair caused for disabled passengers began to surface in the media. The *Mirror* told the story of multiple-sclerosis sufferer Helen Newton, who claimed airline staff told her, 'We don't cater for the disabled.' Helen was travelling from Dublin to Manchester with her sixteen-month-old baby in October 1999, and the family arrived at the airport in good time for the flight so they could borrow a wheelchair to take Helen to the plane.

'We were at the Ryanair terminal at 4 p.m. for the 5.55 p.m. flight to Manchester Airport,' said her father, Dermot Richardson. 'They said she would have to pay eight pounds for one and then they just refused to give her a wheelchair because she had no identification to say she was disabled. Her ID was with her car at Manchester Airport so she could keep it parked in the disabled car park while she was visiting us. And it is more than obvious that Helen has MS ... After about forty minutes they agreed to give her a wheelchair but Helen was close to tears at this stage.' After a long wait the wheelchair arrived and Helen was taken on to the runway and left at the bottom of the steps. 'Helen was able to climb the stairs but no one even attempted to help her. She will never fly with Ryanair again. It was a shocking way to treat a human being. Our travel agent had warned us that they had a very poor reputation with the disabled but we had no idea they would be so bad.'

Responding to the story, a Ryanair spokesman refused to comment on this passenger's experience but once against stated its policy in relation to wheelchairs. 'If a passenger is not a wheelchair passenger and is therefore capable of walking to the airport, Ryanair would expect the passenger to walk through the airport to board the aircraft.'

Another MS sufferer contacted the *Guardian*'s consumer champion column, 'Ask Anna', with details of her experience of travelling Ryanair. Patience Owen, from London, did not use a wheelchair but found it difficult to walk and had asked Ryanair to convey her to and from the plane in an airport wheelchair. She was horrified to find out that she would be charged £48 for the privilege. 'No other airline charges for this,' she said. 'Ryanair told me it's because it's a no-frills operation. Since when has a wheelchair been a frill?' When contacted about the complaint a spokeswoman told the newspaper wheelchairs are hired from an airport contractor and the fee goes to them, not Ryanair.

The level of complaints about the airline was so vast that newspapers began to dedicate specific columns to the grievances of Ryanair customers. Barbara Tanner from Watford wrote to *The Times*' Ryanair postbag outlining her similarly unpleasant experience. 'Despite booking wheelchair assistance, I had to ask a fellow passenger to push me to the departure gate for my Ryanair flight from Stansted to Biarritz. And, upon my return, I sat for an hour waiting for assistance on the plane, getting colder and colder. The crew waited with me and later we were joined by a replacement crew. Eight people stood around as I begged someone to help. I am elderly and with a heart condition – but I was told they were not insured to help. I knew a taxi would be waiting for me and I was worried about my luggage. Ryanair did not seem particularly geared up for disabled passengers, to say the least.'

When contacted by the newspaper, Tanner had just returned from another Ryanair flight on the same route and reported that exactly the same thing had happened again. This time, though, she had to wait an hour and fifty minutes to leave the plane. She said she was both 'exhausted' and 'astonished' – because Ryanair had apologised to her in writing for the first delay and promised her, again in writing, that it would not happen again. The paper asked Ryanair to explain its behaviour, and wanted to know whether it would compensate Mrs Tanner for the £30 in extra mini-cab fares she had to pay as a result of the two incidents.

Ryanair replied: 'The Ryanair crew members involved rightly stated that they are not insured to help with the movement of disabled passengers and therefore, while regrettable, they could not have assisted Mrs Tanner to and from the plane themselves ... we apologise again for the distress and upset it must have caused.' There was no offer of a refund for the extra taxi charges or the inconvenience.

Richard Wood, chief executive of the British Council of Disabled People, said he had never come across this sort of discrimination before and, as a member of the government's task force on rights for the disabled, he would be ordering a full inquiry. 'It reflects very badly on Ryanair,' he said. Tim Jeans responded to this criticism, again justifying Ryanair's stance and pointing the finger of blame at the airport authorities. 'We are a no-frills service. We have made this decision in the interests of our passengers, not to pass on the airports' charges for wheelchair services to the majority who don't use the service. We do think it is outrageous people should have to pay, but this is an issue that should be faced by airport operators who actually make the charges, rather than us,' he argued.

The Air Transport Users' Council, the consumer watchdog attached to the Britain's Civil Aviation Authority, said it had received a large number of complaints from the disabled about Ryanair. O'Leary had dismissed this body as a 'bunch of halfwits' and adopted a policy of ignoring any correspondence or contact it would make with the airline on behalf of disgruntled passengers. Politicians were also getting exercised. British MP Margaret Hodge said the airline could face legal action for charging disabled people for the use of wheelchairs. 'I can't believe they cannot spread that cost across the passengers in an aeroplane and still make a profit for shareholders.' Hodge said that all British airlines had taken a collective decision to absorb such costs and not pass them on to passengers and that Ryanair was discriminating against the disabled. 'If someone needs assistance to get from the desk to the aeroplane and they have a disability, it's not right they should have to pay more than the rest of us for their trip.' Jeans said Ryanair had held many discussions with disability groups and was 'happy' it was not discriminating against the disabled.

Equality authorities began to consider whether the airline was in fact breaching legislation and should be obliged to pay compensation or alter its policies. Fifty British passengers joined to take a class action against it and the British Disability Rights Commission began to prepare to take a case against Ryanair and the British Airports Authority. BAA said it was surprised to be included in the claim as it provided wheelchairs for free to passengers until check-in. At its Scottish airports the cost of wheelchairs was divided among the airlines using the airport from a communal fund, it explained, while Aer Rianta insisted it was Ryanair's responsibility to assist disabled passengers to board its aircraft.

In Ireland the Equality Authority was investigating a 'substantial number' of complaints from passengers. A letter to *The Irish Times* suggested there has been some improvement in the airline's treatment of less mobile passengers. Dr Anne Clancy from Dublin, who was physically disabled and used a wheelchair, complimented the airline for its treatment of her and her blind travelling companion. 'Ryanair dealt with us extremely well,' she said. 'I know that Ryanair have had some bad press in the past for how they have dealt with disabled people, but our treatment was almost flawless. Almost? My blind companion was offered a newspaper to read on disembarking!'

Another 'frill' that briefly disappeared in 1998 was ice. Cabin crew were alerted to Ryanair's ice ban in a memo that explained the initiative would save the airline about £40,000 a year. Ryanair had had a row with its in-flight catering firm, which had told the airline it would no longer supply ice for free; sources suggested that Gate Gourmet, which also caters for British Airways and British Midland, wanted to charge about £800 a week for providing and delivering the ice. When the order was cancelled the crew were left to make up excuses for passengers.

A subsequent memo informed staff that Gate Gourmet would deliver ice to Ryanair's aircraft once every morning, leaving flight attendants to wonder how they would make one bag of ice last from six in the morning until ten at night. 'We are told to use it sparingly as it has to last all day and not to give ice with soft drinks,' said one cabin crew member, who didn't want to be named. 'We have had to make jokes about the delivery van not making it to the aircraft and try to make light of it, but it is really embarrassing. We have a lot of frequent fliers and if we keep saying "Sorry, we have no ice today" they will soon realise it is happening all the time.' Many afternoon and evening flights had no ice. Charlie Clifton, Ryanair's director of ground operations, insisted to the media that Ryanair had the capacity to take ice in one delivery to last all day, but later that week passengers on some evening flights who wanted ice in their drinks were told by staff that there was none available. 'Other colleagues have had trouble on flights when people wanted ice with Baileys and gin and tonic but there was none,' said the crew member. 'Ryanair expects you to pay £3 for these drinks and then there is no ice. Passengers don't want to buy a drink when we don't have ice. Sales are being affected.'

The dispute with the supplier was eventually resolved and ice was reintroduced on all Ryanair flights. O'Leary was victorious. 'Gate Gourmet was attempting to put up the charges so, as we say with most of our suppliers, we are not bearing the increased charges,' he explained. 'So we took it off. They didn't believe we would fly without it. They lost the business and then came back and we reached a satisfactory agreement for continued supply of ice without a cost increase. Everybody thinks when we say we are going to do something that we are bluffing, as did our ice supplier.'

People gradually came to realise that when they were flying with Ryanair they could expect little support or assistance when flights were cancelled. In 1996 hundreds of passengers were forced to spend the night at Luton Airport when three return flights between Dublin and Luton were cancelled. The airline said the situation had arisen due to technical problems and that it didn't have any alternative aircraft available to operate these flights. At first the 300 people who arrived to check in were told that the Ryanair flights were delayed. Then at about 7 p.m. the information screens went blank and passengers were told there would be no flights. They had to form a queue to return their duty-free goods and take back their luggage and then try to ensure they were booked on flights out of Luton the next morning. Ground handling staff at Luton advised passengers who lived nearby to go home for the night. For those less fortunate, though, the message was simple: there was no accommodation and they would have to spend the night in the terminal building. A Ryanair representative said it was unable to find accommodation for its passengers left in Luton and offered the weary travellers a £5 food voucher in compensation. Another 200 to 300 people were also stranded in Dublin. Some were transferred onto flights to other British airports, others went home and the airline provided accommodation for the remainder.

One man, travelling to Dublin with his three children, vowed never to fly with the airline again. 'Ryanair has not even had the decency to send a representative to Luton and explain to us what is happening,' he said. 'They just keep passing messages to us through the airport staff and all they have given me is £5 in compensation.' Some passengers had to spend much of the following day at the airport waiting to get on flights.

Four years later it was clear that the public had still not fully grasped the 'no frills' concept. When Ryanair was forced to cancel flights from Beauvais Airport outside Paris due to bad weather, passengers were stunned at the way Ryanair treated them. The airline offered a refund to those who wanted to return to Paris, and laid on a free bus to ferry them back – but they would have to wait two months to get their money. Those who just wanted to return to Ireland queued up to get their names on standby lists and then learned that the terminal building closed at ten that night and they would have to find somewhere to sleep. There was some relief when the airline referred to nearby accommodation – until people realised where they would be spending the night. One of the 264 passengers, David Gibbons, gave a description: 'The accommodation we were offered for the night was in a hangar in the airport with beds like army cots and no showers. Anybody with any money went into Beauvais.' He had paid just £5 for his ticket to Paris and booked into a two-star hotel in the nearby town at a cost of £30, spending another £10 on taxis. Speaking to the media, he acknowledged that his ticket had been very cheap but insisted that Ryanair's customer care had been appalling. Passengers were horrified to be initially told that they might have to spend more than one night, even up to a week, on stretchers in an airport hangar. And a near-rebellion began when they realised that Ryanair wouldn't be offering them even a cup of tea: as far as the airline was concerned they could either starve or buy their own drinks and snacks at the airport café. Through sheer stealth they eventually managed to push the ground staff to provide 'a roll and a thimbleful of tea', Gibbons said. Some passengers phoned the Irish media in a desperate bid to highlight their plight.

O'Leary robustly defended Ryanair's customer service on national radio, managed to annoy even more people in the process. 'No, we don't provide accommodation for people if their flight is cancelled,' he said. 'It's not part of our service. It's unreasonable of passengers to turn up at the airport and expect to be provided with a free cup of tea. People got an apology and the airport restaurant was open.' He said the airline had chartered an aircraft the following day to bring all of the passengers home. His trenchant response drew harsh criticism throughout the week, although Ryanair refused to make any further comment on the matter. But some passengers had no intention of letting the matter rest, and seven took the airline to the Irish Small Claims Court. The judge upheld their claim and ordered Ryanair to pay £2785 in compensation for their inconvenience.

The airline immediately appealed the decision to the Circuit Court. There Judge Liam Devally said that given the bad weather Ryanair shouldn't have left it until the last minute to inform passengers of the likelihood that the flights would be cancelled. He ruled that there had been a 'lack of candour' by the airline with passengers, and while it had otherwise met 'almost all' of the passengers' contractual obligations he ordered Ryanair to pay the compensation.

Passengers on Ryanair's FR901 flight between Stansted and Cork were distressed and angry about the siege-like conditions they had to endure while the plane was grounded on the tarmac for hours in bad weather conditions. When the flight arrived, six hours behind schedule, the harassed travellers spoke about their ordeal. A woman travelling with a young baby said the crew wouldn't let her change the baby's nappy. 'They wouldn't even let me walk up and down the plane,' she said. Another mother complained that her child, a diabetic, was unable to take medication because of the delays in getting food. Sandwiches were finally offered for sale at £3. One man, who objected to paying after the delays they had experienced, took one from the trolley without paying. His actions were reported to the airport's security staff, who escorted him off the flight. 'The man was not a bit aggressive but did refuse to put the sandwich back,' a passenger who sat behind him explained.

Ryanair spokeswoman Ethel Power defended the airline's action. 'The situation is that a delay does not entitle anyone to steal,' she explained. 'Just because there is a delay, it does not mean that people can break the law.' She reiterated that Ryanair did not have any responsibility to supply free food: 'With adverse weather conditions, the airline is not responsible for feeding people, but if the delay was the airline's fault and was longer than four hours then the airline is responsible.'

For an airline that specialised in point-to-point travel Ryanair wasn't always the most reliable when it came to carrying bags. Passengers on a flight from the City of Derry Airport in Northern Ireland to Stansted in 1999 were stunned when, in an announcement made just minutes before the plane took off, the pilot announced that they had offloaded forty-six items of luggage as a result of a 'bad runway' and 'high temperatures'. Journalist Eamonn McCann, on board at the time, commented, 'I was surprised by his undiplomatic choice of words, given that we were sitting on the tarmac and were just about to take off.'

'It was a major inconvenience as many people were only staying for the weekend and did not receive their bags until the following day,' explained one of the passengers. 'I felt sorry for one couple who were due to attend a wedding the following morning, but all their clothes were back in Derry.' Ryanair insisted there were no problems with the airport's facilities but that it had been forced to alter its service due to weather conditions. 'All decisions taken are in the interests of the safety of passengers and crew on board.' The spokeswoman told the *Belfast Telegraph* that she had been unable to contact the pilot involved to question him about his comments.

One couple whose bags went missing after travelling from Manchester to Dublin in the days before Christmas just managed to get them back in time for the festivities – with the help of the Taoiseach, Bertie Ahern. Their neighbour, Peadar Byrne, made a flurry of phone calls to politicians and to Ryanair seeking assistance, and even left a message on the answering machine at

Ahern's constituency office close to Dublin Airport. On Christmas Eve, the Taoiseach returned Byrne's call and promised to help. 'I was absolutely gobsmacked when the Taoiseach called me back,' he said. 'I told him I couldn't believe it was him. Mr Ahern was very nice to us and said that he would do all he could. Shortly after that, I got a call from the manager of Aer Rianta at Dublin Airport and from a Ryanair supervisor. The long and the short of it is, Ryanair found the bags for the family and sent them down to us by courier express.' A spokesman for the Taoiseach said that Ahern was delighted the bags were found in Manchester and returned to their owners. '"He wasn't sure what he could do to help Mr Byrne, whom he had never heard of, but decided to give it a go. The Taoiseach contacted the airport and airline authorities and is delighted the missing bags turned up.'

The airline also became the first to recruit passengers to work as baggage-handlers. As those on board flight FR287 from Stansted to Dublin settled into their seats the captain came on the intercom to ask for volunteers to load luggage. After a moment of surprised silence, passengers assumed it was a joke and began to laugh. But cabin crew soon made it clear that the captain was in fact being deadly serious. The company contracted by Ryanair to provide baggage-handlers was running short and the pilot had been told he would have to wait two hours to take off. Three passengers came to his aid and stepped onto the tarmac and began to throw the bags into the hold, allowing the flight to get airborne only fifty minutes behind schedule. A Ryanair spokeswoman confirmed that passengers had been recruited as baggage-handlers and thanked them for their assistance. She also commended the pilot on his initiative and pointed out that the volunteers were bought drinks for their trouble.

Consumers could not help but wonder whether baggage-handling would be the next 'frill' to go. Was it now just a matter of time before O'Leary made passengers load their own luggage?

CHAPTER FIFTEEN

The Fourth Secret of Fatima

'It's amazing what lengths people will go to, to fly cheaper than Ryanair,' the Irish airline declared in a 1996 advertisement released only days after a Sudan Airways flight with more than a hundred passengers and crew on board was hijacked and flown to Stansted Airport. The aircraft had been diverted to the UK from its journey to Jordan by seven Iraqis armed with bottles disguised as hand grenades, and sat on the tarmac at Stansted for twenty hours, during which the hijackers threatened to blow up the aircraft and shoot the passengers. They eventually surrendered peacefully and the traumatised passengers and crew were released unharmed.

Airline pilots were shocked and disgusted by the advertisement. The International Federation of Airline Pilots' Associations lodged a complaint with the Advertising Standards Authority in Ireland saying Ryanair had acted in 'bad taste'. The pilots felt it was wrong to capitalise on the misfortune of another airline and to exploit the trauma suffered by passengers; some even considered the advertisement an incitement to commit crime. Ryanair was delighted and revelled in the controversy, arguing that it was just building on the increased public awareness of Stansted Airport sparked by the hijacking.

However, the Advertising Standards Authority took a dim view of the situation, ruling that the advertisement contravened its code, even though Ryanair offered reassurances that the offensive advertisement was very much 'of the moment' and would not be repeated. In any case, it was a massive publicity coup in terms of bringing Ryanair to the public's attention, and a taste of things to come. Three years later, in 1999, when the battle to commandeer Europe's skies was in full swing, the carriers vied for publicity through their outrageous advertising. All turned their guns on British Airways. Virgin, delighted to attack its arch-rival, launched a campaign declaring 'BA does not give a shiatsu.' A week later Ryanair stepped into the fray, branding BA 'expensive ba****ds!' in a full-page advertisement in the London *Evening Standard* alongside comparisons of Ryanair and BA's fares.

Incensed, BA immediately sought an injunction to prevent a repeat performance. It instructed its lawyers to pursue a legal action against the upstart airline and also complained to the Advertising Standards Authority that the advertisements were offensive. Ryanair's Tim Jeans fuelled the publicity by explaining to reporters that the campaign was meant to be tongue-in-cheek – 'BA has definitely lost its sense of humour over this.' BA claimed Ryanair had misquoted its prices; a spokesman said, 'We are taking out a writ because of the advert's inaccuracy, not because of the knocking words in it.' The Advertising Standards Authority upheld BA's complaint, agreeing that the headline was likely to cause serious or widespread offence, and asked Ryanair not to use this approach again. Ryanair retorted that it had simply used the advertisement to catch readers' attention and didn't believe it had been offensive. BA continued the battle in the High Court, but, to Ryanair's delight, Justice Robin Jacob threw the suit out, saying the campaign was honest, comparative advertising. 'The real reason BA does not like it is precisely because it is true,' he said.

These publicity stunts, coupled with special promotions and massive seat sales, were certainly drawing the public's attention to Ryanair. Each promotion would trigger thousands of bookings; indeed the level of demand could be so high that on some days customers would have to call Ryanair Direct's number several times and then hold for lengthy periods before finally managing to book their tickets. Often, though, customers were disappointed to discover that they couldn't actually get the advertised bargains, and some complained that Ryanair's advertising was misleading.

One woman complained to the ASA about a promotion headed 'HOW TO BOOK £49 FLIGHTS' which claimed that the advertised fare also included the £10 UK government tax charged to passengers. When she called Ryanair Direct to book flights from Stansted to Paris, she was told twice by the airline's reservations staff that her flight would cost £46 plus £15 tax. When asked to explain this, Ryanair told the ASA that 44,000 passengers had availed themselves of the £49 offer price, and that over 6000 had purchased the advertised fare on the Paris route. The airline supplied a copy of an issued ticket to demonstrate that flights had been sold at the advertised price of £49 plus £2.40 French tax. It also submitted a computer printout of seven prices available, one of which was for a flight to and from Paris on weekdays for £49 plus local tax. Ryanair did not show how many flights were sold at the advertised price or how many seats had been made available for the offer price on each flight.

The ASA expressed concern that the complainant seemed to have been quoted a price for weekend travel although she wanted to travel out on a Thursday and return on a Tuesday. It concluded that Ryanair had not supplied adequate evidence in support of the advertised price claim and reminded the airline of its obligations to comply with advertising standards. The Air Transport Users' Council (AUC) also criticised the advertising of extremely cheap deals that then proved difficult to purchase, and called for regulations to be introduced to prevent consumer deception. 'Our concern is that these airlines may be misleading people,' a spokesman said. 'On days when they know there is a trade fair or football match on and demand will be high, the public has no way of knowing whether there is a reduction in the number of seats available at the lowest advertised fare.'

The AUC regularly received complaints from customers who, when they called to book a seat at the lowest rate weeks in advance of travel, were told that the flight was not yet open and they should phone back the following week. When they did, they were told that the cheapest seats had already gone. 'We believe there should be a reasonable chance of obtaining a seat at the lowest price and think all the airlines should say how many are available and on which flights,' it said. Ryanair responded by saying that 50 per cent of its seats were sold at the lowest fare and a further 20 per cent at the next lowest.

The following June, Ryanair was unamused when one of its

aircraft, carrying 126 passengers, was impounded at Manchester Airport in a dispute over £500,000 in unpaid landing fees. The flight arrived in Manchester fifteen minutes ahead of schedule at 8.15 a.m. but airport staff refused to let the passengers disembark. Instead, the pilot was ordered to taxi to an area reserved for impounded planes and Ryanair was told it would only be released following an undertaking from its bank that the debt would be cleared. Jim Stockton, the airport's financial manager, boarded the flight and presented documents giving him the right to ground the aircraft until the airport's demands were met. Ryanair's spokeswoman, Ethel Power, described the airport's action as unwarranted and unjustified, and said the airline had met all of its payment obligations to the airport over the past five years. She acknowledged that a payment made two weeks earlier was incorrect, but said this was immediately corrected, blaming a 'clerical error' for the problem. The airline had left large debts at Manchester Airport in the 1980s and had recently been trying to negotiate better terms in the same way that it had in Dublin and Stansted. Jim Stockton explained that the aircraft was impounded 'as a last resort'. He told reporters, 'I agree the powers we exercised were severe but they were justified in the circumstances. We have been unable to resolve certain financial matters over a substantial period of time. We would not have taken this most rare action over an insignificant sum.'

The passengers were allowed to leave the flight after a short time, while those waiting to board the return flight to Dublin had to wait until almost 11 a.m. to get airborne after Ryanair had put arrangements in place to clear the slate. 'It seems there was a ransom on our heads,' one passenger complained. 'Surely there was a better way to resolve this than to inconvenience us?' Ryanair said it regretted that Manchester Airport decided, without warning, to exercise the 'draconian power' of aircraft detention. Eamonn Croke wrote a letter to *The Irish Times* saying that Manchester Airport's actions suggested that it had 'learned the cut of Ryanair's jib'. He wondered if perhaps he too should have attempted to impound the plane that was supposed to fly him from Dublin to Stansted last year, but instead left its passengers high and dry in Luton. 'Ryanair subsequently refused to take any responsibility, or to pay the £9 bus and train fare to get to the destination I had paid them for,' he said. Later that week Ryanair was presented with the 'Best-Managed National Airline' award at the Paris air show.

Michael O'Leary was very sore about its treatment in Manchester and instructed the airline's lawyers to pursue a legal action against the airport. Some months later, though, this was abandoned and Ryanair became the first airline to sign up to the airport's new millennium pricing policy, effective from January 2000. This featured lower charges for airlines seeking to operate routes to destinations currently under-served or not served at all from Manchester. Following the agreement, Ryanair increased its schedule from four to ten flights daily between Manchester and Dublin, with fares starting at £5.

Ryanair's new aircraft were now arriving from Boeing in Seattle and it announced more low fares to new European destinations from Stansted: Genoa, Ancona and Turin in Italy, Biarritz and Dinard in France, and Denmark's second biggest city, Aarhus. Ryanair was also ready to muscle in on the busy London to Frankfurt route, which linked two of Europe's biggest financial centres and was dominated by a new enemy, the mighty German flag-carrier Lufthansa. Ryanair began to offer flights to Frankfurt at £69.99, although those who bought them quickly discovered that they would in fact land at the former US air force base of Hahn, some 128km from the city. From there, passengers could take a coach into Germany's financial centre – a journey of two hours on a good day.

The region had been deathly quiet since the last of the F-16 fighter jets headed back to the US in 1990. The airport's owner, the German airport operator Fraport, began to encourage Ryanair to fly there in the late 1990s, although it wasn't really convinced that it could persuade the Irish airline to operate scheduled flights from such a remote spot. The airport's managing director, Andreas Helfer, still recalls Michael O'Leary's response. 'That's bullshit,' he said. 'People will go there just because airfares are cheap.' Helfer said it offered Ryanair 'whatever it wanted to hear' in terms of discounts and arrangements, saying 'We just wanted to get them started.' During the negotiations the Ryanair team arrived in waves. Bernard Berger, its route development manager, led the way. 'He is the terrier who bites on

80 per cent of what's on the table,' said Helfer. When the airport was close to agreeing a deal, Michael Cawley and O'Leary arrived to seal it, and in 1999 Ryanair began operating two flights daily between Stansted and Hahn. Passengers from London arrived to collect their luggage from a small shed-like structure that was the old Officers' Club. British newspapers pointed out that Ryanair's claim that it was flying to Frankfurt was equivalent to telling tourists they were flying to London, only to dump them out in Swindon or Peterborough.

Some customers complained to the ASA that Ryanair's advertisements failed to mention the exact destination – as well as Hahn, the airline flew to airports in Italy, Norway and Sweden which could be up to two hours from the advertised city. The ASA said there was a simple solution to the problem: Ryanair should make the exact destination clear in all of its literature. 'All they have to do is put the city involved, such as Frankfurt, with Hahn in brackets afterwards,' a spokesman suggested. 'That would be fine. All we are asking the flight industry is to make things completely clear.' Ryanair insisted, however, that it would not be changing its advertising policy. 'We don't feel we've done anything wrong,' the airline's spokeswoman said. 'When passengers book we make it clear where they will be flying and tell them about the coach journey.' She suggested that landing at Hahn could actually save passengers time, by keeping them away from congested runways and arrival lounges. 'They save so much time collecting their baggage and getting through the controls they can be on the coach in twenty minutes.'

Ryanair was certainly operating a very different service from its rivals and its policy of flying to obscure airports was increasingly noticed by the travelling public. In a humorous letter to *The Times*, Bill Colegrave wondered why BA hadn't adopted such a policy: 'You charge much less for the tickets and then take the passengers somewhere they did not really want to go. It does not matter precisely where you take them, so long as it sounds right – so long as the reservations team can answer "yes" to questions such as "Do you fly to Stockholm, Frankfurt, Paris, etc?" As a result, all over Europe places are changing their names to satisfy airline executives. Just a few months ago a sleepy South Sweden town, with a rudimentary airport, called Nykoping (roughly pronounced "no shopping", and very aptly named) discovered that it was really called Stockholm South, even though it is not much closer to Stockholm than it is to Copenhagen. Meanwhile, a disused airbase not far from Luxembourg has become Frankfurt (Hahn), and it is only a short 747 hop from Frankfurt itself, or a two-hour drive in good conditions.' Colegrave joked that this phenomenon had inspired him to consider getting into the aviation business. 'Wait for my airline,' he said. 'Reno will become Los Angeles West (Denver East at weekends); Bermuda will be more profitable as New York (Hudson River Extension Terminal); and London (Goodwin Sands) is under construction, courtesy of the spring tides.'

While Ryanair was trying to encourage more of its passengers to book their seats directly with the airline rather than through travel agents to save money, its telephone booking system was often overloaded and proved very frustrating for those trying to book flights. Caroline Green, who headed Ryanair Direct, favoured adopting a new booking system, and after much discussion O'Leary eventually agreed to purchase the US Open Skies system, which unknown to him included an online booking facility. O'Leary always believed in keeping things simple and would dismiss proposals that he believed would complicate his business model. He didn't know how to use a computer and his colleagues knew that he wouldn't accept the need to set up a website unless he was convinced of its success. 'The staff didn't tell O'Leary about the Internet booking facility in the system in case he would tell them to take it out and pay less for the system,' an employee said. 'They tried to get it in as a trial, and tried to keep its budget low enough that it would be kept it below Michael's radar. He would be afraid it would complicate the business. It was introduced by sheer stealth.'

Eddie Wilson, Ryanair's personnel director, made contact with two students to design the front page of Ryanair's proposed new website through a contact at Gateway, the US computer manufacturer based close to Dublin Airport. John Beckett, a seventeen-year-old secondary-school student, and Thomas Linehan, a twenty-two-year-old dentistry student at Trinity College Dublin, had spent the previous summer working in its technical support division. Wilson offered them £15,500 to work on the design – at the same time as the airline had received a number of proposals from specialist Internet firms that priced the contract at up to £3.5 million. In an interview, Linehan said Ryanair's top priority was to get the website up and running. 'Ryanair wanted their site done yesterday. They knew every day they didn't have a site they were losing money.' He said that it would usually take about ten weeks to design a site but Ryanair wanted the job to be done in three. 'We could do this, with a design they liked at a price they liked. Although we did have to fight for every last penny,' he said.

In August 1999 Ryanair announced a new seat sale to kick-start its winter bookings, offering a million seats to twenty European cities for fares starting from £15.99 one way. This time, customers were told they could book these flights either by phoning Ryanair Direct or by logging onto Ryanair.com. The airline was delighted with the number of people who began to book flights over the Internet. No one was more surprised by the response than O'Leary. 'Suddenly O'Leary became the man who discovered the Internet,' one colleague remarked wryly. Beckett and Linehan turned down the opportunity to work in Ryanair to develop their site further. 'For me, this is just a hobby. The money is not important,' Linehan said. Over the next few months the site was refined and Ryanair employed staff to enhance the booking facilities and make it easy for its customers to use.

Ryanair's business model was thriving. Its low cost base combined with soaring passenger numbers was yielding healthy profits for the Irish airline at a time when British Airways' profits were slumping. On 8 November 1999 BA announced a 77 per cent decline in profits to £89 million sterling in the six months to the end of September. The following day Ryanair announced a 17 per cent rise in profits to £43 million, its ninth successive year of profit, and said it was on target to carry 6 million passengers. In response to its waning fortunes, BA announced a switch to smaller aircraft and dropped twenty European routes as part of a repositioning exercise to concentrate on serving premium and full-fare passengers. O'Leary, delighted with BA's new strategy, said Ryanair would chase the passengers who could no longer travel with the British airline. 'The more BA cuts back, the more we get to carry the great unwashed,' he claimed. 'We're not proud.'

Since 1995 Ryanair's profits had grown by about 33 per cent a year and it was now Europe's biggest low-fares carrier and, according to O'Leary, aiming to double its passenger numbers within four years. It was more profitable than its role model, Southwest Airlines, despite flying to a network of far more remote airports than its Texas-based counterpart. These obscure airfields offered Ryanair extremely cheap landing charges and contributions towards the airline's promotion costs, in deals mostly agreed for ten to twenty years. Staff numbers were kept to the minimum with just two flight attendants serving passengers on each 130-seater aircraft. These attendants would sell expensively priced drinks and snacks during the flight and even ask passengers to take their crumpled newspapers and other rubbish with them to save on cleaning costs.

Ryanair's fleet of Boeing 737 aircraft brought huge efficiencies but its most significant achievement was perfecting the twenty-five-minute turnaround of its aircraft, only possible at quiet, uncongested airports, which allowed it to squeeze up to two more flights in a day. O'Leary often professed that this was the key lesson he learned while he looked around Southwest Airlines in the early '90s. 'It was the road to Damascus,' he claimed. 'This was the way to make Ryanair work.' But others liked to claim credit for the practice's introduction too. Conor McCarthy said that he first raised the notion of turning aircraft around so swiftly but that the suggestion drew a cool response from O'Leary. 'I explained that it would mean that we would get an extra flight every day and could take off at better times, say on the hour or the half hour.' McCarthy remembered O'Leary saying there was no need to change its operations in this way; it might disrupt its flight schedules. 'He told me I would fuck up the operations,' McCarthy recalled. Whoever had the idea, O'Leary decided to see whether it would work. 'He told me to try it and warned that if it didn't work he would have my bollocks,' McCarthy laughed. 'He can be so refreshingly honest.'

All the while Ryanair was aggressively expanding. It opened more routes into Germany, flying to Hamburg – or rather to Lübeck, an hour and a half away. It also put on flights from Glasgow and Shannon airport to Hahn. It expanded in Italy, ferrying passengers to Brescia, about ninety minutes from Verona, and began flying to Perpignan and Montpellier in the south of France and the Swedish city of Malmö.

By now Ryanair.com had proved its worth, with more than 20 per cent of all new bookings coming in over the Internet. The airline decided to formally launch its website in March 2000, offering further discounts for passengers who booked online, and within weeks claimed it had been visited by more than six million people. The airline recognised that the website had the potential to shave millions off its cost base if it could get more and more passengers to book their flights in this way. Ryanair would not only save on commissions but also be able to closely manage the prices charged in response to the demand. O'Leary pledged to turn the site into a one-stop travel website selling travel insurance, hotel accommodation and car hire. He claimed that within a few months Ryanair.com was getting 50,000 bookings a week; it had already generated sales of £3.5 million sterling and he predicted that this would rise to £350 million by the end of the year.

The website was launched at the height of the Internet boom and raised expectations in the City that Ryanair.com could be floated on the London Stock Exchange, raising many millions in fresh capital for the airline. But O'Leary said he had no plans to float despite the website's success. 'We want to concentrate on being Europe's largest low-fares airline,' he said. 'Selling tickets online will help us cut some £10 million in costs, but there is scope for using Ryanair.com to sell a variety of products. We were approached by lastminute.com, the travel site, but we turned them down because we want to sell Ryanair tickets ourselves.' Colleagues remember O'Leary learning how to use a computer around this time, and soon he was constantly logging into the site.

The airline's flair for advertising once more came to the fore in May 2000, when it created a huge furore with a full-page advertisement that poked fun at the Catholic religion. The Vatican had just released details of the 'third secret of Fatima', a prophecy said to have been revealed by the Virgin Mary to three Portuguese children near the town of Fatima in 1917. Under the heading 'Exclusive – Pope reveals Fourth Secret of Fatima', Ryanair's advertisement featured a picture of the Pope whispering to a kneeling nun; a speech bubble above his head contained the words: 'Psst! Only Ryanair.com guarantee the lowest fares on the Internet.' It would prove to be Ryanair's greatest publicity coup, reported across the world. The Advertising Standards Authority in Ireland was inundated with complaints, particularly from the Irish clergy, arguing that the advertisement was tasteless and a gratuitous insult to the Pope and to the millions of practising Catholics, and that it made a joke of the Fatima experience, which was the focus of devotion for many. Critics also pointed out that advertisers needed written permission from any person portrayed or referred to in an advertisement.

Ryanair robustly defended the advertisement and said there was no evidence of grave and widespread offence. It claimed that it had taken a 'topical subject and portrayed it in an amusing fashion to make a commercial point', arguing that if the airline was deemed guilty of bad taste as a result, then the numerous radio and TV programmes that joked about current news items were equally guilty. But the ASA noted the deeply felt and widely expressed reactions to this advertisement, which had attracted more complaints than any of Ryanair's other campaigns. It concluded that both grave and widespread offence had been caused, and that Ryanair had breached the code by not getting written permission to portray the individuals shown. The authority's chief executive, Ed McCumiskey, said it got about twenty-five written complaints and lots of phone calls about the advertisement. 'I have heard Michael O'Leary laugh about this and boast about the huge amount of publicity it won for him. We were asking why the media would run these ads? They were bound to cause offence,' he commented.

Ryanair initially refused to correspond with the ASA in Britain and the Air Transport Users' Council (AUC), although McCumiskey said it managed to prise a response from the airline. 'There tends to be a lot of correspondence with Ryanair on these issues. They don't take it lying down.' McCumiskey said he usually dealt with Michael Cawley. 'With Ryanair it tends to be a question of attitude. Their attitude is childish rather than childlike. They will always say, "How dare you accuse us of whatever in their correspondence?"' he said. 'They fight their corner but they will always give you an answer. They have a very high profile and like to fight their battles in the general public milieu, unlike other people.' He described Ryanair's style as 'assertive' and said there was a distinctive tone running through everything the airline did. 'You always know where you stand with them. They will always reply ... They have a very clear objective about what they want. It's business and that's it. You are dealing with very imaginative people who are always trying to get an edge over their competitors. Aside from all the funny stuff, its advertising is largely around getting people onto their website.' He recalled the authority's early battles with the airline, about its advertising of fares to Paris and Brussels that didn't state the actual destinations. 'They had to be bullied into being a bit more specific. Ryanair's ads have gotten a lot clearer. It's something we keep an eye on.'

While mocking the Pope was highly effective in diverting thousands of customers to the Ryanair website, some were enraged by what they found online. One man complained that he had been charged three times for a flight when he made the booking. Another, Frank McGurk, wrote to *The Times*' travel column to say that he had finally booked his flight through a travel agent after Ryanair's website twice said that his credit card company couldn't be accessed. It later transpired his card had been accepted but Ryanair refused to refund him the money. When contacted by the column, it apologised over his treatment and a spokesman said the problem was 'unlikely' to happen again. When McGurk's experience appeared in the paper, though, many others wrote in to report similar experiences. Norma McCain said she was charged twice for a ticket booked over the web after the site did not acknowledge the first booking, and that Ryanair's response was deeply unhelpful: 'Their refunds department have refused twice to pay me back, implying that I knowingly double-booked.' Another reader fighting for refunds after being double-charged complained, 'The only way airlines such as Ryanair can offer such low costs is by not having any means of dealing with complaints.'

Simon Evans, of the passenger watchdog AUC, agreed. 'There is definitely an element of getting what you pay for with low-cost airlines, in terms of customer service follow-up.' He also confirmed that booking on the web had provoked complaints from passengers who had been double-charged. 'It is something we have talked about here and is a potential industry problem.' A spokesman for Ryanair said it was investigating McCain's claim but denied the airline has compromised on customer service. He added, 'We have the biggest travel website in Europe, and in 99.9 per cent of cases, everyone is very happy. But maybe there is an element of human error when people have became impatient with the web, logged out and back on again and been charged twice as a result.'

The AUC criticised Ryanair for forcing its passengers to go to 'inordinate lengths' to obtain a refund if their credit card had been debited more than once for the same ticket. A Ryanair spokesman said double-charging of credit cards had been a teething problem but that customers had since been refunded. Other travellers who logged onto Ryanair.com in the belief that they could buy the cheapest fares offered by the airline were disappointed to find out that they could have paid less if they had make their booking by phone. Would-be passengers reported that it was £20 more expensive to book a return ticket from Dublin to Beauvais over the Internet, and £10 more for Dublin to Charleroi. O'Leary acknowledged the problem, blaming it on its Open Skies software systems. 'We are trying to get it fixed,' he said. 'At Ryanair Direct, our agents can override the system and combine the second lowest fare on the way out with the lowest fare on the way back. The software people in America are writing a different program to enable the same facility to be available online.' Despite these difficulties, the traffic coming onto the website had exceeded all expectations and within a couple of months of its launch Ryanair claimed that more than 50 per cent of its bookings were online.

Just as BA was feeling the heat of the relentless price war, two UK-based low-fare carriers, Debonair and AB Airlines, collapsed under the strain. They had long been viewed as the most vulnerable of the new airlines and their attempts to combine low fares with the perks usually associated with high-paying business travellers had proved too expensive. Both blamed 'financial difficulties due to intense competition within the industry' for the failures. EasyJet and Ryanair reacted to the news by announcing offers of free flights and cut-price tickets. Ryanair said it would give away 160,000 one-way flights to ten European destinations over the next three months, while easyJet had a seat sale with

200,000 tickets on offer.

BA's no-frills subsidiary, Go, was also finding the going tough and announced a £20 million operating loss in its first seventeen months. EasyJet and Virgin Express were both profitable, although neither was making as much money as Ryanair. And while two competitors had fallen, two more were limbering up to join the fight, both with significant firepower. KLM, the Dutch national airline, had launched Buzz, another low-fares airline based at Stansted, while Lufthansa, the German flag carrier, was rumoured to be considering a similar move.

And while Ryanair was winning more and more passengers and making more and more money, the airline was constantly in the news for all the wrong reasons. In 2000 the AUC named Ryanair and Air France as the worst airlines for losing passengers' luggage and expressed concern about the way complaints were dealt with by some low-cost airlines. 'We believe that the (low-cost) concept should not be extended to complaints handling,' it stated in its annual report. The AUC said it was pressing airlines to provide a minimum level of assistance to passengers whose bags were delayed but had so far made no progress in agreeing terms about damaged luggage with Ryanair. 'To date the airline has refused to do so [reconsider its position] and it appears that in view of this it may be necessary for the Office of Fair Trading to resort to legal action,' the council said.

Ryanair responded vigorously to the claims, insisting that it was working on the problem but warning that it did not want to become 'the compensator of last resort' for 'inappropriate' or 'badly packed' luggage. 'We hope to formulate a suitable form of wording which provides passengers with adequate protection against negligent handling of their baggage,' the company stated. It argued that it was 'a crazy situation' that passengers flying on airfares of as little as £9 return could make claims for £600 because a wheel on a suitcase had been damaged or a zip had burst on an over-packed bag.

The AUC immediately dismissed Ryanair's claims, stating that 'every complainant, whatever they have paid for their ticket, should be entitled to a courteous, reasoned response and an apology from the airline concerned when they have had legitimate cause to complain'. Ryanair eventually inserted a clause in the small print of its terms and conditions stating that it wouldn't pay out if handles, wheels or straps broke on bags. This again angered the AUC, but O'Leary suggested the council was in no position to be interfering with Ryanair's customer policies: 'This is just an attempt by an organisation that doesn't represent anybody to generate some PR.' He claimed that only six people of the five and a half million they carried that year complained to the AUC, and added, 'Some passengers are carrying baggage which is clearly inappropriate.'

O'Leary's robust 'no refunds' policy was also continuing to anger passengers and the airline was eventually forced to publish new guidance about when refunds were available. Many other airlines had a policy of repaying taxes and some would also repay airport charges as well. But because these policies were not published only those passengers who specifically requested a refund would get their money back. All airlines collect taxes and airport charges from passengers, but these sums are only paid to the airports if a passenger catches the plane. If they cancel, the airlines could keep all taxes and charges, which can amount to more than 80 per cent of ticket price on cheap fares. Some analysts estimated that some airlines were earning up to a million pounds a year from 'no show' passengers. The AUC had spoken to many airlines about refunding the standard £10 air passenger duty in these circumstances and a number had agreed to its request.

Ryanair let it be known that it too was ready to refund the £10 to passengers who did not fly. However, it warned that a single passenger would gain nothing from this policy – because, 'to cover postage and the cost of issuing a cheque', Ryanair imposed a £10 administration fee.

CHAPTER SIXTEEN

'Dear Mary'

I t looked as if Michael O'Leary was about to lose his mantle as Ireland's most eligible bachelor. The thirty-eight-year old, whose shareholding in Ryanair was now worth more than £150 million, was preparing to marry Dubliner Denise Dowling on 1 July 2000. A lavish ceremony was planned, although O'Leary's fierce concern for his privacy meant the couple had never even been photographed together. Then, shortly before the big day, the wedding was cancelled, and they each went their separate ways. In a newspaper interview some months later, O'Leary volunteered: 'I'm not gay before you ask.' He said he had simply 'crashed and burnt. I came very close to finding the one but it didn't happen, so it's kick on and just go back to work'. He described himself as 'depressingly single' and 'living in hope that a woman will find me sufficiently attractive to settle down'.

He had of course been propositioning another woman for many months, namely Mary O'Rourke, the minister charged with the transport portfolio. O'Leary proposed that Ryanair would open new routes out of Shannon Airport in return for being allowed to implement its plan for a second terminal at Dublin Airport. His plan was pitched to win the minds and hearts of Ireland's politicians who, keen to revitalise western Ireland, were strongly encouraging Shannon's growth, even ruling that all transatlantic traffic had to stop over there. But O'Rourke was proving difficult to persuade of the need for a second independent terminal at Dublin Airport. Four years after it was first mooted O'Leary had found some support amongst O'Rourke's government colleagues for his proposal, with Tanaiste (deputy prime minister) Mary Harney and Finance Minister Charlie

McCreevy, who by now had forged a friendship with O'Leary, reported to be favourably disposed towards it. Ryanair had been relentlessly lobbying other politicians and had employed the services of former government press secretary P. J. Mara to win further support for its plan. But O'Rourke, whose opinion was by far the most important, was continuing to spurn O'Leary's advances.

At the same time some of Ryanair's competitors were getting ready to fight the airline on its own turf. Richard Branson's Virgin Express, which had enthusiastically volunteered to replace Ryanair in Dublin if the latter carried out its threat to move to the UK, launched a new route between Shannon and Stansted and was considering adding a second flight to Brussels, not to mention muttering about opening for business in Dublin and Cork airports. Go, headed by the woman O'Leary described as the 'fragrant Barbara Cassani', was also contemplating going head to head with Ryanair in Dublin. O'Leary had been scathing about Go's prospects from the start. 'I know more about flying Concorde than BA knows about flying low fares, which is why Go will not work,' he claimed, promising that Ryanair would undercut the airline's fares. Some people believed that, whatever Go's business feelings, Cassani did in fact bring respectability to the sector, helping to persuade the more sceptical members of the public to try the low-cost airlines. O'Leary himself had said that before her arrival the industry was run by a 'dodgy Greek and a Paddy'.

Cassani believed that an airline could offer cheap fares without being cheap and nasty, a jibe that was most definitely aimed at Ryanair. Tim Jeans said he used to describe Go as a kind of 'middle-class airline. I think they felt about a notch above those rather vulgar people out there in Dublin and I think that they misled the market'. Jeans recalled Cassani likening Ryanair to a 'cheap flying pub'. 'When I asked her what was wrong with spending some time in a flying pub, she said, "But it's the sort of pub where people throw beer over your head,"' he laughed.

The flying pub was a moneymaking business. In June 2000 Ryanair, which now employed more than 1200 staff, announced a 19 per cent increase in profits to €90 million. Its profit margins were the envy of its competitors at about 23 per cent, earned from sales of more than 6 million airline tickets, snacks and drinks served on board and from commissions earned from selling hotel accommodation and car rental through its Ryanair.com website. This was one of the highest margins earned by any of the world's airlines, five times higher than those earned by Lufthansa. In good times the full-service airlines tended to earn margins of between 6 and 12 per cent while big low-cost airlines like Southwest could yield between 15 and 19 per cent. None was as profitable as Ryanair.

The airline claimed that its passenger figures could have been even higher but for the disruption to its expansion plans caused by disputes over charges at Manchester, Liverpool and Kerry airports. Michael Cawley, now its operations director, suggested these disagreements had lost Ryanair some 400,000 customers, up to 300,000 from Manchester alone. 'We were basically resisting cost increases there but happily we came out with a better deal,' he said, announcing the opening of eight new flights from Manchester and Liverpool.

Since Ryanair shares had begun to trade on the international stock markets in 1997, the board of directors had set ambitious growth targets for the airline, aiming for an annual increase in passenger numbers of 25 per cent, up to 7 million in 2001. Already some 35 per cent of its bookings were being made over its website, while its call centre handled another 40 per cent and travel agents sold fewer and fewer Ryanair seats. The airline claimed that 40 per cent of its customers were business travellers and that 55 per cent of its passengers originated within the UK.

In 2001 Ryanair advertised fares from Stansted to Dublin for £24.99, to Frankfurt (Hahn) for £29.99 and to Stockholm (Skavsta) for £39.99. The airline was also preparing to add another route from London and said it was in discussions with its airports in Prestwick, Paris, Brussels, Stockholm, Frankfurt and Pisa about basing some of its aircraft at there. Once again it renewed its now-ritual attack on Aer Rianta over charges at Dublin Airport. O'Leary publicly criticised Irish politicians for supporting Aer Rianta's prices and policies and his frustration with their refusal to sanction his second terminal proposal became increasingly obvious. 'It is no surprise that after ten successive years of record growth, Ireland's tourism has shuddered to a halt,' O'Leary declared. 'There is no point in expecting a monopoly to encourage competition. Ireland needs a second terminal at Dublin Airport and we need it now.'

The chief executive was a prolific letter-writer. Colleagues said he could 'pump out' up to thirty missives a day and always dealt with correspondence with great efficiency. He voraciously read all documents that hit his desk, including the small print, and his associates quickly learned that he had an incredible capacity to retain detailed information in his head and could readily quote the various official regulations that related to the airline. 'He can look sloppy but he is extremely organised,' one said. And while he had learned to use a computer and regularly surfed the Ryanair.com site, he refused to engage in correspondence through email, believing it wasn't efficient.

O'Leary had written many letters to O'Rourke trying to per-suade her to entertain his proposals since her arrival at the department in 1998. These letters have now been released under the Freedom of Information Act, and give some illuminating insights into the relationship between the airline and the govern-ment. Things started well, with O'Leary signing his initial letters 'with warmest regards'. In July 1999 he wrote to thank the minis-ter for her timely intervention to 'persuade' Aer Rianta to desist from their proposed price increases, and to inform her that he was about to run an advertising campaign under the banner 'Well Done Minister'.

But the relationship soon started deteriorating. O'Rourke informed O'Leary that she was establishing a regulator to deal with airport charges and other matters and that legislation was being prepared to empower the post. Unimpressed, Ryanair's chief executive replied that there was little point in appointing a regulator 'if you are going to permit Aer Rianta to double the charges anyway on what will almost be his first day in his new office'. In November 1999 he wrote telling O'Rourke that her comments and reply to the Dail committee on public enterprise appeared to be based on 'inaccurate information' and 'an incor-rect understanding of Ryanair's proposal'. The following month, he accused her department of reverting 'to the good old days of acting as the downtown office of Aer Rianta'. Nor did O'Leary spare her senior officials. In a letter to the assistant secretary, John Lumsden, he expressed disappointment that 'as the supposed senior civil servant with responsibility you continue to use weasel words in dealing with our reasonable complaints'.

By now O'Leary was writing letters to the minister and her officials on an almost daily basis. In one he asked if the minister could perhaps answer the questions raised, rather than just 'note the contents' of his correspondence, and by December 2000 he was claiming that her 'failed policy' of protecting the Aer Rianta monopoly, at the expense of competition and the consumer, had resulted in a 'long line of failures' which was lengthening on a daily basis. 'As you are already aware our needs are relatively simple,' he wrote. 'We need your support for our proposal to construct and pay for Pier D with correspondingly low costs at Dublin Airport. The planning permissions are already in place, we have the funding, and it can be done within twelve months.' O'Leary added that he would welcome an early meeting to reiterate the nature of Ryanair's proposals and its requirements for launching what he described as the 'single biggest ever investment' in Irish transport and tourism. 'We are now Europe's largest low fares airline. The only people who don't support or believe in Ryanair's ability to deliver growth have been yourself, your department and your appointees in Aer Rianta.'

In this letter, O'Leary set an end-of-year deadline for the minister to support his proposal. He warned that Ryanair was in the final throes of negotiations with other European airports about expanding its services the following summer. 'We need you to confirm your support for these proposals by December 31st, as otherwise the time will have run out for reaching agreement and planning the launch of these routes and basing these aircraft here in Ireland for summer 2001. You backed the wrong plan (Aer Rianta's) last year, there is still time to correct this failed policy in time for next summer.' He ended by saying that he looked forward to hearing from her, and circulated copies of the letter to her colleagues, Bertie Ahern, Mary Harney and Charlie McCreevy.

O'Rourke's department acknowledged receipt of the letter, and four days before Christmas she issued a lengthy reply, addressing O'Leary as 'Dear Michael'. In this O'Rourke explained that the situation regarding the launching of new services was quite simple. 'Any airline is free to launch any service to any destination within the EU and charge any fare it likes. There is no requirement for Government approval or ministerial agreements. If it makes good commercial sense for Ryanair to launch ten new routes out of Dublin and/or Shannon, Ryanair should just go ahead and do it. I will applaud any initiative of that nature and wish it well. Likewise if air services are not working out commercially airlines are free to withdraw them. Above all, this policy is intended to lead to sound commercial decision making and good commercial behaviour on the part of airlines and for that reason I fully support it.'

The minister pointed out that Aer Rianta offered 'very attractive promotional support' for new routes and urged O'Leary to 'explore' these possibilities with the airport operator directly. 'Your proposal as regards Ryanair investing in Dublin airport and obtaining a low airport charges arrangement for Ryanair in return is very different, however. In my view your proposal, in reality, would amount to Aer Rianta granting a special deal at Dublin airport for Ryanair and Ryanair alone. Such an approach would not be permitted by any independent regulator or by the EU Commission.'

O'Rourke noted O'Leary's considerable correspondence and said that new legislation was being prepared to establish an independent commission for aviation regulation that would ensure all charges were transparent and non-discriminatory. 'I have every confidence that the establishment of the Commission for Aviation Regulation and the completion of the new terminal development at Dublin airport will ensure a competitive airport charges regime and sufficient passenger capacity in Ireland for the future,' she insisted. 'These two key ingredients will provide Ryanair, and other airlines, with the ideal conditions for the development of further services from Ireland on a long-term, secure and sustainable basis.' O'Rourke signed the letter 'with kindest regards'.

O'Leary's deadline passed without any ministerial action, and by January he was firing off more letters accusing the minister of refusing to address any of the issues he had raised. He was growing increasingly frustrated with O'Rourke and her officials' refusal to bow to his bullying tactics. As part of the constant quest to keep costs down Ryanair now managed its own advertising, with O'Leary and a small group at head office all contributing ideas and designing its campaigns. 'Michael's main input into the ads was that he wanted a big plane, the price in huge letters and www on the bottom,' one source commented.

He had already promised O'Rourke that he would post a full-page advertisement applauding her efforts if she backed Ryanair's proposals regarding Aer Rianta and Dublin Airport. But he didn't tell her that he was now so frustrated that he had a very different campaign in mind. Almost a year earlier, the minister had recounted in a radio interview how she first learnt of the surprise resignation of Brian Joyce, the chairman of the state's bus and rail company, Coras Iompair Eireann (CIE) – a departure which, according to some, was due to her constant meddling. 'There I was in my bath this morning with the radio on,' she explained to the amusement of the nation. The comment had not been lost on O'Leary. On 15 January 2001 Ryanair launched a new advertisement that depicted a knobbly-kneed O'Rourke in a bubble bath, complete with the headline: 'MARY, MARY, QUITE CONTRARY, HOW DOES YOUR MONOPOLY GROW? IT DOESN'T.' In it Ryanair accused her of 'minding the Aer Rianta monopoly'. One Ryanair employee said O'Leary hadn't needed any creative input from anyone else for this campaign. 'The O'Rourke ads were all his idea.'

It was a shocking tactic, and one that sat uncomfortably with some of Ryanair's directors, who included a former government colleague of the minister's, Ray MacSharry. O'Leary didn't care and was delighted to defend his actions in the media the next day. 'Competition is a very healthy thing and Dublin Airport needs a lot more of it,' he said.

The following week he wrote again to O'Rourke attaching what he said was a 'pathetic letter' from her assistant secretary, and some days later he wrote to thank her for 'the latest meaningless reply' from one of her officials. Her senior advisers inquired about lodging a complaint about the advertisement to the Advertising Standards Authority in Ireland but decided against. Meanwhile, they braced themselves for further attacks. They didn't have to wait long. Within a few months O'Leary struck again, this time depicting O'Rourke as a gun-wielding cowgirl with the slogan 'WELCOME TO DUBLIN, THIS IS A STICK UP!' Under the minister's photograph were the words, 'Ryanair has launched its new European base in Brussels with low return fares to 7 European destinations and 30 flights per day.' It said that these flights were lost to Ireland by the minister and her department, 'who continue to put Aer Rianta's profits ahead of consumer interest. So for at least another year Irish consumers and visitors from Europe will be paying amongst the highest scheduled air fares in Europe'. The advertisement also carried a table of Aer Lingus fares from Dublin to various destinations alongside the corresponding fare charged by Ryanair, and called on the minister to end 'this daylight robbery'. Knowing the advertisement would land the company in trouble again, O'Leary included a starburst with the words 'We would like to apologise to the Advertising Standards Authority in advance – No, we didn't ask for Mary O'Rourke's permission.' This time the department lodged a formal complaint with the authority, which was upheld on the grounds that 'advertisers should not unfairly attack or discredit other businesses or their products'.

Another advertisement designed by Ryanair's creative advertising brains to promote a special £69 return flights offer over St Valentine's weekend had also triggered complaints. The advertisement consisted of two parts, displayed on the same page of the *Evening Standard*. The first was headlined 'BLOW ME! (These fares are hard to swallow!)' and the second 'SATISFACTION GUARANTEED!', with an images of two pairs of feet, one pair on top of the other. The Advertising Standards Authority received complaints that the advertisements were sexually suggestive and offensive, and a similar advertisement in the *Irish Independent* drew more complaints. Under pressure from the advertising authorities, Ryanair agreed that they were suggestive but refuted that they were offensive, arguing that theirs was a humorous campaign in the context of Valentine's Day, which celebrated relationships. But the advertising standards authorities in the UK and Ireland both upheld the public's complaints in relation to these campaigns. The UK authority considered that the innuendo about oral sex was likely to cause serious or widespread offence and asked Ryanair not to repeat the advertisements.

The promotion had also caused great offence to most of O'Leary's colleagues on the board, with Tony Ryan said to have been absolutely appalled by their vulgarity. 'The board went ballistic,' recalled one person close to the company. 'Tony Ryan thought they were so crass and rude. There was a huge row as O'Leary would go mad when he was criticised.'

The only person capable of restraining O'Leary, Ryanair chairman David Bonderman, eventually defused the row. 'David could rein him in. There was good mutual respect between them,' the source explained. 'He might say, "Ah Michael, let me put it in perspective", or suggest that it was possible there was another angle he was missing. On that occasion David suggested that Michael should decide on some line that he wouldn't cross in the future and asked that he might come back and tell the board what that was. Of course he never did. It had gotten to the stage where the board could spent 20 per cent of the time talking about O'Leary's advertising campaigns.' Most of O'Leary's boardroom colleagues just wanted him to tone down his attacks on O'Rourke. Another source suggested that while they disapproved of his campaigns, some actually shared his view of O'Rourke. 'She was a woeful minister. She had to be put in her box. You would have to ask why would you let a schoolteacher run such an important portfolio?'

O'Leary enjoyed a warmer relationship with the Walloon regional government's transport minister Serge Kubla, who was proving much more receptive to Ryanair's advances. In 2001 Ryanair was preparing to establish its first base in continental Europe from which it would launch new routes to its other destinations around Europe. Michael Cawley and Bernard Berger had been negotiating with Belgium's Charleroi Airport, Frankfurt Hahn, Stockholm Skavska and Paris Beauvais, with a view to selecting one as their new hub. Ryanair brought a series of demands to the airport owners, seeking huge financial support and incentives to underpin its expansion plans from these remote European airports. One source said the airline's attitude was that it would need big financial incentives to bring passengers 'to the middle of nowhere'. The airport owners, who had already experienced Ryanair's ruthless negotiating style, knew it would simply select the most attractive deal, pitting the airports against another until it got what it wanted.

In early March 2001 news began to spread of a management overhaul and a restructuring of the ownership of Belgium's

Charleroi Airport. Charleroi had started life as a pilots' training school in 1991, a year before control of Belgium's regional airports was transferred from the federal state to local government. At that time it was envisaged that Charleroi would be a privately run airport, but now its chief administrator, Marie Desseaux, was ousted and the regional government became the majority shareholder in the airport. The local media suggested this unexpected development was linked to a possible deal with Ryanair, and a few days later Ryanair confirmed Charleroi as its first European base. Belgian's daily newspaper, *Le Soir*, described the recent events at the airport as 'surreal', and suggested that Kubla had masterminded the coup. The Walloon regional government was thrilled to have won the Ryanair contract but Kubla's spokesman said there was 'no direct link' between the new deal and the changes in the airport's ownership. 'The airport is not specially dedicated to Ryanair. Ryanair simply arrived at the right time,' he said.

Ryanair, which had been flying to Charleroi since 1997, was the only scheduled carrier using the airport, although other airlines, including Air Algerie, Tunis Air, Virgin Express and Sobel Air (a charter-flight subsidiary of Sabena) were sporadic visitors. O'Leary claimed Ryanair was carrying 250,000 passengers a year into the airport on its routes to and from Dublin, and under the new deal the airline promised to operate thirty flights a day to and from seven destinations.

O'Leary brought a group of journalists to report on its new base at Charleroi. On the plane he boasted that the Walloon regional government had allowed Ryanair to land there 'practically for free' for the next twenty years. He said the airport would also give Ryanair financial grants to offset training costs involved with staffing up its operations there, and again took the opportunity to attack Aer Rianta's uncompromising stance. Ryanair's charges at Charleroi were 'very significantly cheaper' than the £9 per passenger charged in Dublin, O'Leary said, and as a result Ryanair would base up to four aircraft in Belgium and operate flights to Ireland, Britain, France and Italy from Charleroi rather than Dublin. His comments had a hollow ring, though, and one expert was quoted saying that O'Leary was 'stretching the truth slightly' on this issue. 'Ryanair is Europe's biggest low-cost airline so it's obvious that it needs to expand into Europe,' he remarked.

Kubla's spokesman was upset by O'Leary's comments on the Walloon regional government's generosity to the Irish airline and particularly annoyed with the suggestion that it had agreed to let Ryanair use Charleroi virtually free of charge. He said the airline would be subject to the charges applying to airports in Belgium's French-speaking region and added: 'But it is possible that Ryanair found the prices more interesting than those offered by Frankfurt and Stockholm.' Tim Jeans later said that Charleroi had wanted Ryanair as much as Ryanair wanted the Belgian airport. 'It was one of many airports vying to become its European base. It was the best investment in terms of marketing that it ever made and the deal struck became a template for others.' Jeans added that these airport deals were about more than the money on offer, with the level of efficiency and the capacity to turn around the aircraft rapidly also a key factor in the negotiations.

Ryanair's competitors tried to work out the likely terms the Walloon regional government had signed up to. By then the brash airline chief had already switched his focus to Belgium's national carrier, Sabena, promising that Ryanair would undercut its fares by up to 90 per cent. A spokesman for Sabena said it monitored prices being offered by competitors but that this would be only one factor when it came to making decisions on price. 'We fly to one hundred destinations. We fly to Brussels itself, not Charleroi.' Sabena offered a quality product with more space, better catering and better entertainment than Ryanair, he said: 'We have a saying in Belgium. Do no compare an apple with a pear.'

But Sabena was in serious trouble. By this time the airline had been declared virtually bankrupt by the Belgian government, and its future was hanging in the balance. The previous week the European Commission signalled that a €250 million rescue package for the ailing airline could be in breach of EU state aid rules. Swissair had planned to provide €150 million of that funding; the remainder was to come from the exchequer. Branson's loss-making Virgin Express was also operating from Zaventum airport in Brussels but it was the struggling Sabena that came into in Ryanair's direct line of fire.

The two airlines soon became bitter enemies. Ryanair

attacked Sabena's fares in advertisements that featured a provocative picture of the Manneken Pis, Brussels's famous fountain statue of a child urinating. 'PISSED OFF WITH SABENA'S HIGH FARES?' ran the headline on one, while another asked, 'DO SABENA'S HIGH PRICES MAKE YOU WANT TO THROW UP? LOW FARES ARE COMING TO BELGIUM.' Sabena claimed that the advertisements, which appeared in the Belgian press, were 'misleading' and 'offensive'. It demanded that the ads be withdrawn and sought damages for any future violations. Ryanair claimed that its fares to Charleroi were 90 per cent cheaper than Sabena's. A Ryanair spokesman said, 'The adverts are a way of drawing attention to a state institution in Belgium which has been screwing ordinary people for years. Quite how Sabena plans to defend itself in what is a pretty indefensible case will be interesting to see.' However, a Brussels court upheld Sabena's complaint and ordered Ryanair to discontinue its campaign immediately. Ryanair obeyed, but showed that its appetite for conflict was unabated by filing a complaint with the European Commission against Lufthansa, alleging that the German carrier was engaged in below-cost selling on the Frankfurt and Hamburg to London routes. The complaint was not upheld.

This was a mere skirmish compared to the battle that was about to erupt. Barbara Cassani travelled to Dublin to announce that Go would be offering return flights from the Irish capital to Edinburgh from £50 and to Glasgow from £45, including all taxes. The first flight would take off on 19 September. 'It's about time Irish travellers had the opportunity to combine low fares and high quality – Go's here to provide it,' Cassani declared, predicting the airline would carry half a million passengers. If it met its targets, she said, it would consider flying on the Dublin to London route.

O'Leary's was furious at this threat to Ryanair in its home territory. His immediate response to the news was to question the deal Aer Rianta had offered Go and threaten to sue the airport authority if its competitor was to pay cheaper landing charges than Ryanair. Go didn't qualify for a discount on landing charges on the Edinburgh route, because it wasn't a new route – Aer Lingus had been flying it for a year – but Aer Rianta did offer Go some marketing funds and other services to support its endeavours.

O'Leary was incensed. He announced that Ryanair would now start flying to Edinburgh itself, at fares below those advertised by Go. 'This is going to be a disaster because if the best they can manage is £45 as against our £29 nobody will be flying with them except for the passengers they take off Aer Lingus,' he declared. 'At those prices Go doesn't even qualify as a low-fares airline.' He also claimed that Go's schedule was 'crap' and predicted its swift demise: 'Their first flight out in the morning is 10 a.m. We will be out and back at that stage – goodbye Go.'

Three years after its birth, Go had reported a £4 million sterling profit for the year to end March 2001, and had a fleet of fifteen Boeing 737-300 aircraft with plans to add another ten aircraft. It was successful commercially but no match for Ryanair, which in the same period had made a €104.5 million profit and had one of the lowest cost bases of any airline in the world. Ryanair's routes out of Ireland were its most profitable and, contrary to what O'Leary might suggest, were in fact subsidising many of its new European services. EasyJet, which already operated flights between Belfast and Luton, said it too was looking at expanding to Dublin. But O'Leary would do everything to defend Ryanair's home patch against any carrier who dared to cross the Irish Sea for a fight.

And so a fierce price war got underway. Go raised the white flag after just four months, pulling off both Scottish routes after Ryanair launched a frequent service there and savagely undercut its fares. 'We came to Dublin to offer low fares on routes where none previously existed. With Ryanair's changes it makes sense for us to shift our capacity and offer low fares in a completely new area. We thank our customers for their support,' Cassani said when she announced Go's retreat. Aer Rianta called for Go's decision to leave Dublin to be investigated by a government-appointed group examining the tourism sector, and accused Ryanair of launching services on the Scottish routes with the sole purpose of driving its competitors off. 'Ryanair has no interest in Irish tourism. Its only interest is in creating additional wealth for its shareholders,' said Aer Rianta's chairman, Noel Hanlon. Ryanair swiftly rejected the criticism, saying it welcomed all competitors in the Irish market. 'It is clear that this latest withdrawal from Dublin Airport is yet another victim of the high-cost Aer Rianta airport monopoly,' a spokesman told the media. O'Leary and Ryanair staff were euphoric at their victory. One source said that O'Leary considered its price war with Go to have been money well spent. At Dublin Airport, someone had graffitised the airline's abandoned desks, changing its name to 'GONE'.

Speaking about the ordeal two years later, Cassani said Go had misjudged how fiercely O'Leary and Ryanair would react to their incursion into Dublin. 'We got a thrashing on the new route as Ryanair slashed prices even further,' she wrote in *Go: An Airline Adventure*. 'Going head-to-head cost us millions and we withdrew wounded. We learned another crucial lesson about discounting. You can't take on someone with lower costs because they dig deeper than you to lower their prices and still make money while you're bleeding.' The pair have never met, and while Cassani has publicly acknowledged O'Leary's role in resurrecting Ryanair she remains critical of the airline and its concept of customer service. 'I would just never work for them. I wouldn't want to be treated the way he treats people and I wouldn't want to treat customers the way he encourages his staff to treat customers. Our check-in desks at Stansted were right across from Ryanair's and my assessment of Ryanair is that when everything is going well it's fine, but when things go wrong they would literally shut the desks down,' she told *The Irish Times*.

Cassani fundamentally rejected O'Leary's definition of low-cost travel. 'I disagree with Michael's philosophy, which is you pay low prices, you get crummy service, and I actually think he has done a disservice to the rest of us.' Summing her former rival up, she said, 'I think the accountancy association of the world should vote him as their poster boy. This is what you can do even if you start as a bean counter. You can have a mouth like a publican or a drunken sailor.'

CHAPTER SEVENTEEN

Auf Wiedersehen Lufthansa

'There was an atrocity and it was terrible, but your immediate reaction has to be, "We're in the shit now. How are we going to dig our way out of it?"' So said Michael O'Leary two weeks after terrorists crashed commercial aircraft into the Twin Towers and the Pentagon on 11 September 2001, the blackest day in aviation history. 'The only way to defeat terrorism here is not to be standing there whingeing with your aircraft on the ground looking for subsidies. It's to get out there with lower fares and persuade people to travel more often.' Just as he had searched for opportunities to benefit Ryanair in the immediate aftermath of GPA's collapse almost a decade earlier, O'Leary swiftly decided how he would exploit his competitors' vulnerabilities and gain greater dominance in Europe. His response to the tragedies was to announce millions of cheap airfares to encourage people back into the air. 'Despite the efforts of terrorists, normal life continues – with millions of people travelling for normal leisure and business purposes,' he said. 'Other companies are grounding flights, laying off staff ... We are going to fly our way out of this crisis. Our solution is to get back in the air with more passengers and lower fares.'

Ryanair ran posters advertising fares as low as £1 to its European destinations in a send-up of the First World War army recruitment posters headlined 'YOUR COUNTRY NEEDS YOU'. Once again the airline was accused of bad taste but O'Leary didn't care. When asked to comment on the airline's perceived insensitivity at this painful time his response was, 'Screw them. People have been offended by our ads before and that doesn't bother us. What we're about is not lying down in front of these terrorists and letting them win.' One journalist asked if he believed there was any such thing as bad publicity. 'Yes,' O'Leary replied. 'The tragedy that happened in the US was bad publicity and it affected consumer confidence. Safety is always an issue in the airline industry and that is one of the things on which we would not try to seek publicity. But most other things are fair game: politicians, Popes. What we are trying to do is run ads that get noticed, that are controversial and that will get people to pick up the phone and book flights.'

EasyJet and Go followed suit, offering thousands of cheap flights. O'Leary said its lower-fares response to 11 September had been 'wildly' successful, 'so successful it's almost scary'. He said new bookings had reached their highest-ever levels, with low fares available on every seat on every flight, though the Advertising Standards Authority would later uphold a complaint that Ryanair's advertising campaign had been misleading because it had not made it sufficiently clear that the cut-price offer did not apply to weekend flights.

In the US, where the travelling public had grown even more fearful of flying, Herb Kelleher, the man O'Leary regarded as a 'pure genius', had also slashed Southwest Airlines' fares to stimulate demand. 'When I read that about Ryanair I thought that Michael was wise to do that because a low price can even overcome a fear quotient,' he said later. 'You could say, "Boy, I am really afraid to fly at $29 but at $19 I'll forget about my fear and I'll go." We knew we had to get people back up in the air and re-accustomed to flying as part of their lives. We were charging $19 fares on a 250- to 300-mile route. In constant dollars that was probably the lowest fare ever charged in America.'

As a result of prudent management, Ryanair and Southwest were in a much stronger financial position than their competitors when the disaster unfolded. Southwest was one of the few US carriers not to announce job cuts in the days and weeks after the terrorist attacks and could draw on its robust cash reserves to weather the initial fall-off in demand. "We had the lowest costs, the strongest balance sheet and the most liquidity so we were pretty well fixed in the sense of countering any adversity that we might come across,' Kelleher said. 'In the airline industry you have to be that way because you are going to have that type of emergency, twice a decade. You can count on it ... If it wasn't that it would have been something else. So in that sense we were prepared.'

In Europe, Ryanair had the lowest costs of any airline and a €700 million cash pile to cushion the blow. This was one part of the Southwest model that Ryanair had slavishly adhered to and Kelleher believes there is great kinship between the two airlines in this regard. 'We have always been kind of flamboyant from a marketing standpoint and from a sales standpoint and from the public-relations standpoint but we have always been conservative from the fiscal standpoint and I think Michael is doing the same thing.'

As the US government doled out billions of dollars to support American airlines in the aftermath of the terrorist attacks, the major European airlines began to call on the European Commission to relax its position on state aid and allow governments to offer similar financial packages to alleviate their woes. British Airways announced massive job cuts and approached the British government for help in overcoming a hefty downturn in air travel and increased costs after the attacks. O'Leary accused the flag-carriers of 'whingeing' and wrote to Europe's Transport Commissioner, Loyola de Palacio, to urge the Commission not to alter its policy on state aid. If any such aid was considered, O'Leary argued, it should be 'applied equally to all airlines and all passengers by means of reducing passenger taxes or landing and passenger charges at European airports, rather than straight subsidies to inefficient and loss-making airlines'.

Ryanair had already complained about the proposed funding of a rescue package for Belgium's flag-carrier, Sabena, and was equally forthright about the compensation British Airways and Virgin had received from the British government for the losses they suffered as a result of having to cancel transatlantic flights in the four days after 11 September (BA claimed to have lost £48 million for this reason). O'Leary said that airlines like BA and Virgin had been losing money and needed to make job cuts before 11 September, and were being 'disingenuous' in their pleas for state aid. They were exploiting the US tragedy to 'screw' money out of the Government, he claimed. 'I think the airline industry is reflecting more what would have happened anyway. I think there would be large job losses amongst airlines that are already losing money and this event may have just brought it forward.' At the same time Ryanair could afford to keep lowering its fares to keep its planes in the air. 'We will lose less money than we will by sitting planes on the ground and have the begging bowl out to the European government for massive amounts of money.'

But as he publicly railed against state aid it transpired the Ryanair had been the largest beneficiary of the €6.4 billion insurance indemnity that the Irish government had given to Irish airlines after insurance companies stopped providing cover for 'war risk and allied perils' after 11 September. Had the government not stepped in, Ryanair would have had to stop flying. The Department of Transport let it be known that Ryanair had written to it to ask to be included in any proposed state insurance scheme. 'Nobody has come back and said we will now arrange our own cover,' said a spokesman. The low-cost operator denied that the guarantee was a state aid and said that accepting the indemnity did not undermine its position on bail-outs for rivals. O'Leary claimed it had originally offered to pay the Government for providing the additional indemnity, but the Department had declined. 'It is not state aid, because it is not costing the state a penny,' he argued. 'We would be happy to pay in any case.'

The collapse in BA's share price after 11 September had allowed Ryanair to leapfrog its great rival to become Europe's second most highly valued airline on the stock markets, with only Lufthansa ahead. O'Leary told investors that the terrorist attacks would not affect Ryanair's profits and that it was on course to be Europe's biggest airline within five years. It was planning to open twelve new routes and take delivery of eight new Boeing 737s. A month earlier Ryanair had cancelled options it had over five new Boeings and advertised in *Flight International* for fifty second-hand 737s between seven and fourteen years old, either 737⁸300s or −400s from the 1980s or 737⁸800s from the 1990s. Ryanair claimed it was inundated with more than 600 replies, more than 400 of which it received after September 11 as airlines across the globe closed routes and curtailed their operations. 'I think we must be the only airline in the world buying aircraft at this moment,' O'Leary declared, relishing the prospect of the discounts he could squeeze out of these distressed sellers – and that of putting Boeing on the back foot and forcing it to renegotiate its price if it wanted to win a new order.

Ryanair was also one of the world's few airlines to open up another new base in 2001, this time at Hahn in Germany, which had lost out to Charleroi earlier that year in the contest to become Ryanair's first European base. Hahn Airport's main shareholder, the Fraport group, had invested to expand the passenger terminal and lengthen the runway, signing a twenty-year deal with Ryanair. The base was crucial for the airline, giving it a foothold in Europe's biggest economy with its 80 million population. It was also a direct challenge to the mighty Lufthansa. O'Leary flew to Hahn in November to mark the establishment of the new base and promised that from February 2002 Ryanair would operate over thirty flights daily from Hahn to Milan, Pisa and Pescara in Italy, London, Glasgow and Bournemouth in Britain, Perpignan and Montpellier in France, Shannon in Ireland and Oslo in Norway. Ryanair planned to carry 1.5 million passengers in the first year of these services.

'Thanks to Ryanair and Frankfurt Hahn Airport, the era of Lufthansa's high-fares monopoly in the German market is over,' O'Leary declared. 'For many years visitors to Germany have had no choice other than to pay Lufthansa's high air fares, but this monopoly comes to an end on February 14 next.' The Irish airline now claimed to be Europe's largest low-fares airline, with sixty-three routes across twelve countries, and O'Leary promised that Ryanair would offer German consumers 'savings of over 80 per cent' on the 'ridiculously high' fares being charged by Lufthansa.

It didn't take long for Ryanair to bring its incredibly low fares to the attention of the German population and to draw retaliatory action from Lufthansa, which won a court order forbidding its new rival from advertising comparative fares when the two airlines flew from different airports, and stipulating that Ryanair must list the final price of a flight, including taxes, specify that the fares were subject to restrictions, and that the flights were from Hahn and not Frankfurt International. In a statement, Lufthansa said it would 'continue to take legal action to prevent Ryanair intentionally misleading German consumers'.

O'Leary's reaction was predictable. 'It's typical of a monopoly airline like Lufthansa, who cannot match Ryanair's fares and who don't want to offer the German consumers lower air fares, to run into court at the first possible opportunity. They creep into courts late at night without telling anybody and get injunctions that are designed to prevent German consumers being made aware of competition in air travel. The public-affairs department of the courts never told us the case was coming up,' he said, promising that Ryanair would appeal the German court order (as they did, but without success).

Ryanair revelled in the acres of media coverage detailing the various charges and counter charges between the two. When Lufthansa's incoming chief executive, Wolfgang Mayrhuber, entered the fray claiming that low-cost air travel would not catch on in Germany, O'Leary was incredulous and accused him of being 'eighteen months behind the times'. Ryanair then filed a second complaint with the EU Competition and Transport Commissioners that alleged Lufthansa was using 'dirty tricks' to prevent Ryanair from 'exercising its right to freedom of speech in Germany'. O'Leary protested that 'the only thing that Lufthansa have not yet got an injunction on from the German courts is to prevent Ryanair calling itself Ryanair'.

The Irish airline found no succour from the Commission, which suggested the complaint was a matter for the German courts, while a court in Hamburg issued a ruling to stop Ryanair accusing Lufthansa of a 'dirty tricks campaign'. By then, though, it had thought of another tactic to taunt 'Lufty', O'Leary's pet name for his German enemy. Ryanair had begun to imitate Southwest Airlines by painting advertising images on its aircraft to generate extra revenue and promote new routes. It had negotiated deals with Jaguar and Guinness and others to promote their brands on its aircraft and decided to use this platform to upset its litigious competitor. Soon thousands of Ryanair passengers arriving and departing from Hahn were filing on and off aircraft emblazoned with 'AUF WIEDERSEHEN LUFTHANSA'.

In the midst of the skirmishes with Lufthansa, O'Leary was still firing off salvos in the direction of the Irish government and Aer Rianta, which he described as a 'national disgrace'. 'This new German base means that four more aircraft, two hundred new jobs and over one million tourists have again been lost to Ireland by the high-cost Aer Rianta monopoly,' O'Leary claimed. When asked why he persisted with what seemed like increasingly futile attacks on Irish politicians, he explained that he had to 'shout' at the Government every couple of weeks 'to keep them awake'.

Things were going more smoothly in Italy, where Ryanair had just claimed the slot as the market-leader on flights between London and Venice, leaving BA and Alitalia in its slipstream. 'Not bad for a Mickey Mouse airline, eh?' O'Leary gloated, saying that Italy was Ryanair's third biggest market after Ireland and the UK. Again Ryanair had made its presence felt through provocative advertising, with an aircraft painted specially for trips to Italy that said, 'ARRIVEDERCI ALITALIA'. Alitalia had suffered more than other European airlines in the wake of the terrorist attacks. It had sustained huge financial losses as passenger numbers slumped by up to 30 per cent and was continuing to focus on key routes where it could charge high fares. Stock-market analysts suggested the Italian flag carrier was 'in denial' about low-cost carriers, whose cheap fares were being enthusiastically purchased by Italians, especially young people who were used to the Internet. 'People were growing accustomed to low fares because of Ryanair,' said one source close to the airline. 'Ryanair was like a god in Pisa.'

'Most of the young people think of London as their dream destination but would not normally have flown there until Ryanair gave them the chance to go at a low cost. They were immediately part of an elite group,' said Paolo Pietrogrande, a top Italian businessman who had joined the Ryanair board of directors. 'People have started thinking of going to London as a much less expensive trip and much more of an opportunity. Our planes were full.' Pietrogrande said that older people tended to know that Ryanair was an Irish airline but many of its new customers thought it was British. 'People my age know it's an Irish airline. We would tend to think of Ryan as an Irish name as we remember a movie that was very popular in Italy in the '70s [*Ryan's Daughter*]. Most of the people that have used it to go to London may be confused whether it is Irish or British – indeed there is no great sense that it is foreign. Many people have asked me where its headquarters are based in Italy.'

Pietrogrande, the former chief executive of Italy's huge electric-power generating company ERGA and a director of the motorcycle-maker Ducati, was just one of the successful business figures from Germany, France and Italy to be invited onto the Ryanair board to support its aggressive expansion in Europe. David Bonderman had worked closely with Pietrogrande at a time when the former's Texas Pacific Group had invested in Ducati and engineered a profitable turnaround of the business. The Italian businessman said he was surprised by the invitation given his very limited experience in the marketing of goods to consumers. But he quickly formed the view that the Ryanair chairman was more interested in the experience he could bring to the airline's operations. 'He mentioned that there were many similarities between running a utility company and an airline,' Pietrogrande said. 'He was extremely interested in the fact that we grew very fast, we had double-digit growth and that our per- formance was based on maniacal attention on the operational detail. We were mostly working in an environment where an increase in costs meant an increase in tariff. We were operating in a sector where competition had been slow to materialise and where big national players were protecting their businesses, so in many ways my company and Ryanair were similar. We both had to break the rules, be extremely effective on cost control and somehow anticipate timing.' Pietrogrande said Bonderman was 'very demanding' of directors and was always incredibly well informed about what was happening at each of the companies he was associated with.

Back in Dublin, the board members were considering whether to buy secondhand or new aircraft to underpin the next phase of the airline's expansion into Europe. They mulled over the hundreds of offers received, weighing them up against the possibility of placing an order for new aircraft with Boeing. Spec- ulation began to mount in the stock markets that Ryanair would seek to raise money from investors to buy new planes, fuelled by a report on the company by the London stockbroking firm Credit Suisse First Boston. The report raised short-term concerns about the funding of a new plane order and its comments depressed Ryanair's share price. O'Leary rubbished the sugges- tion: 'Some fellow added two and two together and got 5225… Are we in discussion with the owners of used aircraft? Yes. Are we in discussions with the owners of new aircraft? Yes. But we won't make any decision until the price is right and that could be soon or it could be months away.'

Yet just days later Ryanair announced that it had placed one of the biggest-ever orders for Boeing's 737 series aircraft. The company said it would purchase one hundred Boeing 737⁸800 aircraft in the next eight years and had taken options on fifty more planes, claiming that Boeing's offer was 'exceptionally competitive'. Ryanair said the 'catalogue value' of the deal was $9.1 billion, but refused to disclose the extent of the discount it had negotiated. Airline industry observers, aware of the US aircraft manufacturer's desperate need to win the contract, speculated that it amounted to between 30 and 50 per cent. Boeing had been forced to sharply reduce its aircraft production and to lay off up to 30,000 workers as it struggled to stave off a financial crisis in the wake of the terrorist attacks.

Some people who know O'Leary and Tony Ryan well suggest one of their great similarities is their ability to 'corner their prey'. O'Leary said Ryanair had by then decided it would going to be the 'biggest airline in Europe and then the biggest airline in the world' and needed the planes to do that. Speaking of his own part in the negotiations, he said he came to the table with some 'terrific natural advantages. One of them is that I grew up in Mullingar and farmers know that the time to buy is when everybody else is selling and the time to sell is when everybody else is buying. It was quite simple. We had money. Boeing and Airbus couldn't give away planes. So we went and bought up about two years' worth of productions.' O'Leary later emphasised the attractiveness of the Boeing deal in typically forthright language, telling investors, 'We raped them.' Again the deal was sweetened by America's Export Import Bank, which despite the fact that secondhand aircraft values were on the floor once again agreed to provide Ryanair with loans at interest rates of less than 5 per cent.

O'Leary claimed the expansion would create jobs for 800 pilots, more than 2000 cabin crew and 400 engineering and operations staff. Within the next decade he pledged the airline would operate more than fifty routes and carry 40 million passengers each year, vowing, 'Ryanair is going to be a monster in Europe in the next ten years.'

O'Leary's conviction was buoyed by the company's stunning financial performance. In a year when terrorist threats overshadowed the industry and the outbreak of foot-and-mouth disease depressed travel, particularly between Britain and the rest of Europe, Ryanair recorded a 40 per cent increase in profits to €172 million. Its cheap fare promotions had contributed to a 38 per cent leap in passenger numbers to just over 11 million, and despite an 8 per cent cut in the average fare its profit margins had swelled from 23 to 26 per cent, soaring higher than any other airline. O'Leary's ruthless cost-cutting had ensured that Ryanair had the lowest costs in the airline business and was 70 per cent leaner than the other dominant force in the low-fare sector, easyJet. Ryanair needed to fill just over half of the seats on each flight to break even and as passenger numbers increased it was able to squeeze more and more profits out of each one.

O'Leary was cock-a-hoop. 'People look at 20 per cent margins in the airline business and they assume you are smuggling drugs or doing something naughty with the figures,' he laughed. Even the most sceptical analysts couldn't fault the airline's performance, but some harboured doubts about whether Ryanair would be able to fill all of the planes it had ordered in the longer term. Those with long memories recalled how GPA's massive aircraft order a decade earlier had ultimately contributed to its demise, and wondered whether Ryanair was flying too close to the sun.

Swissair and Sabena, flag-carriers of Switzerland and Belgium respectively, had now collapsed altogether as the result of the airline crisis, but O'Leary was on top of the world. 'We are a small Irish company, out there stuffing it to the biggest airlines all over Europe, and of course that feels good,' he declared. In the run up to a general election in Ireland he promised that he would continue to 'bore' the public with his tirade of abuse against Minister O'Rourke in the hope that she would not return to haunt him. He said he hoped 'she goes to Education or Health where they deserve her', and when one journalist inquired about Ryanair's next priority he replied, 'European domination in five years and after that we'll reassess.' The biggest risk to Ryanair's growth, he said, was 'an accident either by ourselves or by some other low-fare carrier in Europe. The other one is ill-discipline, doing something stupid.'

The airline chief was showing no sign of battle fatigue or of moving on to new ventures – unlike easyJet's forty-one-year old founder, Stelios Haji-Ioannou, who was diversifying into car rental, Internet cafés and cinemas, amongst other businesses. O'Leary said he had no plans to leave Ryanair for the next five years. 'When the industry is as exciting and interesting as this, I would be crazy to go anywhere else.'

CHAPTER EIGHTEEN

Buzz Away

Before Stelios departed to set up his new ventures he launched his most outrageous attack against Ryanair, accusing his rival of putting passengers' lives at risk to increase profits. In what one analyst described as a 'bitter and rambling' letter to the *Financial Times*, Stelios said that Ryanair's profit figures carried a health warning and claimed that half of Ryanair's fleet was made up of secondhand aircraft, some of which dated back to the early 1980s, and that this could compromise safety standards. Stelios further asserted that O'Leary had copied his business formula and questioned the airline's accounting methods, implying that investors should be wary about the factors driving Ryanair's strong performance. The use of older aircraft, he said, meant that it carried minimal depreciation charges on its profit-and-loss account, and he also highlighted Ireland's lower corporate-tax rate as a factor influencing its profits. 'Combine a low-cost airline with old aircraft and the odds of your reputation surviving an accident are against you,' Stelios warned, citing what happened at ValuJet, the American low-cost airline easyJet had modelled itself on, which lost half its business and was forced to change its name after a crash in 1996.

O'Leary, a prolific letter-writer himself, swiftly dispatched a reply to the newspaper in which he emphatically denied Stelios's claims. He said Ryanair adhered to the 'highest standards of international safety' and reminded the public about its massive order for new-generation Boeing 737s. 'What surprised me was that he would put his name to such nonsense,' O'Leary commented. 'It would seem that those of us who sell the lowest airfares just get on with it, and those who do not, write whingeing letters to newspapers.'

This battle was a new departure for Europe's two biggest budget airlines, which had collaborated for years in attacks on the mighty flag-carriers. EasyJet was finalising a £374 million takeover of Go – not unanimously welcomed by investors, who had concerns about its future growth potential – and O'Leary taunted his Greek opponent by saying that easyJet would end up imitating British Airways or Lufthansa. Stelios might have hoped to make the City think twice about Ryanair, but the letters only seemed to raise doubts about himself. 'Stelios has lost the plot. It doesn't matter how old aircraft are – it's whether they are maintained properly,' said one analyst, adding that his attempt to disparage Ryanair's safety record was a desperate measure. 'Stelios has broken the golden rule in airlines – you never hit out at rivals over safety because you never know when it might happen to you. The letter smacks of desperation.'

The contretemps fuelled worries amongst the public about how safe it was to fly with an airline that was charging ridiculously cheap fares. The so-called peanut airlines could only survive by ruthlessly cutting costs, and it wasn't unreasonable to wonder whether their parsimonious tendencies extended to the maintenance and operation of their aircraft. The spat was magnified when it emerged that an unnamed air-traffic controller had complained that pilots from at least one low-cost airline were disobeying instructions from air-traffic control. The controller, who raised his concerns in the Confidential Human Factors Incident Reporting Programme (Chirp), believed that pilots were cutting corners because they were under pressure to meet tight schedules: they allegedly tried to save time by approaching airports too fast and had to abandon landings after coming too close to the aircraft in front. They also ignored flight path instructions and gave 'overly aggressive responses' to controllers because of 'extreme pressure on the flight deck'. The complainant explained, 'I would not like to give the impression that anarchy has broken out or that this problem is occurring more often than not; at the present time, it remains the exception rather than the rule. However, it is occurring with increasing frequency and, in my judgement, is due in part to the aggressively commercial ethos that exists within some airline companies and which probably translates into extreme pressure on the flight deck to achieve programmed sector flight times.'

The airline pilots' union, BALPA, said it believed that the report, which didn't identify an airline, was aimed at one in particular, and added that its accusations were unfounded as far as the British low-fare airlines with which it had arrangements were concerned. The Irish-registered Ryanair also dismissed the report as being without foundation. O'Leary went even further, describing the controller who filed it as a 'loony' and mocking the whistle-blowing body as 'the equivalent of the PPrune chatroom', the Professional Pilots Rumour Network website where pilots exchanged industry gossip. In fact, Chirp is an independent and widely respected body run by a former RAF officer and sanctioned by the Civil Aviation Authority (CAA); its methods are copied in other European states. It was established as a result of concerns within the industry that staff were reluctant to bring problems to the attention of managers for fear of being victimised, and one of its central tenets is that it never reveals the names of those who file reports.

A spokesman for the Civil Aviation Authority in Britain said that it could not act on the report because it did not know the name of the airline involved or the location of the alleged incidents. 'If we did, and if it was a UK airline, we would deal with it immediately and regard it as totally unacceptable,' he said. The Irish Aviation Authority (IAA), which regulated Ryanair, said there had been no reports of similar practices in Ireland. It had not been officially notified of the Chirp report but said it would be 'following it up'. O'Leary claimed that the incidents could never have happened as the controller described them in the report. 'The report from one single air-traffic controller is subjective nonsense with no basis in fact or evidence,' he said. 'The controller is duty-bound by procedures to file a report to the Civil Aviation Authority. He's broken the law if he hasn't filed this concern with the CAA.'

O'Leary claimed that the CAA had never raised an official controller's safety report with Ryanair since the airline began flying eighteen years previously and denied that the Irish airline's pilots were under any more pressure than those employed by full-service airlines such as British Airways. 'You can't fly any faster or slower even if you wanted to because there is a two-minute separation between planes going into landing. Our pilots are under less pressure because we don't operate to the busiest airports like Heathrow, Charles de Gaulle or Frankfurt. I don't even know how we would put our pilots under pressure. What do you do? Call him up as he's coming in to land?'

Ken Smart, the UK chief inspector of air accidents, deplored Ryanair's attack on Chirp, saying it was a vital part of the system that kept Britain's air passengers safe. Stelios said he had no interest in cutting back on safety. 'If you think safety is expensive, try an accident,' he cautioned. EasyJet claimed that low-cost airlines had to work almost doubly hard on safety. 'There's absolute zero tolerance on jeopardising or questioning safety,' a spokesman added. Officials at Go also said safety was 'non-negotiable' and promised to launch an immediate investigation to check if any pilot disregarded instructions. A spokeswoman for KLM's budget airline, Buzz, said: 'Passenger safety and flight safety are absolutely paramount and our schedules are decided on what is feasible and safe.'

Ryanair had other staff problems to deal with. A female pilot, Cliodhna Duggan from Dublin, took an action against the airline, claiming that she had been unfairly dismissed in July 2001 after being allegedly subjected to harassment by a Ryanair captain. Duggan, the daughter of Ryanair's then chief pilot, Jim Duggan, claimed in an affidavit to the High Court that she was shaking and terrified after Captain Les Hounsome allegedly shouted at her during a flight from Charleroi to Prestwick. She claimed that earlier the captain had shouted at her a number of times, once when the two had clashed over whether the autopilot should be connected. He told her: 'You'll fly it the way I tell you to fly it, young lady', and after the flight he had allegedly patted her leg and said, 'Good girl'.

Duggan said Hounsome was in the habit of touching her arm and cornering her when talking to her. She also claimed his actions towards her were unwelcome, something that should have been obvious to him, and that in her opinion they amounted to sexual harassment. She told him and her cabin supervisor that she could not fly the return leg with him.

Duggan claimed she was summoned to a meeting on 12 July [two days after the alleged incident] where she was treated in a 'most disparaging manner' by John Osborne, Ryanair's director of group operations. Four days later he read her a letter informing her that she was dismissed. The letter stated that her behaviour during the flight incident and at the disciplinary meeting on 12 July 2001 demonstrated an 'inappropriate attitude, lack of judgment and an unwillingness to learn or accept direction'. She claimed that the purported termination of her employment was a conspiracy between the Ryanair companies to demonstrate the power of Ryanair and to send a signal to pilots that the company would not accept any critical comments.

Ryanair denied the allegations and said that Duggan had never, before 10 July 2001, made the company aware of any difficulties with Captain Hounsome. It also pleaded that Captain Hounsome was the senior captain, with vastly greater experience. The case was settled in 2003 when Duggan and Ryanair agreed to Mr Justice Butler's declaration that, in refusing to operate Ryanair flight FR7922 from Prestwick to Charleroi on 10 July 2001 with Captain Les Hounsome, Duggan had 'acted in good faith, in the best interests of flight safety and in the best interests of Ryanair and their passengers'. The parties also agreed that a counterclaim by Ryanair should be struck out, as should the remainder of Ms Duggan's claim, which included claims of sexual harassment and defamation, and an application for a declaration that Ryanair had failed to implement a policy to prevent bullying and harassment of its employees. Ms Duggan was also allowed the costs of her action.

O'Leary has often said that safety is the only thing that keeps him awake at night. 'It doesn't matter how good you think you are in the airline business. We live every hour of every day with how do we avoid ever having an accident. I never want to have an accident on my conscience or on any of our consciences,' he said. Conor McCarthy, who headed the airline's ground operations, said safety and maintenance was one area where O'Leary was not interested in compromising on costs. The chief executive had always refused to sit in on Ryanair's safety committee meetings and would let one of the non-executives attend instead. 'He would challenge you about having an additional captain in Dublin but when you said you wanted to buy a spare engine for a 737 he would say "Buy two", McCarthy said. 'He would view that as money well spent.' Because the airline was rarely out of the news, thanks to O'Leary's flair for publicity and passengers relaying their Ryanair horror stories, any slight malfunction on one of its flights also attracted widespread media attention. Reports of tyre blowouts, oil leaks and engine fires were all given prominence, even though the airline's safety record is impeccable.

O'Leary said it was not fair to criticise the airline when it had safety approval not just in Ireland but with the British Civil Aviation Authority and the European Joint Aviation Authority. The unnamed controller's report to Chirp suggested that it was the pressure to turn around aircraft swiftly that was causing most tension between the pilots and air-traffic controllers. All of the no-frills operators had adopted the twenty-five-minute turnaround, with pilots often leaving luggage behind rather than delay the next take-off and upset the tight schedule. As a result mishandled or lost luggage was the most frequent complaint made by Ryanair passengers to the Air Transport Users' Council.

The phenomenal success of the low-cost carriers had been a boon for Stansted. Once much criticised as a white elephant, the Essex airport was now almost full. Ryanair was rapidly becoming its biggest customer and in 2002 had moved to its own new terminal from which its passengers could fly to forty-four European destinations, which included new routes to Klagenfurt, Graz and Friedrichshafen. But Stansted was dangerously close to becoming a victim of its own success; it was beginning to suffer from congestion that made it even more difficult for its key low-cost customers to get their planes in and out of the airport within twenty-five minutes. Terry Morgan, the airport's chief executive, said Stansted was beginning to look too small to facilitate Ryanair's future growth plans. 'If you look at Stansted's runway between six in the morning and seven-thirty it will be completely manic as all of the aircraft based here are trying to get out and to get that first rotation in,' he said. 'Ryanair had a fleet acquisition plan which meant that it was going to be receiving aircraft knowing that only a limited number of them could be based here and that more would have to be based elsewhere in Europe.'

Now that easyJet had swallowed up Go, speculation began to

mount about the loss-making Buzz, and whether it would survive a radical restructuring of its parent business, KLM. The Dutch airline came out strongly in support of its subsidiary, signalling that it would be adding new routes; it was particularly keen to open new services from Stansted into France and claimed it would break even within twelve months. Buzz, like easyJet, flew into some of Europe's major airports, including Charles de Gaulle in Paris, Frankfurt International and Schipol in Amsterdam. Over the following months it operated flights to twenty-four continental destinations, with fifteen in France including Bergerac, Bordeaux, Limoges, Dijon and Toulon. Moreover, it expressed its ambition to start new routes from one of Ryanair's bases at Scotland: Prestwick Airport.

When Buzz revealed that it would begin flying from Prestwick to Bournemouth Ryanair's retaliation was swift and brutal. It dusted off the battle plan that had so successfully driven Go out of Ireland and announced that it too would fly on the same route – but with more frequent flights and cheaper seats. Buzz had advertised a £19 one-way fare including tax; Ryanair offered the same trip for just £9.99, including tax. Buzz, fully aware of Ryanair's firepower, beat a hasty retreat. In a statement it said: 'Ryanair's decision to fly the Buzz route of Bournemouth to Prestwick means it is no longer viable for us to do so. Simple economics will tell you that passenger numbers on this route are not large enough to sustain two low-cost airlines.'

Scotland's members of parliament, who had been hoping that Buzz would also establish a base at Prestwick and increase the range of cheap flights from Scotland, criticised Ryanair's tactics. Brian Donohoe, MP for Cunninghame South and a member of the Commons transport committee, said the loss of the Buzz service was a blow to Scotland which would stifle competition and limit choice. 'There is no doubt that Ryanair is an aggressive player,' he added. 'They operate at a very low cost and can beat the others to pulp.'

Buzz's extensive network of routes into France had triggered a property boom in those regions as thousands of Britons began to buy second homes there, becoming frequent fliers and helping to boost its passenger numbers to 2 million. But despite its popularity the airline was struggling financially and was on course to report a £30 million loss. It had become an expensive adventure for KLM and following another review of its operations the Dutch carrier decided that Buzz's future should involve either a merger or a strategic alliance with another low-cost carrier.

With Go swallowed up by easyJet, Ryanair was the obvious choice to absorb Buzz. O'Leary had always dismissed suggestions that the Irish airline would acquire another airline to expand, saying this would just prove 'a distraction'. It could simply have continued to undercut Buzz's fares in the hope of prompting KLM to shut it down, but the ailing airline held one key attraction: its valuable slots at Stansted. If Buzz collapsed, all of the airlines based there would have the chance to bid for those slots and there was no guarantee that Ryanair would get the lion's share of them. But if Ryanair bought Buzz it would automatically secure the Buzz slots, giving it 60 per cent of the airport's capacity and opening up huge growth possibilities. Moreover, Buzz's UK operating certificate would allow Ryanair to get round the restrictions that prevented the Irish-registered airline from setting up routes from Stansted to non-European Union countries in Eastern Europe. O'Leary and his associates just needed to batter KLM into agreeing a low price for its distressed progeny.

In January 2003 a KLM spokesman said it was in talks with 'several prospective partners' for Buzz and that it wanted to seal a deal within the next couple of months. Ryanair's spokeswoman, Pauline McAlester, refused to confirm whether the airline was speaking to Buzz but said Ryanair talked to its rivals 'about a number of common issues'. A few weeks later Ryanair confirmed that it had agreed to purchase Buzz, for what O'Leary said was the 'bargain' price of €23.9 million – less than the price of a new Boeing 737. And speaking of Boeing 737s, O'Leary also mentioned that Ryanair had just ordered another twenty-two of Boeing's 737–800 series 189-seater planes and taken options on a further seventy-eight. Boeing's list price valued the deal at £3.6 billion but the airline, which was now one of Boeing's best customers, was again believed to have secured a huge discount; when pressed on the exact terms O'Leary said he wouldn't even disclose them to his priest.

Ryanair was now carrying 15 million passengers a year, making it Europe's fourth biggest international scheduled airline.

When the Buzz acquisition was finalised its passenger numbers would rise to 17.5 million, and O'Leary claimed this would soon climb to nearly 20 million. He offered a ready diagnosis of why its three-year-old competitor had never turned a profit, blaming its parent. 'It got saddled by KLM with the shittiest set of aircraft in the fleet, flying to shitty airports and with a few too many employees for an airline carrying two million passengers.' Now he was planning to revive the airline with his trademark strategy of ruthlessly efficient cost-cutting; he warned that his plans would provoke 'hell, brimfire and damnation'.

O'Leary intended to dismember Buzz, axing more than 100 of its 570 staff, killing the brand and shutting its routes to 'high-cost' airports in Amsterdam, Paris and Frankfurt. He made it clear that nothing would stand in his way. 'Let there be no misunderstanding about this. If BALPA or any of the others go on strike, it won't be a question of sacking pilots, we'll close down Buzz.' After a year Ryanair would return Buzz's six inefficient BAe146s to KLM, without incurring any financial penalties, he claimed: 'It's fly to Schipol, load the keys in through the window and run.' And he wouldn't be spending any money repainting them with the Ryanair logo in the meantime either. 'That strikes us as a waste of money. We will simply scratch out the Buzz name and scratch in Ryanair.' O'Leary said his drastic restructuring plan would see the airline returning a €10 million profit in the first year, increasing to €40 million in the following twelve months. The takeover was due to be completed by 1 April 2003.

O'Leary's arrival at Buzz was the worst possible outcome for the unions that represented its employees. It was pretty clear from his comments that O'Leary was planning savage job cuts. Jim McAuslan, general secretary of the British Air Line Pilots' Association, was uneasy about the airline's new owner and said he had asked to meet with O'Leary. 'However charismatic he may be, he is not above the law. You cannot go just hiring and firing people. And you don't motivate people by putting the fear of God into them.' The Transport and General Workers' Union also expressed concern and emphasised its 'strong determination to stand up for our members' rights in the face of robust warnings on job losses'. The TGWU were familiar with O'Leary's total antipathy to trade unions and many of its senior members had been horrified by what had unfolded at Dublin Airport five years earlier.

Patrick O'Keeffe, the TGWU's national secretary for civil air transport, said that O'Leary's attitude towards the unions and Buzz's staff was appalling from the start. 'At the beginning when we realised that he was coming into the UK we thought about it as a union, about whether we should welcome him with open arms, should we be cautious or should we be concerned and I think we had a bit of all three,' O'Keeffe explained. 'We saw it as a challenge, we had a concern and we have been proved right. So what we did was give him a cautious welcome and I think we made a mistake. I think we should have challenged him from day one. I think he misread our cautious welcome as a soft touch. The most appalling attitude he showed was when he was talking about naming the new company. Before we opened discussions he said that he thought he would use the name "buzz away". That immediately sent a message out to the trade unions telling us that he doesn't want us. He wanted us to buzz away.' O'Keeffe, who was from County Cork, said he was particularly saddened to see an Irish man showing such hostility towards trade unions. 'I have been involved with unions in the aviation sector for twenty-five years and he is a shame. He is a plague on our house.'

The unions had brought their concerns about the takeover to the Buzz chief executive, Floris van Pallandt, reminding him that the Dutch airline retained control until the formal handover. Within weeks their anxiety was further heightened when O'Leary said that he was now raising the number of redundancies from 100 to 400. He would get rid of a quarter of Buzz's pilots, 80 per cent of its cabin crew and half the ground services staff, and blamed the mounting tensions in Iraq for escalating the scale of the crisis at Buzz. 'The situation is getting worse,' a spokesman explained. 'The airline is presently losing over €1 million a week and radical action is needed as the crisis is being compounded by the prospect of imminent war in Iraq.' Ryanair struck further fear into Buzz's already traumatised workforce by announcing the grounding of all of its April flights until the deal had been formally cleared.

Then it became clear that Ryanair had no intention of paying the full redundancy entitlements to those affected by the job cuts.

The Irish airline had established a new company, called Buzz Stansted Limited, to maintain the business as a completely separate entity from Ryanair. This new corporate structure was designed to bypass the legislative requirements designed to protect employees who were being transferred from one company to another. 'He was acting within the law but he was effectively dismissing those previous Buzz employees who had built that airline,' O'Keeffe said.

O'Leary told the unions it was pointless for them to mount a legal action against the new company, since it had no money and was totally separate from Ryanair. But he eventually agreed to meet Buzz's 570 staff late one Monday night. There was an air of trepidation at the packed meeting as everyone waited to hear what he had to say. Jo Jakes, the TGWU representative at Stansted Airport, said O'Leary made a fairly basic presentation, explaining how he was going to save the airline. 'He sat there with his entourage and gave a slide presentation. His argument to all three unions was that he was saving Buzz, that it was going to be shut down anyway because it was an unprofitable organisation. He said he was doing a fantastic thing by offering these people work. He didn't mince his words and his language was fairly flowery. He said if they didn't like it they could fuck off.'

Jakes said O'Leary refused to entertain any discussion, telling people they should be grateful to see him and that their views were of no concern to him. 'At one point we did say to him that we couldn't believe that he wasn't being carried along shoulder high in the streets of Stansted because he was such a wonderful man,' she said. 'He did laugh at that.'

O'Leary had already said that he was going to issue new contracts to the hundred or so employees who would keep their job. But few of the Buzz staff were impressed with the terms on offer. Jakes said the overall reduction in the pay and benefits represented a serious loss of income for cabin crew. 'They would have to pay for their uniform, with the amount being deducted from their monthly pay by the airline for the rest of their employment. They had to pay for their car parking, which had been free, and they had to pay for the airport pass.'

The union was also concerned about the basis on which Ryanair would select its new employees, a subject on which the airline steadfastly refused to go into details. 'He then went through a process of issuing forty contracts at a time to cabin crew,' Jakes explained. 'I don't know how the selection happened but I think it was based on service. He would then wait to see how many he got back by a certain deadline. If they hadn't returned the contract by that time someone from Ryanair's personnel division would phone them to ask why and they were told if they didn't sign the contract they were resigning. If it didn't get sufficient take-up in the first round of offers it would issue more contracts while at the same time it had also been issuing redundancy notices. One minute they were being made redundant and the next they were being asked to sign these contracts. People didn't know where they stood.'

At the meeting O'Leary reminded those in attendance who had been fortunate enough to receive new contracts that the deadline for acceptance was looming. One source who attended the gathering recalled him saying, 'Unless you sign my fucking contract, I will shut the fucking airline down on Friday.' Most of the beleaguered employees held out on signing a new employment contract until proper redundancy payments were forthcoming. Ryanair had made it clear that it wouldn't be footing that bill and the unions piled the pressure on KLM, which eventually capitulated. 'We were prepared to take this all the way and I think KLM realised that,' Jakes said. 'We had told KLM it was the employer and that it had given over all of the details of their staff to Ryanair to do exactly what they wanted with them.'

When the final terms of the sale were announced, it emerged that Ryanair had reduced its price for Buzz and would now acquire it for €20.1 million with 130 employees. KLM retained the 400-plus of the staff previously dedicated to the Buzz operation who were facing redundancy. Ryanair later disclosed that it had incurred an additional €26.6 million in excess lease and other costs associated with the acquisition, which were largely related to Buzz aircraft. So overall Buzz cost Ryanair €46.7 million.

About thirty cabin crew signed the contracts and began working for Ryanair. They each took a pay cut equal to about £4000, and lost their service and their pension rights as Ryanair doesn't provide pensions. 'The base salary was about £16,000, which O'Leary claimed was a pay increase, but in fact by the time you took everything off it wasn't,' Jakes said. 'Many of the cabin crew just didn't want to work with him. It was a bad time for all of them.'

Ryanair's policy of making its customers pay for as much as possible also extended to its employees. It charged staff £175 a year for uniforms, and anyone who left the airline after less than a year would have to pay back £500 for their uniform. The new Ryanair employees also had to pay £65 for a security vetting procedure and £15 for a criminal record check, and another £15 a month for parking. When asked about the airline's policy of charging staff for their uniforms, a spokeswoman replied: 'We'd just like to point out that Ryanair staff are very well paid and enjoy generous share options and lots of travel allowances.'

The TGWU lost a lot of members following the demise of Buzz and those who moved to Ryanair found it hard to adjust to the airline's abrasive culture. 'O'Leary didn't recognise seniority so you had people with thirty years' service, especially the pilots, starting at day one. Cabin crew who had years of service were put on twelve-month probationary contracts. Within those twelve months he got rid of some without any reason. I suppose it was because they didn't do what he wanted,' said Jakes. 'His language shows that he has no respect for anyone. When you see that type of aggression you have to be fairly brave to challenge it. He is a total bully and he has gotten away with it, for now.'

Sales of tickets on Buzz's proposed new routes from Bournemouth to Amsterdam, Paris, Belfast, the Spanish resorts of Malaga and Murcia, and Bergerac and La Rochelle in France were all halted. It was a huge blow for Bournemouth, which had been preparing to build a new terminal building to accommodate the Buzz expansion. The thousands of disappointed passengers who had expected to travel with the airline from Bournemouth were told that they could choose between a refund and replacement tickets to another of the airline's European destinations. Ryanair said it still had to decide which other routes from the Buzz summer schedule would be dropped. Tony Ryan's brother, Kell, who was Ryanair's corporate accounts manager in Britain, travelled to Bournemouth but made it clear he was only there to promote a new route to Prestwick and was offering no consolation for angry Buzz customers who arrived to make a protest. He laughed at the 'Ryanair Sucks' sign that had been placed beside the airline's desks. 'What have we got to apologise for? It was Buzz that sucked. They weren't our passengers. They were Buzz passengers and they came into the fold,' he explained. 'I wasn't going to the airport with a bag of money and giving them their money back. We don't do refunds [if Ryanair is not at fault] – it says that very clearly in our conditions of carriage. People buy their tickets. They know what they are getting. You know exactly where you stand with Ryanair.'

It was a particularly stressful time for the thousands of families who had bought properties in remote parts of France such as Bergerac, Limoges, and Dijon, who now waited to hear whether these airports were to be deleted from Ryanair's Stansted schedule. O'Leary was unsympathetic: 'Please don't ask me to feel sorry for rich people with second homes in France.' The Air Transport Users' Council said: 'It's an appalling way to treat passengers but that's what we have come to expect from Ryanair, sadly.' Some won a reprieve after Ryanair negotiated a cheap deal at Bergerac Airport, one of the most popular destinations for Britons with properties in the Dordogne region. The route was re-opened, with Ryanair saying it was delighted to be able to deliver good news to the people of 'Dordogneshire'.

CHAPTER NINETEEN

A Perfect Storm

' It's a complete fuck-up which is going to overturn twenty years of competition in air travel, but it wouldn't be the first time the EU has made a balls of an investigation. It looks like they are trying to come up with some communist rules, which means that everyone pays the same high costs and charges the same high fares. This is an attack not just on Ryanair but on the entire low-fares sector.' It was February 2004, and Michael O'Leary was ranting again. Denouncing the European Commission as an 'evil empire', he explained to the world that the 'Eurocrats' had just dealt a crippling blow to his industry. Dressed in his best checked shirt and jeans, the head of Europe's biggest low-fares airline started to cry as he bravely held his 'EU BANS LOW FARES' banners aloft for photographers.

The news that had so distressed O'Leary had come from Europe's Transport Commissioner, Loyola de Palacio, who that morning had ruled that the money given to Ryanair when it established its first European base at Belgium's Charleroi Airport in 2001 amounted to illegal state aid. Ryanair would have to repay just over €4 million to the Walloon regional government, which owned the airport, and negotiate a shorter contract there. Palacio claimed that the new arrangements would have a fairly modest impact on Ryanair's costs, adding no more than €3 or €4 to its fares. It was a good decision for low-cost airlines and for regional airports, she argued, explaining that it would level the playing field and end the 'secret sweetheart' deals that had been so beneficial to Ryanair. 'These agreements were totally confidential. I am not saying they cheated but it was at least hushed up and this may have abused the good faith of others,' she said. 'I feel there has been a clear lack of transparency and other carriers were not being offered the same conditions.'

But O'Leary couldn't see any silver lining in de Palacio's decision. He invited Europe's media to Brussels' Crowne Plaza hotel, a few hundred yards from the 'evil empire', to denounce the ruling, which he had already ordered Ryanair's lawyers to challenge. 'We consider this to be a disaster for consumers,' he declared. 'It's a disaster for low-fare travel all over Europe and it's a disaster for state-owned regional airports.' According to O'Leary, there was no way that the payments it received from Charleroi could be described as subsidies or that Ryanair could be seen as enjoying preferential treatment over other airlines. 'We don't accept that we have received any state aid at Charleroi. All we received were discounts, just like Tesco would receive discounts from its cheese suppliers.' That same deal could have been negotiated by any other airline, he claimed. Ryanair just happened to be the first to clinch it.

As for its being a 'secret' arrangement, O'Leary was just amazed, describing Ryanair's arrangements at Charleroi as 'the most publicised deal in aviation history'. He had certainly boasted about it at the time, telling the media that Ryanair could land at Charleroi 'practically for free', and he had mentioned in interviews that the airport was giving Ryanair financial grants to offset training costs involved with staffing the base.

Ironically, it was O'Leary's own comments that had led the European Commission to question the deal. Many European airlines had long suspected that Ryanair had been getting similar deals at other publicly owned airports, and, despite Ryanair's vigorous campaigns against government subsidies to the big flag-carriers, its rivals now believed that the Irish airline had become the single biggest recipient of state aid. They were convinced that these arrangements were handing Ryanair an unfair advantage and contributing to its phenomenally low cost base, more than 30 per cent lower than any of its rivals'. Airline chiefs across Europe who were being taunted by O'Leary in their home markets and losing customers to Ryanair were increasingly crying foul. So they seized on O'Leary's comments about Charleroi, and within a few months Brit Air, a subsidiary of Air France, filed an official complaint to the European Commission.

After two years of investigation the Commission revealed the full extent of the Walloon regional government's generosity towards Ryanair. It established that the airline paid just 50 per cent of its published landing fees and was indemnified against any losses it might suffer if airport taxes were to rise during the fifteen-year contract. The airport also handed over €1.9 million for the opening of three new routes, €768,000 to defray the cost of recruiting and training Ryanair's pilots and crew and €250,000 towards providing hotel accommodation for Ryanair staff, not to mention further contributions for the purchase of office equipment. In addition, Ryanair was charged only €1 per passenger for the use of the airport's ground handling facilities, a 90 per cent discount on the advertised price of €10. In its official journal the Commission noted that while it was not unusual for airlines to negotiate a discount, in this case the price charged didn't cover the cost of the service. It concluded that the arrangement allowed Ryanair to operate in 'entirely stable conditions' that were 'sheltered from any commercial risk', putting it at a distinct advantage to other airlines. 'These measures are specific, they are granted using State resources, they are liable to distort competition and intra-community trade, and they constitute State aid,' the Commission stated.

In the months before the ruling appeared, O'Leary had played down the possible effects of the Commission's investigation, which he described as Ryanair's 'Waterloo'. Reports appeared in various newspapers suggesting that the airline had brokered a deal and would not have to repay its grants, though at other times Ryanair's chief executive warned the Commission that the airline would vigorously challenge any adverse ruling and shut down its Charleroi routes. O'Leary had met with de Palacio a number of times during the course of the investigation and constantly tried to pre-empt the outcome through the media. After one meeting, he explained to journalists that the Commission was unlikely to seek a repayment, although he conceded that the length of the arrangement might have to be altered.

De Palacio's spokesman, Gilles Gantelet, was taken aback when O'Leary suggested that he had managed to negotiate a favourable outcome, and said that no such discussion had taken place. 'You must never believe Ryanair,' he wearily explained.

'Ryanair believed that because it was in robust financial health it should get state aid. We had to ask, would it be in such good health if it were not getting these subsidies? Ryanair has shown that it was possible to make money by flying into these remote airports yet some of its competitors would say that it is not profitable. They believed that Ryanair was only making money because of the state aid it has received.' He concluded that while Ryanair 'used to laugh' at the Commission, as the investigation progressed the airline had become 'afraid' of Europe's politicians.

Ryanair's biggest fear was that the Commission would force it to renegotiate the deals it had with other publicly owned airports, which amounted to about 20 per cent of those it used across Europe. If all of these deals became more expensive then Ryanair's costs would rise. David Bonderman and some of the airline's other directors, such as the former European Commissioner Ray MacSharry, had fully grasped the potential impact of an adverse ruling from Brussels and had been trying to restrain O'Leary from hurling insults at these influential politicians. One source familiar with the case said O'Leary had been told to 'maintain radio silence' as the Commission progressed towards a decision. 'If things had gone badly against the airline it could have taken a big hit,' the source added. 'It was potentially very bad news and could have done serious and irreparable damage to Ryanair. O'Leary is a very difficult character. He is impetuous and doesn't easily take advice. The board was trying to keep him under control with Bonderman, MacSharry and James Osborne attempting to sit on him. He was told to "shut his mouth" and not to upset anyone but of course there was the odd squeak.' One of those 'squeaks' upset Belgian commissioner Philippe Busquin, who finally snapped and declared that O'Leary was 'terribly irritating and irritates commissioners'.

Ireland's European Commissioner, David Byrne, had taken up the cudgels and was fighting Ryanair's corner in Brussels. The Irish government was less supportive; one source in Brussels suggested that it 'didn't lift a finger' for most of the investigation. There were signs that Bertie Ahern, whom O'Leary likes to insult by calling him 'Prime Minister' rather than Taoiseach, wasn't pulling out the stops to save Ryanair's skin. O'Leary had been famously rude to Ahern during the 1998 strike at Dublin Airport and since then had lampooned him as 'Dithering Bertie' in advertisements and publicity stunts criticising the government's refusal to sanction a second terminal at the airport. He had even called for the return of Charlie Haughey, the former Taoiseach whose lavish lifestyle was found to have been funded by wealthy Irish businessmen. 'He may have been crooked but at least he got things done,' O'Leary complained.

Some people who have been associated with the airline for many years would say that Ryanair never had a good relationship with any Irish government and had found few friends amongst politicians since its foundation. 'Jim Mitchell [the minister who first awarded Ryanair its licence in 1986] and Seamus Brennan were the two best ministers as far as Ryanair was concerned,' one source said. Brennan, the minister who had saved Ryanair from bankruptcy by controversially awarding it exclusive rights on routes into Stansted in the late 1980s, had now returned to the Department of Transport and intervened to try to limit the damage for Ireland's budget carrier. When the ruling was announced he claimed some success. Brennan said the blow was 'softer' than it might have been and highlighted the fact that in the worst-case scenario Ryanair could have ended up having to repay more than €15 million. Brennan believed that his key achievement was in persuading de Palacio not to use the ruling to issue Europe-wide guidelines that could have imposed sweeping changes and forced Ryanair to undo all of its deals at publicly owned airports. Brennan said he was 'greatly relieved' that that Commissioner listened to him and other transport ministers in this matter.

In December 2003 a French court had ruled illegal a €1.4 million payment to Ryanair from Strasbourg Chamber of Commerce, as part of a joint marketing deal at the airport there. Ryanair lodged an appeal, and in the meantime shut down flights into Strasbourg and switched the service to Baden-Baden some 40km away. The Commission had also received complaints about Ryanair's deals at other airports, including Pau in France, and expected to receive further complaints following its ruling.

One source in Brussels said O'Leary's enemies seemed hell-bent on making trouble for Ryanair. 'O'Leary has been so aggressive that many people just can't stand him,' the source suggested.

'He has created a lot of jealousy and a lot of enemies. In some ways Ryanair has become a victim of its own success. Ryanair flew to airports that nobody else went to and put airports into competition with each other for the first time. That began to raise issues about whether public money could be used to favour one company over another. Now Ryanair is viewed as an airline that has to be attacked.'

In the aftermath of the Charleroi ruling, O'Leary was quick to point out that, while Ryanair had received 'discounts', the deal had greatly benefited the airport, bringing prosperity to a region that for years had been an unemployment black spot. Before Ryanair arrived at Charleroi its baggage-handlers were paid to 'sit around like the local job centre. Now two million people a year fly there and it's booming,' he said. 'Ryanair has never received a subsidy. The money we received from Charleroi was money we paid them in the first place. We paid the published charges and they kicked back 90 per cent. We pass that on to the public. We give the public what it fucking wants. The Commission said this ruling will increase fares. In the States that would cause a riot.'

In characteristic style O'Leary also suggested that the ruling was also a disaster for other airlines. 'That is how lunatic this decision is. It is bizarre. It seems to be an attack by the Commission on all the low-cost airlines.' It could affect airports used by easyJet, British Airways CitiExpress and British Midland, he said, claiming that the other low-cost carriers supported his attempts to challenge the ruling. In fact, many of his adversaries were enjoying his discomfort. On hearing that other low-cost airlines were going to support Ryanair, one excutive laughed and said he found it hard to believe that the airline was being supported by 'the people O'Leary wants to put out of business'. EasyJet welcomed the ruling, making no attempt to defend O'Leary's claims. 'Michael O'Leary has been telling everyone that the sky will fall through, but we just don't share that view. We welcome the transparency that the ruling will bring,' a spokesman said.

Few analysts believed that de Palacio had really sounded the death knell for the low-fares airlines. They universally agreed that Ryanair had won the lion's share of any state subsidy deals but believed it was sufficiently robust to weather the storm. At worst the decision would raise Ryanair's airport handling and marketing costs. 'It's a smokescreen,' said one.

Still, it had not been the best few months of Ryanair's history. The controversy about Ryanair's insistence on charging its passengers for wheelchair use, which had been raging for years, finally reached the courts. Bob Ross, a community worker from North London who suffered from cerebral palsy and arthritis, took legal action against Ryanair when the budget carrier charged him £18 for the use of a wheelchair, claiming that the fee discriminated against the disabled. The Disability Rights Commission supported his case with its chairman, Bert Massie, saying that Ryanair's wheelchair charge was a 'slap in the face' to disabled people wanting to take advantage of cheap air travel.

Like many others on his flight from Stansted to Perpignan, Ross had paid just £10 for his fare, but unlike his fellow travellers he had to pay another £18 on his outward and return journeys to cross the half-mile from the check-in desk to the aircraft, a distance too far for him to walk. 'It meant that Ryanair operated a two-tier charging policy, one for able-bodied people and one for wheelchair users,' Ross said. 'It seemed to me that they were charging me simply for being disabled.' At London's Central County Court in January 2004 his legal team argued to Judge Crawford Lindsay that a wheelchair was not a 'frill' but an 'auxiliary aid' to mobility.

Ryanair insisted that it did not charge wheelchair passengers for assistance. Ross was not travelling in a wheelchair; instead he had used the wheelchair service at the airport provided by BAA Stansted, which charged the airline. Most airlines absorbed this cost but Ryanair simply passed it on to its customers. Ryanair claimed that most of the airports it used provided this service free. A spokesman said, 'These costs should not be imposed on the airlines particularly when – as in the case of Mr Ross and Ryanair – the fare paid by him to fly to the south of France was just half the cost of providing wheelchair assistance to get him through the terminal building in Stansted.'

But the judge agreed with Ross and ruled on 30 January 2004 that Ryanair had breached the Disability Discrimination Act. He awarded Ross £1336 in compensation, £1000 for injury to feelings and the remainder to cover the money Ross had spent on hiring wheelchairs. It was a landmark ruling, closely monitored by thirty-five other disabled people who had contemplated taking a group legal action against Ryanair.

Ross was delighted, saying, 'I see this not just as a victory for me personally, but for other disabled people, too. The judgment has confirmed that it is Ryanair's responsibility to pick up the costs. I suggest it does this with some humility. It beggars belief that a company with a £165 million profit last year should quibble over meeting the cost of providing disabled people with a wheelchair. Perhaps before counting their pennies, Ryanair should have considered the cost to their reputation and the distress caused to disabled people by acting in such a discriminatory way.'

Ryanair reacted angrily to the defeat, vowing to appeal the ruling. In the same breath it announced that it would impose a 50p or 70c wheelchair levy on every ticket, and duly increased its prices by that amount. With Ryanair predicting that it would carry 24 million passengers in 2004, rough calculations revealed that the airline would earn another £12 million from its new levy – a bonanza that far exceeded the costs associated with providing wheelchairs for disabled passengers. The airline said the levy would be withdrawn if its appeal against Ross was successful.

Ireland's Equality Agency had received similar complaints from disabled passengers, and the Irish Wheelchair Association launched a blistering attack on the airline when the new levy was announced. 'This levy is low and grotesque, even by Ryanair standards. It is sending out a message that it is the fault of people with disabilities,' a spokesman said. 'Society in general has moved beyond seeing disabled people as a burden, but the attitude of Ryanair is really dragging us back. I feel that for Ryanair to put such a stark economic cost on what is an issue of equality is obscene. Other airlines, including Aer Lingus, absorb the cost of wheelchairs. They hire them for their disabled passengers and pay for them.' The draft version of regulations due to be handed down from the European Commission in 2004 stipulates that European airports will have to provide wheel-chairs free of charge to people with disabilities or reduced mobility.

However distressed O'Leary may have been at losing these two cases, they probably proved a welcome distraction. In fact, some observers believed O'Leary's over-reaction to the Charleroi ruling was a deliberate attempt to deflect attention away from the airline's real problems. When O'Leary appeared on BBC's *Newsnight*, Jeremy Paxman seemed puzzled by his distress, pointing out that Ryanair shares had actually risen on the stock market after the ruling was announced.

Any rise in the share price was good news, since a month earlier, on 29 January 2004, Ryanair had stunned the stock markets by warning that instead of a 10 per cent increase in profits for the twelve months to the end of March 2004, its profits would be 10 per cent below expectations. It was the first time since its flotation as a public company in 1997 that Ryanair had delivered disappointing news to its shareholders, and the first time Ryanair had been forced to admit that it had sustained injuries in the raging fare wars it had fuelled so aggressively. The announcement immediately sent the shares crashing down by more than 30 per cent.

O'Leary, who was the airline's single biggest shareholder, attempted to allay concerns about its much-vaunted business model, stressing that it would still bring in a profit of €215 million. But even the airline sector's greatest motormouth couldn't bolster Ryanair shares once they started to tumble. In Dublin the shares sank from €6.75 to €4.86, to hover at lows last seen immediately after the 11 September terrorist attacks. The crash wiped more than €1 billion off Ryanair's value, and O'Leary's own pockets were suddenly some €80 million lighter. He insisted there was nothing to fear: the airline had simply hit a brief patch of turbulence.

Flag-carriers like British Airways and Aer Lingus, and its low-fares rival easyJet, had been firing off salvos in Ryanair's direction for months now, offering millions of cheap flights to destinations across Europe. They had forced Ryanair to slash its fares to try to compete with these offers and its response had eaten into its profits. O'Leary admitted as much. 'There is a lot of stupid competition out there losing money. We are not reducing our low fares because we are a charity. There is some below-cost selling – easyJet, British Airways, everyone is at it. It's part of the land-grab going on in Europe and we will always be lower than anyone else,' he explained, though his claims that his rivals were engaged in below-cost selling have never been proved.

In the previous three months Ryanair's average fare had been just under €36, with the airline predicting that prices would fall by another 5 to 20 per cent over the next twelve months. It was determined to continue to flood the market with cheap deals in its bid to dominate Europe's skies. 'We had been saying fares and margins would fall. What we didn't foresee was that they would come down this bloody quickly,' O'Leary conceded. This was a remarkable admission from the man who had always sold the Ryanair story with such great conviction. Some commentators were surprised to have discovered a chink in his armour, and one analyst commented that Ryanair had been 'scratched' for the first time: 'O'Leary wasn't impressive. He wasn't able to speak with as much conviction as he has in the past.'

But O'Leary shrugged this off, even suggesting that some tarnishing of his image might be a good thing. 'There is absolutely no harm in losing the mythical horseshit that we can walk on water,' he said. 'Given that it was our first profits warning, the market went nuts. But there is no point whingeing that everybody has got it in for us. Perhaps we deserved a slap around the head. It was inevitable that at some point in our history profits would stop accelerating. Any chief executive who doesn't have a sense of their own mortality is heading for disaster. They read articles describing themselves as visionaries and geniuses. They shouldn't believe it any more than when the press are calling them gobshites and wankers.'

Despite this setback, he said Ryanair was still on course to become Europe's biggest airline and expected to be carrying 50 million passengers before the end of the decade. It might have to surrender some of its profitability to achieve this goal and to outrun its competitors, but as long as it had the lowest costs in the business it could afford to do so. He was already preparing to wield the axe at Ryanair in response to the fall in profits, suggesting that the airline's two thousand staff would have to accept a pay freeze. Other cutbacks were also under consideration.

In the following weeks O'Leary told staff they could no longer enjoy free tea, coffee or water on board its flights. The airline also abolished its subsidy to the staff canteen and told its employees they were welcome to bring their own drinks and snacks to work – though pilots and cabin crew were banned from using the

ovens on board to heat their food up. This measure was introduced to ensure no additional cleaning costs were incurred,
according to Ryanair.

Pilots were told that in future they would only be issued with
one ream of paper per day for weather and other reports, a measure which some pilots complained would result in paper short-
ages on late flights. They would also have to pay for their own
bi-annual medical examinations, which had to be carried out in
their own time. And, as Ryanair already did with the other cabin-
crew members, the company would now deduct a monthly sum
from their pay to cover the cost of the pilots' uniforms. Their
existing pensions were also to be frozen, while no pension provisions would be made available to new recruits.

Ryanair later relented on the imposed pay freeze but only
after these cost savings had been introduced. O'Leary explained
the reversal to staff: 'Our shareholders would question our commitment to lowest costs if we were awarding ourselves pay
increases at a time when our profits and share price had fallen.
We are taking a big risk by increasing pay at a time of very difficult market conditions and intense competition. But we believe
now is the time to risk the pay increase.'

The company also reminded its staff of its policy in relation
to sick days. David O'Brien, its head of operations, sent a memo
to Ryanair staff who had been absent from work on five or more
occasions in the previous twelve months. In it he claimed that
over 10,000 days has been lost to Ryanair through absenteeism,
which equated to seven un-crewed aircraft every day. O'Brien
stated that this 'high frequency' of absence couldn't be sustained,
as it meant that other people had to take on additional work. 'All
absences in the future will be closely monitored and I need to see
a dramatic and sustained improvement in your attendance in the
months ahead,' he wrote. These employees were asked to confirm
to him that they had received the memo and to outline in writing
the measures they would take to prevent further absence from
work.

At the same time the airline scaled back its immediate expansion plans, saying it would now slow from growing at more than
50 per cent a year, as it had in the previous two, to a more man-
ageable 22 per cent. It also signalled some slowdown in the

number of new aircraft due to arrive from Boeing, but promised it would still acquire more planes and open more routes across Europe. 'It is our job to show that this is a bump in the road and not some hole we have fallen into,' said O'Leary. 'In the next two years we are going to overtake BA and Air France in terms of size. And we are still going to make ten per cent profit margins after tax. No other airline in the world makes that, so is our business model bust? No it isn't.'

Chris Avery, an analyst at JP Morgan, said the airline had been hit by 'a perfect storm' sparked by over-exuberant growth and a thumbs-down from the commission. Others suggested that Ryanair's business model was 'winded' rather than broken. Joe Gill, an analyst at Goodbody Stockbrokers, pointed out that other low-fares carriers had issued profit warnings in the past and staged a strong recovery. 'Southwest Airlines regularly had down days and down weeks and always bounced back,' he said.

One of Ryanair's most sceptic observers, Andrew Lobbenberg, an airline analyst at ABN AMRO, continued to harbour doubts about its business model, in particular its use of out-of-the-way airports. Even though Ryanair was offering rock-bottom fares, nearly one third of its seats remained unsold. It seemed that even though the cost of flying had hit an all-time low, people still needed a reason to take to the skies. Lobbenberg suggested it was even harder for consumers to find a reason to fly to Ryanair's obscure destinations and that the airline would find it increasingly difficult to fill the 189 seats on each of its new Boeing 737-800 aircraft. 'Flying from London to nowhere can work,' he warned, 'but flying from nowhere to nowhere is a challenge, particularly with large aircraft.' Perhaps Ryanair's business model had reached the limits of its capacity.

CHAPTER TWENTY

The Ryanair Generation

I n the twenty years between 1960 and 1980 the number of
people travelling between Ireland and Britain each year had
remained static at about 800,000. When Ryanair's first
fifteen-seater aircraft took off from Waterford in 1985, carrying
seventy-six people a day to London's Gatwick Airport was a magnificent achievement. Almost two decades on Ryanair is on
course to carry 24 million passengers in 2004. It has eleven bases
in Europe and believes this could ultimately rise to about forty.

The low-fares phenomenon championed by Ryanair has revolutionised air travel. One travel agent remarked that if you had
advertised 'cheap' airfares ten or fifteen years ago the public
would have shied away from the offer for fear that the plane
would fall out of the sky. 'Now you can't sell a seat unless it's
cheap,' he said. The airline's greatest rival, Aer Lingus, has
reversed its fortunes by copying Ryanair's low-fares formula. Ireland's Transport Minister, Seamus Brennan, suggests that you
could now buy ten Aer Linguses for one Ryanair. 'They have
shown the way and everyone has followed them.'

O'Leary is proud that the airline has made air travel afford-
able for everyone and has promised that in the future more and
more of its seats will be offered to the public for free. 'Even the
unemployed can afford to fly Ryanair,' he boasts.

Ryanair has certainly attracted passengers from all walks of
life. Britain's Prime Minister, Tony Blair, with his wife Cherie and
their four children, flew with Ryanair to Carcassone in southwest
France for a holiday in 2001. Downing Street's press office
explained it was 'more convenient' for the family to fly with
Ryanair than to take an RAF aircraft. The seats were thought to

have cost about £125 each and Ryanair insisted they wouldn't get any special treatment. 'If they want a cup of tea or a sandwich they will have to pay for it; this is a very egalitarian airline,' a spokesman said. Her Royal Highness Princess Margarethe Ambler, sister of Sweden's King Carl Gustaf, has flown with Ryanair from its Stockholm base at Skavsta to London's Stansted Airport. Media reports in Sweden said her Royal Highness was 'very satisfied' with her Ryanair trip, and the airline immediately issued a press statement claiming that Ryanair was 'Europe's No.1 for low fares, on-times and customer service – even for royalty'. A spokesman added that Princess Margarethe Ambler had chosen Ryanair's low fares over the 'high fares charged by SAS and the other rip-off cowboys'. Other celebrities who have used Ryanair's no-frills service include the Jordan Formula 1 team and Arsenal Football Club.

Over the years the Irish airline has sustained many a long-distance relationship. On hearing of Michael O'Leary's forthcoming nuptials to Dublin banker Anita Farrell in 2003, the *Irish Independent*'s Single File said it was happy that the man who had helped to improve so many people's sex lives had finally found love. Thanks to Ryanair, it said, 'a gorgeous German or stylish Italian is just a few hours away, with a flight more cheaply bought than a return rail ticket to Cork. We have dated judges from Norway, teachers from Trieste and engineers from Amsterdam'. Ryanair is a favourite for groups heading away for stag and hen parties and has been blamed for the influx of carousing revellers to Dublin, which many believe has given Ireland's capital city a bad name as a tourist destination.

Ryanair has also contributed to more significant social changes. Friends of Tony Ryan and his family say they are very proud of the way Ryanair has benefited so many people. 'Tony is exceptionally proud that Ryanair is a very dynamic company that is revolutionising aviation,' said a friend of Ryan's. 'In the Irish context, though, the thing he likes best is that the airline eliminated the word emigration forever. It was a big word in Ireland in the sixties, seventies and eighties but now it's gone.' Another person who has had close links with the airline for many years still recalls a documentary made by the BBC in the 1980s that showed a mother saying goodbye to her son, who was emigrating from Knock Airport in County Mayo. 'She said, "Promise me that you will spend your first pay packet on the Ryanair flight back."'

The young man in the documentary was just one of the thousands of young people forced to leave Ireland to get work in the 1980s and early 1990s to earn a living. Unlike the millions who had made that same journey years earlier, Ryanair's cheap fares and regular flights set them free to fly home as regularly as they liked, and they became known as the 'Ryanair Generation'.

Ryanair has also been responsible for fuelling a housing boom in regions of France, with its regular flights spurring thousands of Britons to buy second homes there. In the most popular areas, such as the Dordogne, estate agents advertise properties for sale saying 'Ryanair 40 minutes'. O'Leary has flatly warned these homeowners that they have no guarantee that Ryanair will continue to fly to these destinations and shouldn't be buying property based on where the Irish airline will carry them. If these routes aren't profitable O'Leary will abandon them without a second thought.

Ryanair has been rolling out new routes at breakneck speed. In 2003 alone it opened services to fifty new airports from its bases in Britain and continental Europe, which now also include Stockholm Skavsta and Milan Bergamo. In spring 2004 Ryanair offered flights to 125 European destinations. Yet despite its formidable advance into Europe, the airline is still hugely reliant on its traditional routes linking Ireland and Britain, which effectively subsidise much of its European network. According to documents Ryanair filed with the New York Securities and Exchange Commission, its Ireland and Britain flights accounted for 44 per cent of its total revenues in 2002 and 36 per cent in 2003. The report told investors. 'So long as the company's operations remain dependent on routes between Ireland and the UK, the company's future operations and growth will be adversely affected if this market does not grow and if there is increased competition in this market.' The substantial profits Ryanair still earns on these routes explain why O'Leary waged such a bloody battle against Go following its incursion onto its home turf in 2001 and suggest that he will repeat this type of assault whenever new airlines come to Dublin.

Executives at Aer Rianta enjoy highlighting the importance of the Irish routes to combat O'Leary's years of complaining about its high charges. In 2004 the Irish airport operator was still under siege but from a new combatant, the Transport Minister Seamus Brennan. Almost a decade after O'Leary first began his campaign to end the Aer Rianta monopoly, the minister decided to break up the company into three competing entities that would independently operate Dublin, Cork and Shannon airports, and to move forward with the construction of a second, independent terminal at Dublin Airport – another O'Leary demand. These initiatives put the minister on course for a head-on collision with the trade unions representing Aer Rianta employees, and O'Leary seized every opportunity to raise the temperature. He was already looking forward to playing the three new airport operators off each other to secure the cheap deal he had been chasing for years and that would enable him to open new routes into Europe.

Relationships with unions have never been O'Leary's strong suit. His conflict with Ireland's biggest trade union, SIPTU, during the 1998 strike at Dublin airport was a disaster for both sides. By brokering improved pay deals with its pilots Ryanair also managed to keep the Airline Pilots' Association out of Ryanair, and O'Leary broke the Association of Transport and General Workers' Union's stranglehold at Buzz. But just as Europe's big airlines are causing trouble for Ryanair on various fronts, there are signs that trade unions across the continent may yet combine to wage a battle against Ryanair. Unions in various European states have received approaches for advice from some of the airline's staff and are also monitoring how Ryanair's cheap deals are reducing the earnings of their members.

Patrick O'Keeffe, the TGWU's national secretary for civil air transport, said the union will challenge O'Leary's refusal to allow an independent voice for Ryanair's workforce. 'If O'Leary believes that he is so in tune with his workforce then why are people asking us to join our union for their voices to be heard within Ryanair?' he demanded. 'We are not going to accept his methods of non-involvement with the workforce in industrial relations matters.' O'Keeffe said that despite O'Leary's victory at Buzz he will have to greatly improve the pay and conditions of the airline's workforce if he wants to keep the trade unions out of Ryanair. 'He had to pay money to Ryanair pilots to discourage them from joining a union of their choice. If that is the way he is going to play it then he will have to pay all of his staff a living wage and pensions and provide benefits that are beyond his competitors and I don't think he will. He will do it for the pilots because he needs them.' O'Keeffe says the TGWU wants to talk to Ryanair about standards and partnership. 'You can use people to a certain degree. Ryanair has a very clever age profile, as most of its employees are young and happy-go-lucky. But when people have to support their families, their partners and have a wider commitment they also want a say in the company. That is what mature people want. He has to understand that.'

For all of the trade union's harsh words, the airline claims to be inundated with applications from pilots and staff seeking other positions at the airline. Indeed the volume of applications from pilots is so great that O'Leary insists that they must pay a €50 application fee to cover the airline's administrative costs, refundable if their application is successful. Those who pass the initial interview then have to pay another, non-refundable €200 to undergo a simulator assessment. During periods when there are no vacancies some pilots have been invited to join the airline as members of its cabin crew, serving its expensively priced drinks and snacks to its passengers. The highest turnover of staff tends to be within the crew ranks, as some tire of the long hours while others use the opportunity to travel and then move on to other careers after a few years.

When Ryanair flights first took off in the mid-1980s its staff were encouraged to provide high-quality customer service and told that being rude to a passenger was a sacking offence. Under O'Leary the airline's priorities changed. He was obsessed with providing a functioning and efficient airline and cared little about pleasing its passengers at any other level. But as the airline expanded and the wave of customer complaints swelled, some of his lieutenants attempted to address these issues. Conor McCarthy, the head of the airline's operations, recalled holding focus groups with staff and customers to address some of the recurring problems. However, he said that Ryanair's strict policies in relation to excess baggage and its refusal to offer any support or succour when flights were delayed or cancelled largely rendered this a futile exercise.

His colleague, Caroline Green, who had headed Ryanair's reservations operations before becoming its director of customer service, was constantly trying to seek improvements in the way the airline dealt with its customers. 'She is a very capable person and was always trying to get O'Leary to accept the need for customer responsibility,' McCarthy said. 'She had to fight for everything.' Green has since introduced retraining for its flight and ground attendants in customer service and has offered to pay a special €150 bonus to those who go out of their way to be charming and helpful to Ryanair passengers. The airline will even be dispatching mystery passengers who can recommend bonus payments for crew members who go 'beyond the call of duty'. When asked about Ryanair's more customer-friendly policy, Green replied, 'What does it cost to welcome a passenger on board and be nice to them during their flight? That is what this is all about. The things we are doing differently don't cost a thing, but they could make all the difference to a customer and their experience of the airline. We want people to start going the extra mile in their work.' Ryanair has also started to distribute surveys asking passengers what their views are on the airline and how it might improve its service.

The Air Transport Users' Council in Britain, which O'Leary once branded as 'a bunch of halfwits', has also reported a thawing in its relationship with Ryanair, and some of the airline's senior staff have attended meetings with the council to discuss passenger complaints. Investment analysts also report that the company is beginning to face up to the need to repair its tarnished customer-service reputation. It has now adopted a customer charter and one analyst suggested that as the airline continues to dominate in Europe it may evolve into a more passenger-friendly company. Its role model, Southwest Airlines, strives to provide the lowest fares and the highest quality of service, and its founder Herb Kelleher says this has always been the cornerstone of its success.

Ryanair continues to claim that it receives a very low level of customer complaints and enjoys boasting about its consistently low fares and its punctuality. Its pilots frequently announce that Ryanair flights will arrive up to fifteen minutes early at their destination and when things are going well passengers waiting for return flights know that once the incoming aircraft lands on the tarmac, within twenty-five minutes they will be airborne and on their way home.

Ryanair's success is largely due to the vision of a few people, all of whom have benefited hugely from their involvement. Its founder Tony Ryan is still a director of Ryanair and remains actively involved with the airline. He is now resident in Monaco and spends time at the Lyons Demesne, in County Kildare, which is owned by the Ryan family. They have extensive interests in the bloodstock industry, with Shane and Cathal both involved in breeding racehorses at Kilboy House in County Tipperary and Swordlestown stud in County Kildare. Tony Ryan owns one of America's greatest studs, Castleton Farm in Kentucky. He was awarded an honorary doctorate from Trinity College Dublin in 1987, for his achievements at Guinness Peat Aviation, and his associates refer to him as 'Dr Ryan'. Ryanair has made a fortune for the Ryan family. Tony Ryan and his three sons, Cathal, Declan and Shane, have raised more than €500 million through the sale of Ryanair shares and still have another almost €300 million-worth of Ryanair stock. Cathal and Declan, who are no longer involved with the airline, sold €44 million of Ryanair shares in early 2004. Declan heads the family's investment vehicle, Irelandia. Some estimate the Ryan family's wealth at more than €1 billion.

Ryan's close friend James King believes that Ryan always believed in the airline's potential. 'Tony doesn't give in easily,' he said. 'Michael would have given up but Tony wouldn't give into that. He knew inherently that he was right. He just kept at it. He had dark days in the early days of GPA too trying to get financing for it but he would just keep at it. I think he saw Ryanair exactly where it is today ... I don't think people have ever recognised the dimension of Tony's vision. I never thought that GPA would have grown to where we did. I never thought that Ryanair would get to where it is today. Now I take my hat off. It's not Tony Ryan who has achieved that, it's Michael O'Leary. Tony had the idea, the vision and in his own messy way got around to the right structure and the right way.' O'Leary has always said that it is Ryan who deserves the credit for having supported Ryanair as it veered close to bankruptcy in the 1980s and early 1990s, when O'Leary himself believed the Ryan family should cut their losses and shut the airline down.

Paolo Pietrogrande, who is a boardroom colleague of Ryan's, said that everyone who attends board meetings is very keenly aware that the airline bears his name. 'Michael clearly listens to Dr Ryan,' he said. 'Even though they act completely differently Dr Ryan is Michael's reference point. One wears a tie and the other dresses very informally but this is more a reflection of what you see than the way they act. Dr Ryan is very open with Michael during those meetings,' he said. One less diplomatic source said that Ryan and O'Leary regularly have fierce rows at board meetings: 'They would bully each other. Tony would lash out at Michael. They do have respect for each other but I think Michael's respect for Tony is somewhat tongue in cheek. Tony Ryan made Michael O'Leary, he gave him a platform to perform but Michael is not grateful.' O'Leary has always admitted that the pair have had an uneasy relationship and while most people would say it has worsened over the years the pair still regularly meet for dinner. Colleagues greatly admire Ryan's huge energy and great passion and enthusiasm for whatever venture he is involved with, and speak of his great ability to engage colleagues and associates with his ideas. One person said that Ryan is much better at dealing with people than O'Leary.

Whatever tensions emerge between them during board meetings are ably defused by David Bonderman, the corporate raider who helped them realise their fortunes. Bonderman had led the group of US investors that purchased 19.9 per cent of Ryanair in 1996. The group, known as Irish Air Partners, included members of Bonderman's Texas Pacific Group and other investors whose part-financing of the transaction was managed by the US investment adviser Farallon. They had paid the equivalent of €1.27 million for their stake in Ryanair and advanced a further €30 million of loans that were repaid after the airline's stock-market flotation in 1997. Within two years the group had sold most of their Ryanair shares, realising a profit of more than €150 million, and the partnership was dissolved in 2001.

Bonderman now holds a less than 1 per cent shareholding in Ryanair in trust for his family. When asked about his lucrative association with Ryanair, the man reputed to be worth more than $6 billion, who paid the Rolling Stones $4 million to play at his sixtieth birthday bash in Las Vegas in 2002, said it had been 'a very successful investment. We have had other very successful investments too. I guess it's not a question of which one is better, but this one was great'. Bonderman said that in 1996 he had been impressed with Ryanair's business model and its management team. 'The airline was small but looked like it had the potential for rapid growth. We liked O'Leary and his management team. We understood the business model from Southwest and other airlines in the States when I think people in Europe didn't. We were in the airline business through Continental and America West and having seen Southwest and other low-cost carriers in the US we were in a better position to evaluate this than some other folks.'

Bonderman and Ryan had forged business links many years earlier and it was no surprise when in 1998 his Texas Pacific Group took a major shareholding in the former GPA, which had been restructured and renamed Aerfi. Two years later, when Aerfi was sold to DaimlerChrysler for $950 million, Bonderman's group walked away with a $370 million profit. Ryan, who still retained a shareholding in the company he founded, pocketed $40 million in the deal.

In 2003 Bonderman and Ryan joined forces with Singapore's national airline to establish a new low-cost carrier, Tiger Airways. The new airline will be closely modelled on Ryanair, offering no frills and low fares to destinations in Malaysia, Indonesia, India, Thailand, China and Vietnam. Several of O'Leary's lieutenants have also taken the low-cost message elsewhere, having cashed in their share options and left the airline very wealthy men. Charlie Clifton, the fifth person hired by Ryanair and who headed the airline's in-flight operations, went to help establish Tiger Airways in 2003. Conor McCarthy, the former Aer Lingus executive who managed Ryanair's operations, left to set up PlaneConsult, offering his advisory services to other airlines. McCarthy is also involved with Air Asia, a new Malaysian low-fares airline that will be a direct competitor of Tiger Airways. Tim Jeans, who had led Ryanair's charge from Stansted into Europe, departed and emerged in 2003 at MyTravelLite, the low-cost airline established by the British MyTravel group. The airline has courageously taken on Ryanair, with Jeans promoting flights to Birmingham from Dublin and Knock airports.

Even though Bonderman is no longer one of Ryanair's major shareholders he remains committed to his role as the airline's chairman and travels to Ireland several times a year to attend board meetings. He says he can't see any reason why Ryanair can't grow five- or ten-fold over the next two decades and predicts that it will be one of just two substantial low-cost carriers in Europe. 'There will always be minor players here or there because the nature of this business is that anyone with new airplanes can start a carrier and there are always surplus airplanes. But there will probably be two, maybe Ryanair and one other, that will survive as successful low-cost guys.'

Bonderman and the other directors believe that the biggest challenge facing Ryanair in the future is managing its rapid growth. 'When you grow you tend to become a little more bureaucratic and that would kill Ryanair. The challenge is not to get too happy about the growth and to retain the spirit that Ryanair has,' Pietrogrande explained. 'When I joined the Ryanair board I thought that Michael was the business. Now I think there is a management team that is the business. They all have a similar style and are able to replace one another which is very unusual.' Pietrogrande suggests that even if O'Leary had a much less successful career he would still be the best controller he had ever met. 'The way he looks at numbers, the way he understands concepts and statistics is very impressive. He is very analytical in his approach and he is very personable.'

O'Leary above anyone else is responsible for Ryanair's extraordinary achievements. Some at the airline have described him as the 'ghost in the machine', the presence that makes Ryanair work. 'He is very clever. He knows where the fault lines are. He is always testing the temperature. He would have his ear to the ground,' said one. 'He regards the pilots as key to the operations and has recognised that he had to keep them happy. He also loves to point out individuals who have rapidly climbed up the ranks, baggage-handlers and cabin crew who became pilots or senior managers.' Others mentioned that he could glance through a list of Ryanair staff and point out the 'troublemakers' and 'union heads'. He still helps with baggage-handling and plays soccer on Thursday evenings. Colleagues laugh at these antics, which they say he does for public notoriety. 'He is such a show-off. You know he is into theatre,' one commented with amusement.

O'Leary has taken the aviation world by storm. He is a brilliant communicator and much sought after as a speaker at prestigious investment conferences and business gatherings, where entrepreneurs from across the world listen intently to his words of wisdom and laugh at his withering insults and humorous asides. His daring publicity stunts and his outrageous comments are lapped up by the media, a body he claims to loathe, though he has courted certain journalists as acquaintances over the years.

O'Leary claims not to care what people think of him and shrugs off criticism from any quarter. 'I am entitled to get a lot of criticism,' he has said. 'I am opinionated, I am certainly not shy about holding forth on my opinions but regardless of whether I am being criticised people in Ryanair are doing such an outstanding job. They get far too little credit in Ireland for what is by far and away and if not the most successful Irish business in the last twenty years.' Acquaintances insist though that he craves public admiration and affection. 'He likes to be popular. He can't abide not being the people's champion,' one said. 'Sometimes he pushes the envelope of getting people to love him a little bit far,' according to another.

Pietrogrande suggests that Bonderman regards O'Leary fondly. 'I think David Bonderman likes Mike,' he said. 'He has this energy and it's like he's your son or something. I think that there is an affection there which is very unusual as they only got to know each other in recent years.' Bonderman describes O'Leary as a 'mad genius' and the best chief executive in the airline business. 'He is a little bit like Herb Kelleher at Southwest was in his younger days. I think wretched excess is his style and so there will be people looking to shoot at him, but there is nobody in this business who is better than Michael.' Bonderman says that O'Leary has been fundamental to Ryanair's success and that he 'sure expects' that he will stick around for a very long time. 'Nobody is irreplaceable but having Michael here gives everybody confidence,' he said.

O'Leary remains the airline's single biggest individual shareholder with a holding of just over 5 per cent, a fact that gives the board and other investors great comfort. 'Michael is always acting in the interests of the company because he is a shareholder. I think this is a company that Michael has invested everything in. Frankly I think there is no reason why he would leave a successful project like this,' Pietrogrande said. 'I think Michael also has the capability of enjoying life besides work. I know very few people who can enjoy both their business and their personal life. I think in this respect Michael is mature beyond his years. I don't think he would be looking around to start a new Ryanair. I think he would not be able to leave Ryanair and still feel content. Aviation is part of his personal history as well as his professional history. I really cannot think of Mike going to bed without considering Ryanair's market share on the routes into Venice.'

Michael Cawley, the airline's chief operations officer, and Howard Millar, its financial officer, were both promoted to the rank of deputy chief executive to work closely with O'Leary during Ryanair's rapid expansion. Some analysts suggest that either of them could ably replace O'Leary, though some sources familiar with the airline's operations suggest that nobody is being groomed for the top slot. 'Ryanair needs another maniac to run it but they are not there,' one said. 'Howard Millar is too conservative. Michael Cawley doesn't have the killer instinct. Neither have the ability to do what he does. They would have to lean on people around the organisation.' Others suggest that O'Leary will simply step back from the day-to-day operations rather than walk away, and some believe that might happen within a couple of years. 'He's got everything he wants in life now,' one source said. 'He is an extremely wealthy young man. He still enjoys going to the office. I can't see him staying at home for a while counting the cattle but chief executives don't go on forever.'

Some sources at Ryanair believe that if O'Leary left the airline would collapse. 'When he is on holidays or is not there you can tell. Ryanair is driven from the top down and this doesn't happen when he's not there. He runs the place by kicking people in the head. At the same time he has a finger in every pie. He has the pulse of the place.' In terms of running the business, his single greatest skill is driving costs down. 'This is the first thing he thinks about when he wakes up in the morning,' an associate explained. He has banned post-it notes and highlighter pens and told staff to steal biros to save money. 'I tell the staff not to buy them. Just to pick them up from hotels, legal offices, wherever. That's what I do,' he explained, showing off his collection from the Ritz Carlton and the Great Southern. 'When he goes they will start getting colour printers and things like that and the costs will gradually creep up,' one remarked. One investor says the airline can continue to thrive using its tried and trusted formula for success. 'The system is in place now. O'Leary has got the controls in place. It's just more of the same from here on. It's the same old advertising, the same low fares, and to keep driving the costs down and that is O'Leary's greatest skill.'

O'Leary is identified as closely with Ryanair's success as Kelleher is with Southwest, and the departure of either of these airline legends would trouble investors. Kelleher said that being personally linked to the airline's fortunes can be a burden if you view this as a responsibility but is more lightly borne if you are on a power trip. 'If it's a matter of title and prestige and power you can never let go because it's your soul. It's a rotten soul but it's your soul. I think that makes a difference.'

More than thirty-five years after Herb Kelleher helped to found Southwest Airlines he is still leading its charge. He attempted to step back from the business in 2001 but changed his plans after 11 September and said he is happy to be still on board. 'I absolutely enjoy it and Michael O'Leary does too. I don't know if he would tell you that but he does,' said Kelleher. 'I am in a different position than some other people because I was there at the birth of Southwest Airlines. It is kind of like, you never forsake the responsibility for your children no matter how old they get. When they get to be twenty you don't say, "OK, you are twenty, I never want to see you again." I have got that kind of familial attachment to Southwest Airlines. There are a lot of people who just hop from one corporate job to another and it doesn't give them a lot of heartbreak or angst to move onto another company or to take a multi-million-dollar severance allowance to go and pleasure themselves. But if you've helped to procreate then I think you have a very different feeling towards your offspring.'

O'Leary has dismissed any suggestion that he may soon disembark and claims that the airline's problems with the European Commission and with the stock markets have merely made his life more interesting. 'Of course I'm only here if the shareholders want me, but I don't plan to go anywhere.' Speaking after these setbacks, O'Leary said he was happier than at any time in the past fifteen years: 'It is much more fun when the world is falling apart than when things are boring and going well.' He is fully aware of the formidable enemies who are waiting to clip Ryanair's wings at every opportunity but still relishes the fight. 'Undoubtedly there are people I irritate, who find me feisty and confrontational. Some people will believe that my handling of the [Charleroi] case has caused this, and I would find it hard to disagree with elements. If that is the case, then the ultimate responsibility rests with me,' he told investors. He is determined that Ryanair will become Europe's biggest scheduled airline. Given Ryanair's achievements in the past decade, few would argue this is a fanciful notion.

O'Leary has more enemies than friends in the aviation industry and has pledged to 'destroy the airline business as we know it'. He suggests there are only three reasons why Ryanair might fail – 'nuclear war in Europe, a major accident or believing our own bullshit'. For him running Ryanair is 'the most fun you can have without taking your clothes off'. He is obsessive about the airline. When he is away for a weekend or on holidays he will arrange for the its daily operations reports to be faxed to him, and when he arrives at Ryanair's Dublin headquarters the first thing he looks for is the average amount of money, or yield, the airline will take from each passenger and the load factor – the number of passengers on each flight that day.

He has made a vast fortune from Ryanair. His shareholding in the airline alone is worth around €190 million and he has taken more than €150 million out of the company through share sales over the years. Some who know him suggest his current wealth far exceeds this figure, with some suggesting he could have assets worth more than €500 million. He says money is important when you are trying to make the first million, 10 million, or even the first 50 million. 'After that it doesn't so much matter. But if you take it all away tomorrow, I will be really pissed off.'

He claims to puts his money in the Post Office but is known to have invested in properties in Britain and the United States and to hold a substantial share portfolio. One source said

O'Leary is fundamentally very cautious about money and that he wouldn't be surprised if the bulk of his wealth was tied up in secure Government bonds. 'He probably keeps €30 or €40 million to play around with and to invest in bloodstock and property.' O'Leary has joined with his brother Eddie to breed race horses at Gigginstown. One, called Economy Drive, has made a number of outings at race meetings but has yet to establish its form. Another, War of Attrition, enjoyed some success at Cheltenham. Having shunned sunnier tax havens to live in Mullingar, O'Leary is one of Ireland's biggest individual taxpayers, and has no qualms about revealing the size of his annual tax bill. In 2003 he held an oversized cheque for more than €14 million aloft outside Ireland's Government Buildings to publicise his contribution to the state's coffers.

Imaginative as ever, O'Leary caused a furore when it was discovered that he had converted his blue Mercedes into a taxi to beat the traffic congestion around Dublin and to shorten his commute from Mullingar. The taxi plate had cost €6000 and allowed the car to travel in the bus lanes. Taxi drivers were incensed by his sheer chutzpah while the public mostly laughed as his latest stunt. Reports about Ireland's newest cabbie circulated across the world, even making it into the *South China Morning Post*, which quoted O'Leary saying, 'I was always a transport innovator.'

Up until shortly before his wedding Gigginstown House was registered as a heritage home to allow O'Leary to offset some of his taxes against the cost of repairing, maintaining or restoring the property. In return he was obliged to open his home for public viewing for at least forty days a year, and officially visitors were welcomed on mornings between April and June, charging adults €3 and concessions €2. But it was never easy to get inside O'Leary's residence – the phone was often unanswered when tourists tried to make a booking, and others arrived to find that nobody was home. One journalist did manage to get a tour and described O'Leary's collection of portraits of bluebloods from the seventeenth and eighteenth century, hanging in ornate gilt frames along the hallway, and the 'Who Wants to Be a Millionaire?' game in one of the main reception rooms. The airline chief was said to be so incensed by the story that shortly afterwards he de-listed his home, preferring to pay his taxes rather than to suffer such invasions of privacy.

He claims that he still works a six-day week, although colleagues say he no longer works crazy hours and generally will arrive mid-morning at his office and leave by seven. One remarked that it had taken him a long time to decide that he needed a driver to bring him in from Mullingar and had wondered if 'maybe he didn't want to have to work in the back of the car'. Soon after his marriage he dismissed speculation that he might slow down. 'My experience of most married men is that after marriage and children they tend to spend more time at the office than they did before,' he has said.

After many years of hard work and devotion to the airline, Ryanair's forty-three-year old chief executive appears to have found happiness in his personal life. 'I was rude, worked too hard, I am probably a bit offensive; I am certainly not charming. I don't do nightclubs. I was too busy working through my thirties to meet someone. I got very lucky, met someone lovely. I couldn't be happier.' His wedding to Anita Farrell was a lavish affair hosted at his Mullingar home. Mary Harney and Charlie McCreevy attended, along with Tony Ryan and his family and David Bonderman, who flew in from the US for the occasion.

People who have come into contact with O'Leary said he can be 'very nice' and 'great company', though some who know him suggest he doesn't have any friends. One said, 'I like him but I keep my distance.' He doesn't cultivate relationships within Ryanair and is close to few people beyond his family. Others say that he can be fatherly and loves to be asked for advice. His favourite greeting is 'Howya lad'. When inquiring about how certain ideas and initiatives might play with Ryanair's female staff, he has been heard to ask, 'What do the dollies think?', though staff said this was never said in a disrespectful way.

Ireland's most successful entrepreneur seems set to continue to live a low-key life when not running Ryanair. Since his marriage he has purchased a €6.5 million home in Howth, in north County Dublin close to the airport, but says that Gigginstown House will still be his main home. 'Having grown up on a farm I would like my family to grow up on a farm. Like most people today I need to work harder and harder to make wealth for my family. I live in great fear of spending my eighty years and not making a difference.'

But Michael O'Leary is sure he has made a difference. As he said, 'Even if you only pissed people off at least you made a difference.'

Index